IRISH COSMOPOLITANISM

UNIVERSITY PRESS OF FLORIDA

Florida A&M University, Tallahassee
Florida Atlantic University, Boca Raton
Florida Gulf Coast University, Ft. Myers
Florida International University, Miami
Florida State University, Tallahassee
New College of Florida, Sarasota
University of Central Florida, Orlando
University of Florida, Gainesville
University of North Florida, Jacksonville
University of South Florida, Tampa
University of West Florida, Pensacola

IRISH
COSMOPOLITANISM

Location and Dislocation in James Joyce, Elizabeth Bowen,
and Samuel Beckett

◇
◇
◇
◇

NELS PEARSON

University Press of Florida

Gainesville · Tallahassee · Tampa · Boca Raton

Pensacola · Orlando · Miami · Jacksonville · Ft. Myers · Sarasota

An earlier version of chapters 1, 3, and 6 appeared respectively in *Modern Fiction Studies* 57.4, 2011 ("'May I trespass on your valuable space?': *Ulysses* on the Coast"), *Twentieth-Century Literature* 56.3, 2010 ("Elizabeth Bowen and the New Cosmopolitanism"), and *Irish University Review* 40.2, 2010 ("Beckett's Cosmopolitan Ground").

This book may be available in an electronic edition.

22 21 20 19 18 17   6 5 4 3 2 1

First cloth printing, 2015
First paperback printing, 2017

Library of Congress Cataloging-in-Publication Data
Pearson, Nels, 1969– author.
Irish cosmopolitanism : location and dislocation in James Joyce, Elizabeth Bowen, and Samuel Beckett / Nels Pearson.
pages cm
ISBN 978-0-8130-6052-1 (cloth)
ISBN 978-0-8130-5463-6 (pbk)
1. Cosmopolitanism in literature. 2. Modernism (Literature)—Ireland. 3. Joyce, James, 1882–1941. 4. Bowen, Elizabeth, 1899–1973. 5. Beckett, Samuel, 1906–1989. 6. English literature—Irish authors—History and criticism. I. Title.
PR8755.P43 2015
820.9'9415—dc23
2014030823

The University Press of Florida is the scholarly publishing agency for the State University System of Florida, comprising Florida A&M University, Florida Atlantic University, Florida Gulf Coast University, Florida International University, Florida State University, New College of Florida, University of Central Florida, University of Florida, University of North Florida, University of South Florida, and University of West Florida.

University Press of Florida
15 Northwest 15th Street
Gainesville, FL 32611-2079
http://upress.ufl.edu

For Emily, Rachel, Phyllis, and Harry

CONTENTS

ACKNOWLEDGMENTS

In many ways, this book is about the continuums of thought and feeling along which innovation occurs: the unceasing process whereby the past, assembled from and shaping each moment of experience, generates things we paradoxically call "new." My most enduring gratitude is to my family; they have not only supported the long creation of this book but also comprise the core of feeling that evolved into its ideas and convictions: Emily Orlando, my wife, intellectual companion, and friend for life; my mother Phyllis, whose passions for music, theology, and ideas inhabit my own; my late father Harry, professor of Economics at Bennington College, whose indomitable, compassionate mind is my cynosure; my Godmother Gail Kirby, a rescuer with abiding intelligence and wit. Most of all, I thank my late sister Rachel (1971–1989), whose enduring presence has allowed me to understand simultaneity and hence to write this book.

Many concepts in this book first came to life amongst the vibrant community of students and faculty at the University of Maryland. Particular thanks are due to Brian Richardson, *il miglior fabbro*, who consistently inspired my thinking about modernism, pushing me beyond easy conclusions and through difficulties, not only then but now. I am also deeply grateful to my friend and colleague Rob Doggett (Professor of English, SUNY Geneseo), who has not only read and offered invaluable advice on drafts of the book but has also, in what seems like one unending conversation extending across the years, contributed a great deal to its arguments. My wife and colleague Emily, in her capacity as astute editor and collaborator, has also read, supported, and given numerous crucial suggestions to this project from our days at Maryland to our days on the faculty at Fairfield. I am grateful, too, to Sangeeta Ray, who first suggested that I look deeper into contemporary theoretical developments in cosmopolitanism and cosmopolitics.

Many colleagues in modernist and Irish studies have also read and/or heard versions of what became chapters in the book, contributing helpful suggestions and much needed support. I am especially thankful, in this regard, to Johanna Garvey, Elizabeth Loizeaux, Nicholas Allen, Joseph Valente, John Brannigan, Kate Costello-Sullivan, and Gregory Castle. To Mark Facknitz, my life-changing mentor at James Madison University, and his colleague Mark Hawthorne, who first taught me the depths of Joyce, I owe more than I can say. The Faculty Support Center at Tennessee State University assisted me with a valuable release time grant in 2007, and many colleagues at TSU, especially the irreplaceable Erik Schmeller, inspired me to keep working on this project through challenging times.

Finally, I am grateful to my dear friends and colleagues at Fairfield University, to Fairfield's College of Arts and Sciences for a research leave that allowed me to focus solely on this project, and to our research librarians Jonathan Hodge and Curtis Ferree, who helped secure many important materials. Without the spirited, supportive community of this lovely college on a hill in southern Connecticut, this book would not have been possible.

ABBREVIATIONS

Abbreviations used in chapters 1 and 2 for works by James Joyce

CW	*The Critical Writings of James Joyce*
D	*Dubliners*
CP	*Collected Poems*
OCP	*Occasional, Critical, and Political Writing*
P	*A Portrait of the Artist as a Young Man*
UL	*Ulysses*
FW	*Finnegans Wake*

Abbreviations used in chapters 2 and 3 for works by Elizabeth Bowen

BC	*Bowen's Court*
CI	*Collected Impressions*
HD	*The Heat of the Day*
HP	*The House in Paris*
LS	*The Last September*
MT	*The Mulberry Tree: Writings of Elizabeth Bowen*

◇
◇
◇

Of Coast and Cosmos

Locating Irish Expatriate Modernism

I said, the sea is east, it's west I must go, to the left of north. But in vain I raised
my eyes without hope to the sky.

Samuel Beckett, "The Calmative"

The title of this book is somewhat paradoxical. After all, if a "cosmopolitan"
is one who pledges allegiance to humanity at large, rather than to a specific national or ethnic collective, then what is the need, or rationale, for
designating an "Irish Cosmopolitanism"? Much of the rationale stems from
changing ideas about the term "cosmopolitan." Over the past two decades,
since an animated debate in the *Boston Review* in 1994, intellectuals from a
variety of disciplines have questioned the Western inflections and biases of
the concept of cosmopolitanism and deliberated whether it can be reimag-
ined for a postcolonial world in which experiences of the nation, in space
and time, not only vary widely but also involve volatile, layered relationships to a "global" sphere that has typically also been imperial.

One outcome of this debate has been the growing awareness that, for
what may be the true majority of peoples, relationships between national
and international, homeland and world, cultural roots and universal humanity are not simply dialectical and sequential—following a presumably
"natural" inclination to move from more local to more global aspirations—
but intricately overlapping, tangled together from the outset, and difficult
to prioritize. Any genuinely egalitarian ideal of humanity must therefore
be global in scope, yet also vigilant against imperialistic pretensions of universality, skeptical of generalizations about national feeling, and willing to

forgo the teleology of global "unity" in the process of understanding cultural particularity.

The book is so titled, then, because it aims to demonstrate how these new discourses of cosmopolitanism, and new critical approaches to global democracy, can enlighten questions of place and identity in the substantive Irish expatriate contribution to literary modernism. It focuses mostly on the works of James Joyce, Elizabeth Bowen, and Samuel Beckett, stylistically innovative writers who left Ireland to live and work primarily in capital cities of international modernism (Trieste, London, and Paris). Each of these authors became immersed in international culture and notions of ecumenical modernity while still processing, still assessing, his or her connections to an Ireland that, in the midst of a long and turbulent decolonization, was itself unsettled and contingent. This paradox of being an international expatriate without having an established or default sense of patria is not just an important historical context of their modernism but also one of its generative philosophical dilemmas. To examine this phenomenon, *Irish Cosmopolitanism* builds upon postcolonial approaches to modern Irish literature but also brings them into a richer dialogue with discourses of transnational humanitarianism and the universal human subject. The book posits that these authors' modernisms—in content, intellect, and form—arise from a rigorous, nonhierarchical, and mutually transformative interplay of national and global consciousness.

When the concept of international modernism was in its midcentury, critical heyday, the evolution of the nation-state also appeared to be at a crossroads, destined either for more centralized and totalitarian iterations or, in certain intellectual circles, for gradual extinction under the pressures of universal humanitarianism. A cosmopolitan critical discourse thus grew up around international modernism, and especially around its Anglophone writers, that interpreted the movement's aesthetics not so much as "a-historical" as deeply invested in the idea of historical *aftermath*: a new poetics, forged in and against the cauldron of nation-state violence, that seemed to posit an absolute break with prior, orthodox modes of historical and cultural-geographic identification. As Richard Ellmann and Charles Feidelson put it in *The Modern Tradition*, international modernism was identifiable by its emphasis on "historical discontinuity," "disinheritance," and the "inborn challenge to established culture" (vi).

When this powerful notion of historical and cultural negation was combined with the equally formidable idea that Ireland symbolized the dehu-
manizing effects of nation-statist preoccupations, Joyce and Beckett came
to be seen as the definitive "supranational" experimenters—avatars of the
link between aesthetic innovation and a vast, cosmic, postnational perspective. Ironically enough, it could therefore be argued that Joyce and Beckett
would not have been so triumphantly hailed as universal artists were they
not Irish. Meanwhile, and regrettably, this same constellation of ideas fu-
eled the dismissal of Bowen as a less innovative, more "locatable" realist—a
belated Victorian whose work, especially in its frequent revisiting of Ascendancy culture, seemed to be invested neither in high experiment nor in
ideas of the postterritorial cosmos.

Postcolonial approaches have supplied a much-needed counterpoint
to this overly idealistic, postnational image of Irish expatriate modernism.
They also, however, have tended to locate the primary impetus or generative
conditions of that modernism within the national context of decolonization. That is, in order to dislodge and overturn prevailing assumptions about
the international aspirations and universalist aesthetics of Irish modernism, these approaches have tended to focus on the ways that it dismantles
specifically imperial and nationalistic constructs of Irish identity. We see
this, for example, in Enda Duffy's argument that *Ulysses*, by "deconstruct-
ing the interpellating narratives [of] the oppression of Ireland as a colony"
(26–27), becomes "the starred text of an Irish national literature" (2–3) and
in Andrew Gibson's claim that Joyce's experiments "work towards a liberation from the colonial power and its culture" (13). We see it, too, in C. L.
Innes's seminal argument that Bowen's fiction "problematiz[es] notions
of nation and gender, largely through the use of multiple perspectives and
dislocations of narrative" (173). David Lloyd memorably situates Beckett's
modernism "against the state" by arguing that its "aesthetic domain emerges
in the need to resolve contradictions which subsist both within the subject and in the relationship between each individual subject and the state,"
hence Beckett's "way of manifesting absence, of incarnating [that] emptiness" (*Anomalous* 55).

My aim is not to contradict such groundbreaking studies but to push
their conclusions further by exploring the ways in which the anticolonial
contexts of expatriate Irish modernism are dynamically related to the ways

in which it imagines the universal and global. Indeed, *Irish Cosmopolitanism* proposes that postcolonial interpretation ultimately obliges us to renovate our understanding of how these writers engage internationalism, to recognize how they complicate abstract and deracinated images of global unity, and to appreciate their call for a more historically continuous, less idealistic model of the human experience beyond states. My approach therefore focuses more on the ways in which colonial experience both inspires and shapes one's image of the world or cosmos, as well as on how the incongruous experience of moving "outside" a disputed homeland influences the *types* of international being one experiences.

I will also often concentrate on moments and sites of departure, as well as of return and crossing, in order to show how the literal and conceptual borders between Ireland and the broader world become contradictory and, in a sense, mobile or ineluctable spaces. I hope to show that Irish expatriate modernism does not so much ingeniously deconstruct, as much as express and make evident, the intellectually and psychologically demanding relationship between colonial and international identity. Emergent discourses of cosmopolitanism, which highlight the severe limitations of global teleology as well as the nonsequential, potentially nontranscendable place of national affiliations in postcolonial geopolitics, can aid substantially in these considerations. Seen through their lenses, international Irish modernism emerges as an important challenge to presumed oppositions between national location and global dislocation, historical rootedness and temporal displacement, the familiar terrain of tradition and the strange new world of the modern.

Stephen Dedalus and the Irish-Cosmopolitan Paradox

As a product of the classical and neoclassical West, cosmopolitanism has typically denoted an enlightened decision to pledge one's primary allegiance to global human society over its lesser, presumably reductive copy, the nation-state. As Immanuel Kant reasoned in 1795, human society ought rationally to matriculate from a geopolitics whose best-case scenario is "a law of equilibrium [between] secure . . . state[s]" (257) to one whose best-case scenario is an "international government [without] precedent in world history" (257, 260). Driven by their inherent capacity to empathize beyond the "established state," humans would thus reify, via the concrete political form of a global democracy, the "universal cosmopolitan condition, which Nature has as her ultimate purpose" (260).

For many who reside in developing nations, postcolonial states, and partitioned homelands, and for the millions who emigrate from them, however, this theoretical move from the established socio-geography of the "secure . . . state" toward the spatial abstraction of the universal can result in a paradox. The paradox is that one must be "international" before ever fairly knowing what it is to be national. That is to say, many minority transnational subjects have not yet experienced the situated state of social-collective autonomy that is the a priori of Kantian cosmopolitanism, the previous political form from which it evolves. Nor is such a form of achieved sovereignty ever likely to take place—at least not in the same way as it has been imagined and experienced in the First World—because modern global and transnational realities have already transformed irreversibly the spatial and temporal image of the homeland. The impact comes not only in the form of the "dislocating intersections between local and global processes" wrought by imperialism's uneven import of global capital (Cleary 121) but also in the form of the native population's engagements in transcultural processes at home and abroad. The postcolonial nation, the idea of which must ironically commence after this transculturation, is thus always deferred as a concrete, organic habitus. In turn, postcolonial national identity ends up being imagined and constructed not prior to but at the same time as international identity. Postcolonial national identity cannot therefore be isolated from extra-national relationships in time or space, for the former is neither prior to nor elsewhere than the latter. Ironically, however, many in the developing world who seek to enter a so-called international or "multicultural" milieu are compelled to make this false separation, to transform their contested and already globalized origin into a fixed object, an "established" national terrain.

In the final chapters of A Portrait of the Artist as a Young Man, Stephen Dedalus finds himself squarely in the throes of this paradox. In the series of epiphanies that foreshadow his departure from Ireland, Stephen, drawn to the shoreline and gazing across the sea, feels called to join a human family whose resemblance lies in the established sovereignty of its otherwise distinct cultures: "[O]ut there beyond the Irish Sea [lay a] Europe of strange tongues . . . valleyed and woodbegirt and citadelled and of entrenched and marshaled races" (181). Later, as he prepares to take flight from his compatriots, he senses a similarly capacious, Kantian-cosmopolitan vocation. Gazing over the ships in Dublin Bay, he hears the voices of "distant nations" calling out to him as "their kinsman" (275). Try as he might, however, he cannot forge a comprehensive image of the Ireland he is leaving behind— the known, rooted national collective that he wants to set up as the opposite, and the lesser precondition, of his dawning international consciousness.

Stephen spends much of the final chapter of the novel trying to translate particular incidents of his Dublin experience into all-encompassing statements about "the thoughts and desires of the race to which he belonged" (259). But these efforts to totalize Ireland and Irishness come up well short of the mark, and this repeatedly frustrates him. His series of journal entries, which has often been read as a signature example of a cosmopolitan farewell to the particularities and parochial limits of the homeland, is in fact full of withdrawn conclusions and frustrated revisions of previous attempts to summarize Irishness. Several entries simply abandon in obscurity the subjects Stephen cannot resolve into a national or racial generalization. In one, he retracts his earlier dismissal of Emma, his love interest, as an unwitting "figure of the womanhood of her country" (239), then lapses into an almost Beckettian tone of futility as he casts about for a new absolute proclamation: "Then, in that case, all the rest, all that I thought I thought and all that I felt I felt, all the rest before now, in fact . . . O, give it up, old chap!" (275; ellipses Joyce's).

His entry on a peasant "from the west of Ireland" who was recently interviewed for Dublin audiences by a Celtic Revival folklorist ends in similar frustration. Although he tries to use this cliché event to make a case in point about Ireland's insular self-preoccupation, he is too disturbed and disoriented by the image of the old peasant to finish his grandiose claim:

> 14 April: John Alphonsus Mulrennan has just returned from the west of Ireland. (European and Asiatic papers please copy.) He told us he met an old man there in a mountain cabin. . . . Mulrennan spoke to him about universe and stars. Old man sat, listened, smoked, spat. Then said:
>
> —Ah, there must be terrible queer creatures at the latter end of the world.
>
> I fear him. I fear his redrimmed horny eyes. It is with him I must struggle all through this night till day come, till he or I lie dead, grip-

ping him by the sinewy throat till . . . Till what? Till he yield to me?
No. I mean him no harm. (274)

Seamus Deane calls this a "mock obituary . . . for the Gaelic Revival" (329).
I would argue, however, that Stephen's response indicates a haunting awareness of the unassimilated cultural material left in the Revival's wake. For
what he seems to fear, or what he cannot account for, is the grave difference
between the *use* of the peasant as national symbol (an effort to fix the symbols of national culture that is typical of "prestatized nationalisms" [Cheah,
Spectral 6]) and the "redrimmed horny eyes" of the peasant himself—the
old man returning the anthropologist's gaze, refusing assimilation into an
abstract of Celtic tradition, remaining unexplained.[1]

The rural lower classes, as real people, have often frustrated Stephen's
quite genuine desire to understand "the hidden ways of Irish life," or to
comprehend Ireland as a totality of which he is a part (196). From his early
childhood memory of wanting "to sleep for one night in [their] cottage before the fire of the smoking turf . . . breathing the smell of the peasants, air
and rain and turf and corduroy" (17), Stephen has felt at once drawn to
and dislocated by the physical, rooted lives that surround him—lives that
under cultural nationalism are in a sense symbolic before they are real. As
he abandons his imagined wrestling match with the old peasant, he must
acquiesce to the fact that there are numerous phenomena in Ireland that he
does not yet understand—diverse, local realities that resist any sanctioned
national mythology, and that are therefore indifferent to his grandiose re-
jections of the national mythology. Thus his cosmopolitanism, and the stirring of his artistic soul toward "freedom" that attends it, contains within
it a still-unfulfilled inclination toward an uncontrived national belonging,
or toward an unselfconscious feeling of native integration. This inclination
can only be deferred, not curtailed, and must therefore be interwoven with
the new affiliations and processes of identity formation he will experience
outside of Ireland. As he travels abroad, his process of ascertaining an Irish
consciousness can neither be cancelled nor maintained as a distinct and
primary agenda. Rather, it comes to co-exist with, to influence and be influenced by, his developing international consciousness and ideas about the
human universe.

I would offer that Stephen's troubled effort to think globally about Irishness, like Gabriel Conroy's simultaneous weighing of "his journey west-

ward" and the snow falling "through the universe" at the end of "The Dead" (225), pinpoints the generative locus of Irish expatriate modernism: *the border itself*, the vexed and protracted threshold of colonial departure. A modernism that derives not from choosing between national and cosmopolitan sympathies, but from the need to somehow make these concurrent principles: to form the "uncreated conscience of my race" by heeding the call "of tall ships . . . [and] their tale of distant nations"—to create a moral sensibility based in transnational humanity while simultaneously incarnating an abstract sense of racial or cultural origin (275–6). As I hope to show, the compulsion to grasp this simultaneity—and thus to court its paradoxes, tensions, and challenges—is a vital link between Joyce, Beckett, and Bowen.

The book examines the Anglo-Irish novelist Bowen as an equal alongside Joyce and Beckett because her confrontations with the ironies and incongruities of Irish internationalism are at least on par with those of her compatriots, and are often more direct. Her protagonists, many of whom have vague, unresolved ties to Ireland, typically face the problem of blending into a culture of transient modernity when they have neither a patria nor a previous life of tradition against which to contrast that transience. Postcolonial revisions of cosmopolitanism help reveal that Bowen's dissonant grammar and vocabulary of space and time are aesthetic manifestations or stylistic reflections of this contradiction. This new understanding of Bowen's idiosyncratic modernist style in turn illuminates many of the family resemblances between all three writers. Her much-discussed Irish novel *The Last September* (1928) is important in this regard, but equally if not more significant are her less-studied narratives set in London, Paris, and Rome, for in these works Bowen's irresolutely bi-directional psychology, and the language of equally provisional attachment and detachment through which she expresses it, are most fully developed.

Irish-European Modernism and the "New" Cosmopolitanism

These relationships between contingent, deferred national orientation, transnational perspectives, and modernist styles grow in significance when we consider them in light of recent interdisciplinary efforts to define a subaltern or minority mode of cosmopolitanism, as well as critical approaches to global democracy, often referred to as "cosmopolitics." Unlike their classical and neoclassical predecessors, these discourses sustain a healthy postcolonial skepticism regarding the inclination to generalize *both* national and global belonging. Attempts to revise ecumenical humanism from minority and postcolonial vantage points have many differences and trajectories, but common to most of them is the argument that early twentieth-century ideals of world citizenship were predicated on moving beyond the preexisting, sovereign state, whereas any viable global ethics today must stem from the experiences of mobile, transnational subjects whose orientation relative to sited cultural origins remains actively unresolved. As Sheldon Pollock observes, "nationhood . . . may be the common currency of world culture and international politics, but its varied geopolitical histories have demonstrated . . . the terrible asymmetries of the idea of modernity itself." "[T]oday's cosmopolitans," he contends, "are often the victims of [this uneven] modernity, bereft of the customs and comforts of national belonging" whether they reside at "home" or abroad (6).

Contemporary cosmopolitan theories also grapple with the need to identify and articulate cultural positions that exist in between national and global abstractions, and that reveal the pragmatic inaccuracy of those abstractions. Susan Koshy, for example, has recently proposed the term "minority cosmopolitanism" to denote "translocal affiliations that are grounded in the experience of minority subjects and are marked [both] by a critical awareness of the constraints of primary attachments . . . [and an] ethical or imaginative receptivity, orientation, or aspiration to an interconnected or shared world" (595). Especially relevant for Koshy are those mobile subjects whose sense of home is "partial"—incomplete and still in process—because it is "shaped by the legacies of colonialism and nationalism" that in turn "haunt [present] visions of location and belonging" in general (596–97). Walter Mignolo argues for a "critical cosmopolitanism," which he defines as a project of "imagining ethically and politically from subaltern perspectives" while also resisting "new form[s] of cultural relativism" (181).[2] Cosmopolitical discourse often hinges on a similar point, namely, that neither statist nor poststatist visions of global governance fairly account for the needs of the presovereign majority who exist in dynamic positions between home and world, cultural origin and human ecumene. Indeed, for many of the key voices in today's debates on transnational ethics, the future of geopolitics rests precisely in our ability to mediate the tension between the idea of universal human rights and the need for local iterations of democratic justice to be sovereign and self-generated (Benhabib 70–72).

As Rahul Rao argues, "the language of common humanity operates in ways that are both oppressive and emancipatory, just as the language of community is a source of both repression and refuge." Therefore, "[any] theory that does not seek to hold both in tension," or that does not "speak in mixed registers of universalism and particularity," will ultimately fail us (ii).

As an international literature, expatriate Irish modernism may be more relevant now than ever, for it is prodigiously fluent in the "mixed registers of universalism and particularity." While Joyce, Bowen, and Beckett are unique voices, they are similar in that even as they use international exposure and modern dislocation as conduits of humanistic insight, they also speak to the utter impossibility of choosing to either reject or embrace a national past that remains contested and internationally suspect. For each writer, it is not just that Ireland as a historical, cultural, or geographical entity is always incomplete—an origin-in-process that one can neither unselfconsciously inhabit nor triumphantly depart—but also that going abroad or thinking globally heightens one's awareness of this incompletion. The result is a perpetual and mobile negotiation between (post)colonial and universal perspectives that differs from, and arguably offers more rigorous philosophical challenges than, the more oppositional and sequential relationship between located tradition and dislocated modernity that is often articulated in Anglophone high modernism. In that idiom, authors have at their disposal the ability to depict the disorienting vastness of a postorthodox modern world by contrasting it with a past that was once historically and geographically coherent but is no longer tenable or habitable. As Louis muses in Virginia Woolf's *The Waves*, "the lighted strip of history is past and out; Kings and Queens; we are gone; our civilization; the Nile; and all life. Our separate drops are dissolved; we are extinct, lost in the abysses of time, in the darkness" (225). Stephen's famous promise to "forge in the smithy of [his] soul the uncreated conscience of his race" would seem to embody a different set of ideas, for it assumes no "lighted strip of history" in the past as it goes forth into the uncertainty of the wider world; rather, the ongoing creation of that "former" habitus must become an active part of the traveling subject's wider experience.

To leave an Ireland undergoing decolonization and go to Europe, in an era when nation-states and national identities were an especially valuable international currency—whether as origins to claim, or origins to reject in exchange for cosmopolitan caché—is, after all, to ask a different set of questions: not what does it mean to live "after history," or outside the familiar lights of tradition, but what does it mean to come from a history that has never been objectively illuminated in the first place? What is the "beyond" of a place that is not concretely established? Having never been rooted, in the sense of being unselfconsciously enmeshed in "a culture which has given proof of its existence" (Fanon 209), what is it to be dislocated? At the conclusion of Beckett's *Endgame*, Clov stands at the threshold of the duo's seaside dwelling, one of Beckett's many coastal settings, preparing to depart. He tells Hamm, "I say to myself that the earth is extinguished, though I never saw it lit" (81). It is not that there is no going away or forward or beyond, but rather that, in the Irish Cosmopolitan idiom, such movements do not occasion a distillation of essential from social being—a cataclysmic ontological denuding—because they do not radically alter the disorientation and uncertainty that already exist. These remain in process, even as one moves away and beyond. Importantly, the result is that location and dislocation become equally desired, but equally unverifiable, states of being.

Elizabeth Bowen understood this as well as anyone. In *The Heat of the Day*, she summarizes her heroine Stella Rodney's efforts to extricate herself from the unsettled history and disputed property of her Anglo-Irish family by writing, of Stella's ex-husband Victor, that "she couldn't leave someone who wasn't there" (236). In *The Last September*, Hugo Montmorency, pressed to explain the "side" of the Cork Ascendancy in the troubles, describes the Anglo-Irish as "expressing tenacity to something that isn't there. That never was there" (117).

Like *A Portrait of the Artist as a Young Man*, Bowen's *The Last September* is a coming-of-age narrative (for Bowen, the setting is an Ascendancy enclave during the Anglo-Irish War that resulted in the partition of 1921) that ends with its semiautobiographical protagonist's incipient departure for Europe. Like Stephen's, Lois Farquar's pending expatriation is an extension of the native displacement, or sense of domestic exile, she has experienced from the beginning. Just entering her twenties when IRA soldiers kill her boyfriend, a British soldier, and burn her house, Lois has known only the peculiar combination of rootedness and estrangement that defined the Anglo-Irish gentry. The enervating banality of this strange combination of provinciality and dislocation is not just a matter of context for Bowen but a matter of style, as it inhabits her descriptions of even the most quotidian events: Lois's social routines are expected, yet always "doomed to incompletion" (*LS* 133), she "do[es]n't live anywhere, really" (229), and her return home amounts to "the discovery of a lack" (244). Once wooed by Gerald, the British soldier, she does not feel more aligned with his side but rather an "inside blankness" (127): "[She] saw there was no future. She shut her eyes and tried—as sometimes when she was seasick, locked in misery between Holyhead and Kingstown—to be enclosed in a nonentity, in some ideal no-place, perfect and clear as a bubble" (*LS* 127).

As Joyce does with Stephen, who opens *Ulysses* as a failed expatriate despondently gazing at the Holyhead/Kingstown passenger ferry as it "clear[s] the mouth of the harbor" (1.83–84), Bowen is here locating Lois's vexed emergence into modern self-consciousness in an intermediate, coastal zone between national and foreign territory. Stephen's inability to wake from the nightmare of history, a discovery he makes after having returned to Dublin from Paris, is reflected geographically by his wandering along Sandymount strand amidst Joyce's numerous allusions to frustrated sea travel. Lois's is encapsulated in the irony that there is little difference between being "locked in misery between Holyhead and Kingstown" (literally, ferrying between Britain and Ireland; metaphorically, being Anglo-Irish) and escaping to "an ideal no-place." Her "original" cultural location is *already* "between Holyhead and Kingstown," therefore the thought or act of moving beyond it only repeats its "blank[ness]." Even her subjective reveries—in which she imagines being "enclosed in a nonentity" or traveling to an "ideal no-place"—reiterate the domestic alienation she already knows.

Like Stephen, what Lois is experiencing is thus not the typical modernist trajectory of an increasingly deterritorialized subjectivity—a critical detachment from stable orthodoxies accompanied by an anxious liberation of the capacious, synchronic mind—but the expansion of a subnational or presovereign unbelonging. Herein lies what might be called the generative, twin paradox of Bowen's artistic vision: the desire, on the one hand, to lay roots in ephemeral, contingent places, and, on the other, to transcend one's confining, but incomprehensible, horizons. Both are impossible desires, for one cannot be sure, as Lois never is, whether they amount to the need "to be in a pattern . . . to be related" or the need to seek "unmarried sorts of places" (142–43). And yet, it is precisely because of this contradiction that Bowen's heroines, no matter where they reside, are disinclined to be duped by vague ideals of either patriotism or cosmopolitanism. Like Stella Rodney, in London, they "enjoy the sensation of being on furlough from [their] own li[ves]" (*HD* 103), but like Karen Michaelis, in Paris, they also "hate exile, hate being nowhere, hate being unexplained, hate having no place of [their] own" (*HP* 207). As we will see, this double resistance is also played out in Bowen's prolific contributions—as essayist, journalist, and spy—to both public and intragovernmental discourse on such topics as patriotism, the war efforts of English citizens on the home front, and Irish neutrality.

If, as Susan Stanford Friedman has observed, a truly "spatialized" or sited understanding of modernity requires "a radical rewriting of what critics have called modernism's internationalism" ("Periodizing" 426–28), then it is important to recognize the complex relationships between travel, dislocation, and cultural affiliation that are suggested in these aforementioned, coastal scenes. They imply a transnational consciousness that forms while a sense of national belonging or identity is still in process. If they are cosmopolitan, they are not so in an idealistic, abstract sense, but in the sense of a human "mutuality [that exists] in conditions of mutability, and . . . in terrains of historic and cultural transition" (Pollock 4–5). Embedded in them is the idea that the need to have an origin—to feel a part of a sovereign consensus that pertains to a primary habitus—and the need to contemplate wider scales of the human condition are not sequential points of view through which one matriculates, but simultaneous, interactive needs that are never easily reconciled.

I would argue that no one captures the simultaneity of these needs, at least as they emerge in Irish writing and as they can be expressed aesthetically, more completely than Samuel Beckett. For many lovers of Beckett, this is not, understandably, an easy argument to accept. After all, more so than Joyce, Bowen, or perhaps any twentieth-century author, Beckett is associated with a form of dislocation that is final, a resistance to specific placement that, although applicable as a critique of various and specific ideological positions, is in itself "pure" or absolute. Especially after Beckett moves away from using the identifiable Irish and English settings of his prewar, pre-French period, his irreducibly vague locales are often taken to exemplify his rare ability to depict the human condition at its most fundamental, least culturally specific level. Hence, to think of Beckett as Irish or to read his work in Irish contexts, as a small but significant group of scholars have admirably begun to do in recent years, has continually run up against the charge that to do so is limiting, and is intellectually restricting if not "recolonizing" a writer who is defined by his philosophical significance. I will propose that the philosophical, in particular the practice of ontological questioning as a core human experience, is deepened rather than limited by the role of Ireland, and of postcolonial spatial epistemology, in Beckett's texts.

A perfect storm of cultural history, cultural bias, and the dramatic turning point in Beckett's writing style and reputation has led to a prevailing narrative in which Ireland becomes bordered or bracketed, both as a social, cultural reality and as an experience in Beckett's intellectual development. It becomes a signifier for other concepts and entities that his mature work resists or moves us beyond: national feeling, the state, cultural rootedness, orthodox familiarity, historical or cultural particularity. The details of Beckett's aesthetic development are then mapped onto this bracketing: he officially left Ireland as his primary residence in 1945/46, the same years in which his style took a major leap forward into the unknowing minimalism and abstract settings for which he became famous. Thus the move beyond Ireland is doubled, geographically and aesthetically, as a move toward universality. In complicating this model, my goal will not be to show that it overlooks a historically or biographically Irish Beckett as much as to show that Ireland and Irish identity are not fixed fields relative to Beckett's post-1945 style, and, more important, that they are not fixed fields relative to the philosophical, international, and humanistic relevance of that mature style.

Characterized from the start by displacement, shot through with the contrary wishes to belong and reject, Beckett's experience of Irishness was both less definitive and more continuous than prevailing national/cosmopolitan binaries allow. As today's more nuanced theoretical models of the relations between marginalized societies and global imaginaries help to clarify, his work actually challenges the opposition between historically located and temporally generalized (that is, synchronic) human conditions that is often used to bolster the nation/world binary. Indeed, when we "trouble" the border between Ireland and the secular cosmos of modernity—when we admit the ambiguity of Irish crossings, memories, and traces as they pertain to Beckett's "becoming Beckett" in the 1940s—we begin to see profound correspondences between Beckett's art and the effort to modify philosophical and ecumenical discourse from minority and decolonial points of view.

Rather than working from biographical details about Beckett's Ireland into archeological readings of his Irish content, I will start with the supposedly abstract or placeless setting itself and examine how its fixation on local displacement, or disorientation as a "grounded" phenomenon, resists both national and universal meaning. The cause of disorientation in French works like "The Calmative," *Molloy*, *Waiting for Godot*, or *Endgame* may well be the *inability* to abstract one's place—the impossibility of comprehending one's native and immediate environment as a conceptual whole. After all, in each of these works, to know "where" one is, or has come from, is never any less pressing a matter, or challenging a proposition, than to know whether one is.

If we consider Beckett's peculiar combination of rootedness and alienation in light of the spatial metaphors often used to differentiate national and cosmopolitan affiliation, we begin to see how deeply Beckett's settings actually complicate the home/world distinction. For scholars focused on the struggle of postcolonial societies to achieve sovereignty, the act of remaining committed to specific processes of nation-building in the midst of vague ideals of multicultural mobility and hybridity has meant being "grounded." In other words, it has meant being alert to the actual locations that pertain to a particular ethnos, or remaining in contact with the material conditions of the national struggle and the violations of human rights that pertain to it. In contrast, to be "international," culturally migrant, or cosmopolitan has typically been associated with being ephemeral, with being up in the air, and with thinking of global space in terms of theoretical abstractions. Defenders of the emergent postcolonial nation-state such as Tim Brennan and Pheng Cheah have repeatedly, and justifiably, cautioned that ideals of "migrancy" and "hybridity" reflect a globalization from above that "reviles modernist detachment" but sees national particulars through the "ironic detachment [of a] cosmic, celebratory pessimism" (Brennan, *At Home* 41), or "from the comfort of the observation tower" (Brennan, "Celebrities" 6). Their point is that cosmopolitanism, even in its new guises, takes a "dismissive or parodic attitude towards the project of national culture" while promoting a "perennial immigration [and] rhetoric of wandering"—a "cosmopolitan embrace [that amounts to] a flattening of influences . . . on the same plane of value" (Brennan, "Celebrities" 7, 2, 4). Hence, national and culturally particular affiliation is figured as rootedness, as tangible and physical territory, while cosmopolitanism, an "unsettling generality" (Knowles 1), is associated with an airy and intangible, merely conceptual sense of place.

One way of disarming the charged opposition between Beckett's historical Irishness and his modern, aesthetic worldliness is to note that his obscure settings evoke *both* of these spatial registers at the same time. For even as they "doom all mapping expeditions to failure" (Ackerley and Gontarski xv), and just as they can almost always be taken to represent the external world in the most abstract, Cartesian sense, so too are they relentlessly physical, local, and material. Unable to be mapped according to any national rubric, they are nonetheless populated by rooted locals who have "never . . . left [their] region" yet remain perplexed by "its character-istics [and] limits" (*Molloy* 65)—denizens who crawl in ditches "rank with tangled growth" ("Calmative" 28), plod through "gnarled roots, boulders, and baked mud" (*Malone Dies* 204), and "press [their] cheek to the ground [and] clutch the grass, each hand a tuft" (*Malone Dies* 239).

Whether it refers directly to Irish soil or not, what is most important about the boggy, hilly, coastal Beckett terrain is that it is abstractly local and inscrutably tangible: an "unfamiliar native land," as the narrator of *The Un-namable* puts it (314). As the narrator of "The Calmative" looks out at "the coast, the islands, the headlands" and prepares to bid a "strange farewell[]" to his city, he looks to the ground, noting that "it was always from the earth, rather than the sky, . . . that my help came in time of trouble" (32). Both alienating and familiar, and often fixated on the interstitial territory of the "invisible nearby sea" ("Ill Seen" 51), the Beckett terrain suggests an unend-ing process, rather than an aftermath, of origin: an interminable transition between the unreconciled home and the human cosmos. Indeed, Beckett's quandary of unverifiable being is perhaps most acutely revealed in the "zone of stones" by the sea, the coastal zone *between* home and away that so many of his works revisit ("Ill Seen" 53).

That space and subjectivity in Beckett's avant-garde reflect a continuous state of transition rather than a transcendence of culturally familiar terri-tory is further suggested by the potential Irish historical and geographical allusions that haunt his post-1945 works. Like the paintings of Jack Yeats, which Beckett deeply admired, Beckett's vague landscapes often evoke Irish places and events in a spectral, half-faded way that could imply either their evanescence or their indelibility—their persistence as a site not yet understood—even as they evoke feelings of displacement and transience on a broader scale. *Endgame*, for example, takes place in a bare two-room dwelling that is located nowhere in particular, set amid a "corpsed," "gray" landscape nearby the sea (30–31). For much of the play, Hamm rehearses his "chronicle" about how he found and adopted Clov. Although we can never confirm the location or truth of this past event any more than we can know where the couple now reside, Hamm's narrative hauntingly links Clov's adoption to famine, emigration, and deportation:

> Hamm: (*Narrative tone*). . . . Where did he come from? He named the hole. A good half-day, on horse. What are you insinuating? That the place is still inhabited? No, no, not a soul, except himself and the child—assuming he existed. Good. I inquired about the situation at Kov, beyond the gulf. Not a sinner. Good. And you expect me to believe you have left your little one back there, all alone, and alive into the bargain? Come now! . . . what he wanted from me was . . . bread for his brat? Bread? . . . or perhaps a little corn?. . . . Corn, yes, I have corn, it's true, in my granaries. But use your head. I give you some corn, a pound, a pound and a half, you bring it back to your child and make him—if he's still alive—a nice pot of porridge. . . . The colors come back into his little cheeks—perhaps. And then? . . . Use your head can't you, use your head, you're on earth, there's no cure for that! (52–53; third ellipses Beckett's, others mine)

Hamm's "chronicle" evokes impoverishment and suffering in a way that is ambiguous, no doubt, but also visceral and localized. It ends in a universal, existential quandary ("You're on earth, there's no cure for that!"), but this conclusion neither supersedes nor fully incorporates the particular, local trauma that it truncates.

For the details that pierce the ambiguity of Hamm's story, as he continually rehearses it into art, are that of a diminishing rural population, refugees at "Kov" harbor (a phonetic spelling of "Cobh"[3]), and the denial of surplus corn to the starved. These details imply, in specific ways, the Great Hunger of the 1840s.[4] Hamm's reply to the pleading man that he "use his head" suggests a general Cartesian crisis, but his argument against donating a pound of corn also chillingly echoes the Utilitarian, laissez-faire principles—couched in the Corn Laws—that perpetuated the famine. Whether or not these trace images and references ought to be firmly linked to Irish history is less important than the manner in which their potential Irish locations always subsist, as specters or traces, within a broader evocation of human alienation. The broader evocation could not, in fact, exist as it does without those traces.

Like the multidirectional nature of Stephen's quayside reveries at the end of *A Portrait*, and the Bowen heroine's simultaneous desire for rootedness and uprooting, the Beckett terrain is particular and concrete but irreconcilable with either a national or a global abstract. Each of these telling examples point to a modernism that arises less from an idealistic, poststatehood cosmopolitanism than from the indefinite deferral of native origin and the contradictory effort to think beyond or "outside" of it. This more continuous condition, not postnational but a move from one statelessness to others, has a different, but no less pervasive, global resonance.[5] By no means intellectually confining, to bring one's native irresolution abroad is to cultivate a rigorously expansive, decolonial and democratic mind, for it involves scrutinizing the dislocations of modernity—alienation, transience, social uprooting, loss—from the standpoint of a preexisting, subnational or presovereign experience of those same kinds of dislocation. Indeed, much of what we hail as "modernist" in the aesthetics and themes of Irish expatriate writing arises from the paradox of bordering an unresolved origin, and from the consequential awareness that the "national" and the "universal" are equally salient, yet equally unrealistic, modes of human experience.

◇
◇
◇
◇

CHAPTER 1

Ulysses, the Sea, and the Paradox
of Irish Internationalism

[I]t is at the heart of national consciousness that international consciousness
lives and grows. And this two-fold emerging is ultimately only the source of
all culture.

Frantz Fanon, *The Wretched of the Earth*

At the conclusion of his essay "On National Culture," Frantz Fanon summarizes the rationale for emphasizing national culture during decolonization:
a meaningful sense of national identity is a prerequisite, or stable conduit,
for reciprocal belonging in a broader global society. But this famous proclamation also reveals the tremendous challenge that many developing societies experience in identifying the relationship between their national and
international phases. Lingering beneath Fanon's taut biological metaphor is
the vexing reality of the unsynchronized and spatially uneven relationship
between these two stages or states of emergence.

Although postcolonial studies has often focused on the erosions and
fraught reconstructions of national or indigenous cultures in the wake of
imperialism, equally at stake is the tremendous influence that colonization,
and certain nationalist reactions to it, have on the global-economic and related transnational-cultural life of the subject population. Too often, these
systems conspire to usurp that population's ability to develop balanced
migrations and reciprocal socioeconomic exchanges, turning borders into
sites of surveillance, apprehension, forced emigration, and segregation from
international economic processes. Indeed, when we speak of "development," or the establishment of sovereign postcolonial states, much of what
we are referring to is the recovery from a drastically uneven entrance into

global capitalism, a recovery that does not and cannot follow simple, unidirectional models of movement from regional to universal allegiances, from national to international consciousness.

That the access to and control of ports, harbors, and waterways are vital to the economic and cultural development of a civilization is one of the most secure truths of world history. Yet when we consider development from a global perspective, it is also true that shipping ports and coastal infrastructures are often microcosms of the gross imbalances that exist between one locus of socioeconomic emergence and others, or between the subject populations of imperialism and the broader commercial systems that it aggressively introduces.[1] Especially in the colonies of a British empire for whom "ships and overseas trade were, as everyone knew, the lifeblood" (Hobsbawm 24), local ports, rivers and navigable estuaries have not been vital arteries connecting the national organ to the international body, but sites that reveal the diseased perversion of such potentially reciprocal flows—sites of mass emigration, controlled immigration, embargoes and sanctions, human cargoes, and fiercely exploitive imbalances of labor and capital. In short, maritime hubs offer an important focal point for the stifling, coerced economic dependencies that have repeatedly threatened Fanon's "two-fold emergence."

Throughout the opening chapters of *Ulysses*, which prominently feature the coastline of greater Dublin (including Dalkey, the imperial port at Dún Laoghaire then called Kingstown, Sandymount Strand, and glances north to Howth), Joyce provides crucial insight into Ireland's particular and acute experience of this broader problem. Postcolonial interpretations of *Ulysses*, in their long overdue effort to show "how a text . . . which for years has been gleaned for every last attribute of its [apolitical] narrative theatrics, might have all the time been operating as a postcolonial novel" (Duffy 5), have typically focused on the nation—or potential nation—as the damaged entity on whose behalf Joyce's writing subverts and dismantles imperial discourse. Enda Duffy for example observes that the opening chapters deploy a series of imperialist stereotypes of Irish national and cultural life—the "derivative interpellating narratives [of] the oppression of Ireland as a colony" (26–27)—so that the novel can proceed to deconstruct them (26–27). Vincent Cheng meanwhile notes, in *Joyce, Race, and Empire*, that Stephen's ouster from the Martello tower is "a figure and a parable for Ireland itself . . . a synecdoche for the Irish condition [that] resonate[s] with the home rule question and the longing for Irish autonomy from English occupation" (151–52).

If, however, we shift our attention from symbolic national territory to the importance of coastal setting, and then expand our theoretical framework to include the intervention of pragmatic sovereignty in the dialectic of nationalism and cosmopolitanism, we begin to see that the more insidious crime, for Joyce, is the destruction of a legitimately *international* Irish identity.[2] More specifically, we come to see that *Ulysses* is shaped by its engagements with the challenges and contradictions of postcolonial internationalism, chief among which is the paradox that the insistence on a distinctly national phase of development is both a vehicle of decolonization and a threat to its ultimately transnational socioeconomic aspirations. In saying that *Ulysses* is "shaped by" its engagements with this paradox, I mean that even as it exposes the ways in which the decoupling of national and international modes infected Dublin life, it also reflects Joyce's much more immediate, less conclusive effort to resolve the profound contradictions which result from that decoupling. In what follows, I will first examine the ways that *Ulysses* exposes these contradictions, and then consider how, via the consciousness of Bloom and Stephen, it becomes more intimately entangled in them.

Given its setting of the Martello tower at Sandycove, the Telemachus chapter is of course full of references to the sea, ships, and maritime trade and travel. We begin with Buck Mulligan's classical and romantic homage to the sea—his shouting "Thallata! Thallata!" (1.80) as he looks from the tower across Dublin Bay and proclaiming, in reference to Algernon Swinburne and George Russell, respectively, that the sea is our "great sweet mother" (1.78) and "our mighty mother" (1.85). These reverential pronouncements are ironically undercut in several ways, most compellingly by the episode's references to drowning, a tactic Joyce continues in "Nestor" (as Stephen's pupils read "Lycidas," Milton's elegy for a friend who drowned in the Irish Sea) and in "Proteus," where Stephen reflects at length on "the man that was drowned nine days ago off Maiden's rock" (3.322–23), the same "man who had drowned" with whom he had begun to associate in "Telemachus" (1.675).

These references, combined with the overarching irony of the Homeric parallel—the *Odyssey* is, after all, the tale of a long, serially interrupted effort to sail home and restore threatened sovereignty—help create an initial subtext whose theme is the imperiled capacity for departure and return via the sea. Mulligan's "thallata!" cry in fact alludes to *Anabasis*, wherein a remnant of Greek mercenaries, after being betrayed by their Persian officers, march home through the Assyrian desert and Armenian mountains, then joyously hail "the sea!" as they reach their return route, the Black Sea. The allusion suggests a journey commissioned by another empire that has been fraught with failure, narrow escape, and negative return for traveling labor. All of this attention to threatened sea routes is meant to symbolize not only Stephen's recently ill-fated expatriation, but also the damaged transnational livelihood in Ireland which is the material basis of that failure. This is confirmed when, immediately after Mulligan's energetic cry, Stephen gazes down despondently at the water and notices "the mailboat clearing the harbormouth of Kingstown" (1.83–84). The inevitable mailboat, leaving for Holyhead, indicates foreign control of Ireland's coasts (and its international commerce) just as the point of view from which Stephen "looks down" on the harbor scene, the Martello tower, is a potential vista of transnational aspiration that is in reality a site of imperial surveillance and containment.[3]

Although Kingstown had been made the Irish mail terminus in the late nineteenth century, and although mail did expeditiously and regularly cross the channel from Holyhead to Kingstown, the "mailboat," as it came to be called, was actually a large passenger ferry connecting the two port towns. This cross-channel connection was also a link to the heavily traveled metropolitan rail lines (and, soon, motorways) on either side of the water: in Wales and England, between Holyhead and London; in Ireland, between Kingstown and Dublin. As a 1908 *Handbook to the City of Dublin* puts it, "[t]o the Victorian age the rise of suburban Dublin is to be attributed, which had its beginning in the construction of Kingstown Harbour" (274). Despite this mass transit, and the attendant spectacle of large ships, vibrant commerce, and period fashion that it often brought to Kingstown pier (see figures 1–3), the reality is that this commercial bustle was a classic sign of uneven development—the symptom of a modernized pale whose accrued capital in travel, trade, and culture, already disproportionately distributed within that pale, had also reached only sporadically into the wider Irish society.

It is this economic imbalance, and not just cultural imperialism, which underscores the cultural stasis that pervades the chapter. The only intellectual and artistic goods that Ireland has recently produced, Joyce suggests, are of the static, nonregenerating type incentivized by such unidirectional economic flows. The traveling Englishman Haines's willingness to pay Stephen for his witticisms, the ironic difference between national-ism's symbolic investment in peasant women and the Irish-illiterate milk woman—likely a transplant from rural Ireland[4]—who gets shortchanged, and Mulligan's hedonistic encouragement that Stephen take advantage of Haines's offer so that "the bards [can] drink and junket" (1.467) each rep-resent the decadent cultural caricatures favored by a colonial tourist econ-omy. As Stephen implies, the market for anything else is limited at best: "The problem is to get money. From whom? From the milkwoman or from him. . . . I see little hope . . . from her or from him" (1.497–501). At the end of the chapter, Joyce's famous reference to usurpation (of Stephen's home by Haines and Mulligan, of Ireland by the global designs of others) might, then, be more specifically understood as the appropriation of Ireland's abil-ity to be functionally global, the ongoing denial of its mutually productive exchange with the broader ecumene.

In "Nestor," Joyce more thoroughly develops this theme, and again em-ploys Ireland's appropriated and partitioned coastal territory as a fitting site in which to do so. On multiple levels, the episode plays upon the striking contrast between a British imperial state that has expanded its influence by controlling the seas (as well as the economic exchanges between itself, its colonies, and other nations) and an Ireland that has not been able to cul-tivate an international consciousness because its trade is tightly restricted by England and its extranational self-image is confined to an anticolonial obsession with English culture. The most obvious example of this contrast is during the history lesson on Pyrrhus that Stephen is teaching at a school for boys in the wealthier, Protestant suburbs of Dalkey. When a befuddled student answers with a pun ("Pyrrhus, sir? Pyrrhus, a pier. . . . A kind of bridge. Kingstown pier, sir" [2.26–33]), Stephen responds with the cryptic joke that Kingstown pier is "a disappointed bridge" (2.39). The joke, which the students do not understand and which Stephen fears will make him a "jester at the court of his master" when he later tells it to Haines (2.43–44), of course hints at his own failed exile, but it also implies that the pier, under the control of the imperial British state in both name and function, is a false bridge to the wider world. It is "disappointed" both in the Latin sense that it is "pointed away from" equitable international exchanges and in the legal sense that it is incorrectly "appointed," or deeded in ownership. For Joyce, who saw ancient Ireland as vibrantly and materially cosmopolitan—as a gathering place for Europeans and the center of a culture that "[spread] throughout the continent a . . . vitalizing energy" (*CW* 154)—and who saw modern Ireland as a racially diverse society coerced into attitudes of ethnic essentialism,[5] Stephen's joke about the pier is also symbolic of Ireland's *lost* or forgotten transnational identity. The context and the setting of the joke further substantiate this interpretation.

The context is a history lesson during which Stephen wonders to himself, via Aristotle, about how the possible or potential in human affairs eventually becomes the actual, the recorded events of history that can "not . . . be thought away" because "[t]ime has branded them and fettered [and] lodged [them] in the room of the infinite possibilities they have ousted" (2.50–51). The "disappointed bridge" thus raises the question of whether Ireland was fated—as in Stephen's grim forecast that his riddle will only win condescending approval from Haines—to be fettered as a servant in England's global-oceanic design, or whether there might be a counterfactual trajectory of events wherein Ireland was to continue to develop as a sovereign presence in an international system. A later echo of this effort to think against the self-manifesting, progressive temporality of imperial capitalism is Bloom's question, in "Eumaeus," about how "to meet the travelling needs of the public at large, the average man" without first knowing "whether it was the traffic that created the route or vice versa" (16.537, 567).[6] These concerns also resonate in "Lestrygonians," when Bloom wonders "How can you own water really? It's always flowing in a stream, never the same" (*UL* 8.93–94). These direct and indirect references to the difficulty of discerning Ireland's agency and position within the time frames of global development return us to Joyce's acute awareness of Fanon's paradox: the problem of how the emerging postcolony, which has focused on constructing or reconstructing a distinct national consciousness, is to conceptualize its role in an international system.

Joyce's use of setting in the episode suggests he was also deeply aware that this paradox has a spatial dimension. As Mulligan notes in jest, when Stephen goes to teach in the upper-middle class seaside vistas of "Vico road, Dalkey" (2.24–25), he has crossed one of the many borders that conceptually divide Ireland's urban regions into communities of nationalists and unionists, Catholics and Protestants, the culturally Irish and the "west Britons." Not surprisingly, Stephen can only think of his pupils as the sons of "welloff people, proud that their eldest son was in the navy" (2.24–25) even though he rightly senses that they share his feeling of national-historical disaffection: "For them *too* history was a tale like any other too often heard, their land a pawnshop" (2.46–47; my emphasis). More than just a "cynical [reflection] of [Stephen's] own failed attempt to fly by the nets Irish culture has thrown at him" (Rickard 17), the reference to the misdirected and externally owned shipping pier is therefore part of a broader interrogation of the temporal and spatial logic of "post" coloniality—of when and where such a phase of existence can be positioned if the conditions of achieved nationhood are separated from those of an active and actual internationalism. As R. F. Foster notes, even during the early years of the Irish Free State "98 per cent of Irish exports went to the UK" (522). Given that Joyce was now living in Trieste, where many "well appointed" piers extended from bustling piazzas into the Adriatic and where cosmopolitan culture existed alongside strong factions of irredentist nationalism, it is logical that he would make the critical comparison between the two coastal cities, and increasingly recognize that the separation of the two conditions was a crippling falsehood.[7]

There is much to support the argument that the bracketing out of global flows from the conceptual space and time of the postcolonial nation is a form of false consciousness—a lie of omission delivered via the hegemony of a first world inter-*state* system whose members were able to historicize their nationhood at roughly the same time that they established state sovereignty (or were making the transition from earlier forms of sovereignty). For although there is ample evidence, not to mention psychological and strategic merit, to the idea that an insulated national period must precede international engagement, it does not square with what we know—from de Certeau, Hobsbawm, Bhabha and others—about the time frame in which national histories and traditions are actually constructed. It is antithetical, in other words, to the fact that much of a nation's historical identity is constructed in any given present, typically at the *same time* that the nation seeks to identify itself relative to others (the audience for its self-creation necessarily being both internal and external). Nor does Fanon's injunction that "the mistake . . . lies in wishing to skip the national period" (247) align with what we know, from transnational historians and poststructural anthropologists,[8] about the role of cross-border migrations of labor, capital, and ideas in the production of what are only later imagined as home grown economies and cultures. The same is true of "multiculturalism," which cannot simply be the historical phase that follows a global condition of "mono-culturalism," for what was often lacking was not the conditions of national or cultural plurality, but the ability to affirm or elaborate them.[9]

One might propose, then, that the longer a given nation-state has been settled and established—the longer the national idea has been "bonded to the territorial state" (Cheah, "Introduction" 26)—and the more that the imperial expansion of the state has been naturalized, the easier it is for the subjects of that state to repress these inherent contradictions, and, in turn, project and perpetuate *elsewhere* the idea that the separation of the two modes is natural. In many colonized societies, where this idea, like nation-alism itself, is inherited via the already untimely mode of anticolonialism, the postponement of the territorial state can easily become proportional to the exclusiveness of the conceptual boundaries that are erected around the national idea (as race, ethnos, culture, popular history) which comes to serve as its placeholder. This is why, for example, Eavan Boland has written that "the love of a nation is a particularly dangerous thing when the nation pre-dates the state" (*Object Lessons* 12). Part of the danger is the insidious irony that, under such conditions, the separation of the national and inter-national modes in time, as well as in space (for example, partitions, class enclaves, racial zones), can actually become accepted as the primer for a role on the international stage. One thinks of the uneven playing field upon which Fielding and Aziz discuss nationalism in Forster's *A Passage to India*. Aziz's half-hearted cry for nationhood, "No foreigners of any sort!" (361), uttered even as he is excluded from English society, is a grim foreshadowing of Indian partition.

The problem, in Ireland as in India, is that once this derivative essen-tialism is asserted as conscious design, its inherent contradictions cannot be repressed in the same way that they can be in the achieved or imperial state. Thus, they remain at the surface. As a result, the individual's ability to think of his or her actions as meaningfully involved in a national milieu is constantly assailed by the fact that the conceptual history and geography of the nation remain contested, their inherently constructed nature always too painfully evident, too much of a daily dispute to become "branded . . . and fettered [and] lodged" in collective memory (2.49–50). The national phase or national modality, which despite this fragmentation continues to be gov-erned by an ideal of essential unity, therefore threatens to extend indefi-nitely, all the while postponing an international identity that itself becomes distorted and idealized in the process. Left in an untimely relationship to interstate dynamics and incipient globalization, citizens of the late colony are thus easily caught between the habit of recognizing (or misrecognizing) the local and the daily in terms of competing national abstractions and the inclination to romanticize, obfuscate, or demonize existing extranational and subnational phenomena.

Ulysses certainly diagnoses these problems, often with searing and uncanny objectivity. After all, much of the novel focuses around the Ireland-born son of a Hungarian Jew from "Szombathély, Vienna, Budapest, Milan, London and Dublin" (16.534–36)—"Leopold Bloom of no fixed abode" (15.1158)—who negotiates multiple ethnic affiliations and exhibits cosmopolitan feeling but is repeatedly misunderstood and marginalized by nation-centric cliques. Of the many scenes in the novel involving Bloom that demonstrate the multifaceted political and psychological condition just described, the most notable occurs in the Cyclops episode. In the scene, the unnamed narrator, the Citizen, J. J. Molloy, and Joe Hynes are gathered at Barney Kiernan's pub discussing national concerns, chief among which is the British trade restriction on Irish cattle. Joe Hynes tells the narrator he is going to "give the Citizen the hard word about" a recent meeting of the "cattle traders [association]" concerning "the hoof in mouth disease" (12.62), the infection that British officials had cited as the reason for the Irish livestock embargo.

Their discussion quickly becomes a well-rehearsed tirade about the long history of imperial usurpation of Irish industry and the maritime trading autonomy that was once a sign of Ireland's international vitality and economic sovereignty: "We had our trade with Spain and the French and with the Flemings before those mongrels were pupped," the Citizen boasts,

> Spanish ale in Galway, the winebark on the winedark waterway.
> —And will again, says Joe
> —And with the help of the holy mother of God we will again, ... Our harbours that are empty will be full again, Queenstown, Kinsale, Galway, Blacksod Bay. .... And will again, says he, when the first Irish battleship is seen breasting the waves with our own flag to the fore. (12.1296–1307)

As Joyce well knew, the basic argument here is valid and relevant (in fact, he made similar arguments in articles he wrote on Irish ports and trade for

Irish and Italian newspapers, which I will examine shortly). The problem lies in the men's compulsion to make the present trade crisis an immediate symbol of a vast history of transgressions, thus projecting the weight of accumulated history onto it, a maneuver that they make throughout the episode and that Joyce relentlessly parodies with inflated narrative styles.

The result is a tragically self-manifesting rhetoric of postponement in which the present problem is obscured by idealistic images of the distant past and distant future: "and will again . . . and will again." But the deepest irony of the scene is that as the men bond over this inflated yearning for a restored *international* Ireland, they cast a xenophobic eye at Bloom, who represents both transnational and economic livelihood in a very quotidian, realistic sense. Unable to recognize this, they ultimately revile him as a moneylending, rootless Jew whose only value lies in the possibility that he may have helped Arthur Griffith to devise the plan for Sinn Féin to follow Hungarian models of national self-fashioning.

The question of where Joyce's *modernism* is located relative to the troubling desynchronization of national and international consciousness—or the degree to which the subjective and polyvocal techniques of *Ulysses* can represent an aloof diagnosis of its effects—is a more complex matter, however. We recognize this when we consider the ways in which Bloom and Stephen, Joyce's focal characters, can themselves become stymied by the extremes of the national/international binary, and unable to think outside of its paradoxes. The Cyclops scene is typically understood as opposing the open-minded, mobile perspective of Bloom to the narrow-minded myopia of the nationalist Citizen. This opposition is often interpreted as being reinforced at the level of style, the idea being that Bloom's disruptive interventions in his society are paralleled by Joyce's parallactic, polyvocal narrative styles.

In similar fashion, Stephen's cerebral, critical distance from his environment—epitomized by his claim that "history . . . is a nightmare from which I am trying to awake" (2.377)—has been seen as a gateway into the critical stance of Joyce's modernism relative to historical conditions. As Trevor Williams puts it in *Reading Joyce Politically*, "the development of a critical consciousness in Stephen Dedalus and in Leopold Bloom's . . . persistent silent questioning of the status quo, are the beginnings of a counter hegemony [that is paralleled] [a]t the level of technique" (xiv). But when it comes to the difficulties of developing transnational consciousness, both characters struggle to apprehend the problem to the extent that their own thoughts reveal its symptoms.

In the scene discussed above, for example, Bloom's vision of universal tolerance, his protest against "national hatred among nations" (12.1428) and his disdain for "hatred, history, all that" (12.1481) suggest an overly idealistic, politically abstract brand of cosmopolitanism. This too is symptomatic of the broader problem I have identified, for, *like* the territorial ethnocentrism it contests, it is part of a more pervasive inability to find pragmatic, realistic common ground between national and global concerns.[10] Put more accurately, it too reflects the insipid conundrum bequeathed to "developing" nations by interactive sovereign states: the challenge of locating such a ground amidst widespread belief that the national is territorial and monocultural while the global, which comes later, is nonterritorial and hybrid. The opposition between Bloom and the Barney Kiernan's clique becomes further muddled when we consider that the Citizen and his cronies are not just espousing nationalist clichés, but are also trying in their own way to imagine Ireland *internationally*, as part of what J. J. Molloy boastfully calls "[t]he European family" (12.1202). Joyce's own voice or position is itself split between the two, given that his writings consistently demonstrate both a wish for Ireland to be a recognized, sovereign member of the international community (culturally and politically) and a predilection for imagining universes—moral, psychological, linguistic—that obliterate or transcend national and cultural particularity.[11]

More than a mock-epic battle between myopic, rooted nationalists and the mobile, broad perspective of Bloom, the episode is thus a layered, self-reflexive revelation of how deeply and pervasively the lack of democratic sovereignty impacts the global identity of the colonized. Joyce, who was abroad during the Great War and Ireland's war of independence, and whose nationalist and cosmopolitan perspectives both became more sophisticated in these years, is certainly more aware of this dilemma than his characters. But it is hard to interpret his display of technique in this episode as advocating any particular mode of resistance to it, or as providing an aesthetic analogue for how to counter its hegemony. Once we recognize that it is a key crisis of the chapter, for example, we can no longer rely on the critical trend of linking the multiple narrators and perspectives with Bloom's mobile, open-minded, disruptive interventions in the societal "norm," a trend evident in both high-modernist and postcolonial criticism.

What we might reasonably conclude, though, is that Joyce's national and transnational commitments were *both* becoming more defined, that he was still in the throes of forging a composite in which neither was superseded by the other, and that doing so required him to think along two temporal trajectories simultaneously: the first in which the construction of national identity is leading to a sovereign place in world society and the second in which the impermeable borders of that construction can be disavowed, knowingly conscribed to the nearsighted past. The opinions about national belonging advanced by the Citizen and his cronies, which offer *both* a narrow perspective that Joyce ruthlessly parodies *and* a salient, material counterpoint to Bloom's vague cosmopolitanism, reflect this double-consciousness, as does the monumental effort to articulate and mock cultural nationalist concerns simultaneously throughout the episode. Even the interpolated stylistic parodies embody this tension, insofar as Joyce's own literary project, and its efforts to have Irish culture emerge internationally, are among the things they satirize: "the grave elders of the most obedient city, second of the realm, . . . had taken solemn counsel whereby they might . . . bring once more into honour among mortal men the winged speech of the seadivided Gael" (12.1185–89).

In "Sirens," Bloom's flatulence-interrupted reading of Robert Emmet's claim that he will not "have done" until Ireland "takes her place among the nations of the earth" (1284–94) has been interpreted, in cosmopolitan-modernist tradition, as Joyce's innovative mockery of provincial patriotism. Postcolonial critics, in contrast, have cited it as a rebellion against "the commodification of Emmet's words," and, therefore, as a microcosm for the aesthetic resistance to colonial hegemony that *Ulysses* enacts in its entirety (Enda Duffy 88–89). Both readings assume that Joyce's aesthetic trumps the historical conditions it faces. In the first, it vanquishes nationalist provinciality while in the second it subverts imperialist assimilation by positing a perpetually recalcitrant Irish identity.[12] But given that the material conditions of Joyce's Dublin, and indeed of Emmet's Ireland, include the production and recognition of the international *within* the national, I'm not so sure that Bloom's famous release amounts to an absolute defiance. For we can also read the scene as a manifestation of the very fear that haunts Emmett's compulsion to extend the national struggle: the fear that, despite such extension, Ireland will fail to achieve international consciousness. After all, whether Bloom is a stereotype-breaking, multiethnic Irishman or a postnational, cosmopolitan *flâneur*, the fact remains that he has just been effectively exiled from an esoteric community preoccupied by national debate, just as he is in "Cyclops." Perhaps the historical crisis with which Joyce's art contends is neither a nationalism whose only alternative is exile, nor an imperial takeover whose only alternative is the insubordinate poetics of anticolonial resistance, but the perceived naturalness, in the late colonial environment, of these oppositions themselves.

Partly in response to the desynchronization and exaggerated opposition of national and international modes, but also enmeshed within it, the modernism of *Ulysses* is produced by contending desires and obligations: on the one hand, to construct and articulate an Irish identity not yet recognized by the world; on the other, to dissolve Irish cultural particulars into a synchronic universe of contingent, heterogeneous identities. This double compulsion is elaborated exponentially in *Finnegans Wake*. Indeed, we might speculate that where the paradoxes of postcolonial internationalism are concerned, Joyce's modernism is neither subverting nor transcending them, but emerging in their midst, voicing their inherent challenges. This would not mean that Joyce has been "duped" by history, nor that he escapes its materiality by responding to it on a separate aesthetic plane. It would simply mean that one of the conditions to which his art responds—that of being pulled between a potential world society and a contested colony not yet able to be absorbed equally into any imagined global community—is *already* suffused with profound philosophical obstacles, as well as potential insights about concurrent, plurilocal belonging that are simply not available to those who have not seriously contemplated these obstacles.

The communicative crises and philosophical conundrums that preoccupy Stephen Dedalus throughout the opening chapters of *Ulysses* are a monumental example of an effort to comprehend and negotiate the colony's national/international paradox. His increasingly ironic, reflexive, and cerebral perspective constitute an intense, ultimately inconclusive intellectual response to the postponement of Ireland's sovereign participation in world society, and the simultaneous need to develop and emerge from a distinct national consciousness that comes with it. After all, one of the main things that troubles Stephen, who in *A Portrait of the Artist as a Young Man* could only find "proud sovereignty" via aesthetic reverie (183), is that his art and his international identity do not really exist outside of the realm of imagination and possibility. Like Bloom, his cerebral, critical ruminations upon his society are therefore liable to reflect, rather than transcend, the mutually negating or mutually distorting relationship between home and world which plagues that society.

A prime example of this susceptibility is his inclination to read his situation in terms of a stark opposition between nationalistic generalizations and exilic-cosmopolitan alienation. Stephen proclaims that "all Ireland is washed by the gulf stream" (1.476), declares the broken mirror "a symbol of Irish art," and reads the milk woman as a national symbol. Because he so immediately subjects every local event or object to national abstraction—extending his near-obsession, in *Portrait,* with making totalizing or final statements about the Irish race—he leaves himself no option but to map his internal contemplation onto an equally abstract cosmos: "his own rare thoughts, a chemistry of stars" (1.652–53). This tendency of Stephen's to turn away by turning inward, coupled with his physical departure from Ireland, has been read as either a "cosmopolitan" gesture or a need to subvert both imperialism and its nationalist derivatives, but it might be more pragmatically understood as a mystification or misrecognition of the extranational, a projection onto the world of the epistemic disjunctures that define his perception of Ireland. The "cracked looking glass of a servant," in other words, has also disfigured his image of the world (1.146). Noting that the nationalism/cosmopolitanism binary is itself a factor in delayed postcolonial sovereignty, Pheng Cheah has observed that "the understanding of cosmopolitanism that opposes it to nationalism and sometimes equates it with exilic migrancy only makes sense *after* the nation has been bonded to the territorial state" ("Introduction" 26). Indeed, the struggle between historical nightmare and universal art that many readers associate with Stephen and Joyce can also been seen, in its entirety, as a symptom of the exaggerated separation of national and international modes that accrues during the indefinite transition from colony to state.[13]

Seen in this light, Stephen is plagued by the same general problem as his students, Deasy, Haines, and Mulligan (and the social sectors they represent): the geographical and historical episteme in which he operates has made thinking beyond the nation into an act of the mystical or fantastic. Like Bloom and the Citizen, Stephen and Deasy are opposites on the surface but quite similar insofar as they both inflate or abstract extranational reality in unreasonable ways. For the protectionist Deasy, border-crossing means a diabolical permeability that leads to immigrant masses (especially

Jews) who erode the nation; for the brooding, now-defeated expatriate Stephen, it is a vague, ever-deferred cultural and intellectual space that he imagines as existing beyond the "nightmare" of "history," or outside of the seemingly interminable national modality. If we look more closely at what is often read as Stephen's smug, erudite dismissal of Deasy's bombastic missive against the English embargo of Irish livestock—the central reference to international maritime trade in "Nestor"—the validity of this argument emerges more distinctly.

After lecturing Stephen on coinage and financial conservatism, Deasy asks Stephen to read an editorial that he has composed about the foot-and-mouth disease which is infecting Irish livestock and threatening "an embargo on Irish cattle" in English ports (2.339). Like the heated conversation in "Cyclops," his letter refers to an actual incident that came to a head in 1912 and is thus one of the many anachronisms that, as Enda Duffy has shown, indicate Joyce's investment in contemporary Irish politics while he was working on *Ulysses* in Trieste. The restrictions on Irish livestock had indeed threatened Irish commerce, raised vociferous debates about national economic policy, and, especially as Joyce saw it, exposed the relationship between Ireland's interminable national debate and its uncertainty about how to present itself in international affairs. In the letter, Deasy inflates the issue to symbolic historical status, posing it as the latest in a long legacy of England's conspiratorial subversions of Irish industry, chief among which is the forever delayed nineteenth century plan to build a major transatlantic seaport in Galway.

Stephen's glance through the letter indicates that he sees these arguments as tired clichés: "May I trespass on your valuable space? That doctrine of *laissez faire* which so often in our history. Our cattle trade. The way of all our old industries. Liverpool ring which jockeyed the Galway harbor scheme" (2.323–26). The arguments are indeed tired ones, or truths elaborated by untruths. The Galway harbor, for example, was likely not undermined by competitor interests in Liverpool, but by mismanagement (Gifford 37). Yet there is more to Stephen's reaction, and considerably more to Joyce's own interest in these affairs, than an argument for the artist's ability to outwit the historical status quo.

For one, Stephen at some level sympathizes with the problem Deasy addresses, as did Joyce, even though he harbors deep distaste for the strident, self-invested, and rather exotic solution Deasy proposes. As in "Cyclops," the larger problem is that the cooperative language in which to discuss and elaborate their degree of shared opinion—a *local* discourse beyond national debate—eludes both men entirely. Like the Citizen's diatribe against British control of Irish harbors, the topic of concern in Deasy's letter—embargoes in the east and the denial of transatlantic connectivity in the west—is something Stephen can only partly reject, and that the novel itself must articulate on two levels. At one level, the letter symbolizes the over-rehearsed, national-historical obsession from which Stephen is "trying to awake," while at another, it serves as a valid indictment of the usurped sovereignty that is still unresolved, and which validates the notion that the national history is *not yet finished.*

To be sure, one cannot simply "wake" from such a paradoxical condition. This inevitably divided feeling about the incomplete national phase emerges later in the episode when Stephen, after having wrung free of Deasy, decides to assist him with his anti-embargo letter ("Still I will help him in his fight" [2.430]) and then smirks at the thought of Mulligan accusing him of being "the bullockbefriending bard" for doing so (2.430–31). The subtle epiphany here suggests a symbiotic relationship between domestic tolerance and functional internationalism that is thinkable but realistically unavailable in the prevailing conditions.

In complicating the nation/world and history/art oppositions that pertain to the relationships between Bloom and the Citizen and Stephen and Deasy, I have suggested that the trials of articulating an international Irish consciousness are voiced as much through Deasy and the Citizen's coterie as they are through Bloom and Stephen's efforts to see their environment at a critical distance and from a universal perspective. Another reason I am inclined to think so is that, in 1912, Joyce himself took great interest in both the Galway harbor scheme and the British cattle embargo. He composed newspaper articles on both topics, for Irish and Italian newspapers, and traveled to the Aran islands where he studied the promotional materials for the proposed harbor.

In his article on the cattle trade, for *The Freeman's Journal*, Joyce notes the seriousness of the "national calamity," and assures readers that "Irish farmers and traders . . . have sound and solid reasons for demanding the reopening of the ports to healthy Irish stock" (*CW* 240). But he calls for Irish statesmen to act as confident diplomats rather than covert conspiracy-theorists who will only confirm British suspicions of Irish backwardness, or inwardness, and thus jeopardize "the confidence of the trading public" (*CW* 240). His piece on the Galway harbor, written for Trieste's *Il Piccolo della Sera*, is also concerned with the accumulating crises of deferred internationalism. The article indirectly comments on the harbor through the perspective of weary Aran islanders who have only trace memories of the expansive commerce that once emanated from nearby shores. They have forgotten the "long friendship between Spain and Ireland," writes Joyce, for "time and the wind have razed to the ground the civilization . . . of [their] forefathers" (*OCP* 204). The imagery here is akin to a cultural nationalist's opposition between the ideal past and its erosion under colonial modernity, but the important distinction is that what Joyce sees in the deep past is a multicultural Ireland that did not separate its expansive interactions from its rich local culture—a society of vernacular cosmopolitans who would not have known what it was to decouple or desynchronize the two spheres of being.

Joyce hints that the new port might restore (or "reappoint") this condition by circumventing the destructive one-way flow of Irish commerce across the channel: "[t]he old decaying city would arise once more. Wealth and vital energy from the New World would run through this new artery into blood-drained Ireland." However, in a stronger nod to the present-day problem of postponed sovereignty and externally controlled coastlines, he concludes the piece by comparing the proposed harbor to *Hy-Brasil*, the mystical land of promise that the fishermen of Aran legend envisioned on the horizon of the Atlantic: "Once again, after ten centuries or so, the mirage that dazzled the poor fisherman of Aran . . . appears in the distance, vague and tremulous on the mirror of the ocean" (*OCP* 203). Joyce's suggestion is that just as the ancient mirage, which implies America, has been made ironic by modern Ireland's mass emigrations, so too is the contemporary port a mirage that is ironically destined to be another "disappointed bridge." The pamphlet promoting the Galway harbor, which Joyce had been reading, more than substantiates these grim associations. Its authors envision better access to Canada, whose "recent industrial growth [has made it] the granary of great Britain," as well as a "highway to America, which is the great industrial storehouse of the future." The seaport would thus be "of incalculable advantage to British and American commerce, yet because it is in Galway and in Ireland, this benefit which God intended as a blessing is of no avail to them" (qtd. in *OCP*, 343n).

That Joyce was still caught up—geographically, politically, intellectually—in the effort to address the conundrums of postcolonial internationalism, and that certain aspects of his modernism are an outgrowth of his
own ongoing, inconclusive effort to combat them, is perhaps nowhere more
evident than in "Proteus," the episode which "come[s] nearer the edge of
the sea" (3.265) than any in Joyce's oeuvre. A plausible synecdoche for the
genesis of Joyce's art, Stephen's internal, philosophical meditation as he
walks along Sandymount Strand can be interpreted as an intense effort to
transcend and particularize a location at the same time. It is also densely
allusive, relentlessly subjective, and takes as its theme the cyclical nature
of all life, the shifting physical and material forms in which the universe is
made manifest. As such, I would argue, it constitutes a monumental attempt
to respond to an irresolute dialectic of colony and universe that perpetually
elides a sustainable international consciousness or identity. The most recent
chapters in Stephen's development as an artist, we might recall, attest to
precisely such an elision.

Just prior to his artistic epiphany in section IV of *Portrait*, he had "turned
seaward" from his path along Clontarf Road and crossed the bridge to Bull
Island, in Dublin Bay. From this symbolic, coastal vantage point he had
gazed back upon Dublin—a city "weary [and] patient of subjection" since
the days of the Norse invaders (181)—then turned eastward to look toward
a Europe that he envisioned, in stark contrast, as a world of achieved races,
established cultures, and firmly bordered nation-states: "out there beyond
the Irish Sea [was a] Europe of strange tongues and valleyed and woodbegirt and citadelled and of entrenched and marshaled races" (181). Caught
between the interminable colony and the lure of a Europe that appeared, in
contrast, as an ideal example of how independent nations produce international culture, he had decided to resolve the problem in art. That his art is a
substitute for an active *transnational* reality, or is an effort to forge one in the
mind, is also suggested by the coastal location of his epiphany. It is further
implied in the contradiction of national and cosmopolitan ambitions that
Stephen associates with his art and in the idealistic nature of each contradictory ambition. Rather than being a part of international culture, he imagines
himself transcending the earthly altogether: "A Voice from *beyond the world*
was calling" (181–83; my italics). Yet he will also resolve Ireland's unformed
national self-awareness by seeking, and giving form, to an equally metaphysical origin: the "uncreated conscience of his race" (276).

In "Proteus," having been called back to Dublin and again walking alone on its coast, he is having even more trouble reconciling nation and world. He notes with irony that while in Paris, one of his most significant interactions was with the exiled Fenian Kevin Egan, "unsought by any save me" (3.250). Despite his disdain for this encounter, he does feel a degree of sympathy for Egan. Indeed, the duo's meeting in Paris resonates with Joyce's own still-forming relationship to Ireland in Trieste: "they have forgotten Kevin Egan, not he them" (3.263–64). Thus, as in *Portrait*, he is again at the crux of national and international consciousness, unable to synthesize or actualize the two. In fact, his inclination to seek a resolution of this crisis at the level of philosophical and aesthetic abstraction has only been augmented. In other words, although his reflections *are* "purely" philosophical, their impetus or latent content is his inability to ascertain quotidian transnational actuality. His preoccupation with things returning—"wending back," "fall[ing] back" (3.419), being "call[ed] back" (3.420), "bring[ing] . . . back" (3.83–84), "homing" (505)—arguably manifest this deeper concern. His obsession with "ineluctable modalities" may also be seen as its abstract extension; that is, as a philosophical iteration of the question of whether one can emerge from the colonial nation, or whether it extends indefinitely.

The only way one can affirm that Stephen's abstract queries are *not* an extrapolation of the political situation I have been discussing is by making the smug assumption that the intellectual challenges which pertain to the political are *by their nature more limited* than the philosophical, as opposed to existing *on the same plane* as the philosophical. Stephen's famous question in this episode—"Am I walking into eternity on Sandymount strand?"— implies many philosophical conundrums, but none of these are more intellectually demanding than the political, local question that subsists within it: *does* the modality of postcolonial nationhood end? If not, do its shifting forms reveal the universal, or conceal it?

Homi Bhabha has written extensively about Fanon's formula for international self-recognition, noting the apparent contradiction in its requirement for the simultaneous "emergence and . . . erasure of the conscious of nationness." For Bhabha, this paradox is actually the key to a new postcolonial-cosmopolitan, or "vernacular cosmopolitan," understanding of global diversity. Bhabha reminds us that, for Fanon, "national consciousness is not nationalism," but the awareness of one's actions and interactions as meaningful relative to a national community or context. Therefore, national consciousness never *does* conclude but instead extends into dialogue with international communities "in a temporality of continuance" (43). The international sphere, in turn, can no longer be imagined as an undifferentiated, homogenous space of common humanity, as in Enlightenment ideals of cosmopolitanism, but must be understood, like the nation, as a site of ongoing "acts of cultural translation between here and there, private and public, past and present" (43). To recognize this subidealistic, constant negotiation between what is within and beyond the nation is to affirm the "potentially subversive, subterranean sense of community" that develops in the "disjunctures of space, time, and culture" which exist globally (43). I would argue that Stephen has encountered these communal negotiations and is desperately *trying* to imagine such acts of "cultural translation" between Ireland and Europe but he does not recognize these interactions in anything close to the affirmative and commonplace context that Bhabha does. Nor perhaps can he.

For what may be most important about Stephen's journey along the strand is that he is walking along a border that does not exist and that will remain contested throughout the century: the would-be physical limit of an independent Irish state, the potential point of confident departure into and exchange with other states, the Irish border that would be the "diaphane" of international consciousness itself. When Stephen is walking along it in 1904, this potentially porous threshold of the nation-state is riddled with signs of uneven development and imperial surveillance: harbingers of the restrictive border that it will soon become under the anxious, partial sovereignty of the Free State. In marked contrast to the vistas of Dalkey, a mere six miles south, the strand boasts "unwholesome sandflats" that "breath[e] upward sewage breath" from the polluted Liffey (3.147–48). Jutting into the beach from the corner of Strand and St. John's roads is a wide, imposing Martello tower (see figure 4), a symbolic counterpart to "the police barrack" that, in *Portrait*, he had passed on Clontarf Road, just before heading out to Bull Island. If not as extensively in 1904, then certainly during the 1916 to 1922 heyday of the Royal Irish Constabulary backed by paramilitary forces, this section of the strand would also have been regularly policed.

Given this setting, it is understandable that Stephen's thoughts are more of a hermetic, erotic montage of international culture than a fluid blending or affirmative negotiation of global locations. Linguistically, his mind jumps from Scots dialect to snippets of Italian, German, Hebrew, Hindu, Swedish,

FIGURE 1. Kingstown harbor, photochrome print, ca. 1895. Library of Congress, LC-ppmsc-09881.

FIGURE 2. Postcard of Kingstown harbor, ca. 1920–1930. Courtesy of Postcards of the Past.

Greek, and Latin. Culturally, it scans through images of the sensual in contemporary and medieval European art and the diverse, bohemian, noctur-
nal life that made Europe alluring to Stephen and that is no longer available,
at least without abjection, in Dublin. His recitation of the verses *"Won't you
come to Sandymount / Madeline the mare?"*—an allusion to the sensual wa-
tercolors of fin-de-siècle French painter Madeline Lemaire—encapsulates
the serious threats to Irish-European cultural translation that Stephen faces:
European culture is not only embargoed by a colony that has restricted
moral conscience to the realm of nation-building—a vibrant "Ireland [of]
the Delcassians" that has become "of Arthur Griffith now" (3.226–27)—but
is also idealized and eroticized as a result.

This contrast between an externally possessed coastal border and a cosmopolitanism turned inward, a potentially expansive sociocultural negotiation inverted and transformed into sensual reverie, is striking. To be sure,
it is an apt, formal conceit for the effort to think and act globally from a
location whose genuine and equitable involvement in interstate systems has
been assailed on all sides. Having crossed Ireland's nonexistent border in
both directions, and now walking along it while struggling to synthesize
memories of home and abroad, Stephen is clearly still engaged in a battle to

FIGURE 3. Kingstown harbor, ca. 1930, photo reproduction of postcard.
Courtesy of Postcards of the Past.

FIGURE 4. Postcard of Sandymount Strand, ca. 1950. Courtesy of the James Joyce Museum in Sandycove, Dublin.

perceive the interchange between home and world as something happening in Bhabha's realm of action, in real time and inhabited space. In conclusion, I offer that Joyce's modernism, which "culminates" in Anna Livia's internal, polyvocal, indefinitely postponed effort to reconcile Ireland and the universe in words, to merge the territory of the nation with the unappointed, circumfluent water of the world, also remains, in its entirety, so engaged.

CHAPTER 2

◊
◊
◊

"Forget! Remember!"

Joyce's Voices and the Haunted Cosmos

> Listen, listen! I am doing it. Hear more to those voices! Always I am hearing
> them. . . . Annshee lispes privily.
>
> *Finnegans Wake* 571.24–26

James Joyce's works often figuratively imagine or predict their own genesis.
One of the ways they do so is by using sensual images of voices breaking
silence, or the hearing of voices, as metaphors for the artist's creation of innovative narrative forms, his incipient "revolution of the word." In *Finnegans
Wake*, wherein Ireland becomes "Earalend" (546.33), Joyce relentlessly implies that the text's multilingualism and polyvocality are the result of long-
silenced voices straining to be heard by hearing impaired or sleeping listeners: "Hear, O hear, living of the land! . . . dead era, hark"! (68.19–28); "Hear,
O hear, Iseult la belle! Tristan, sad hero, hear!" (398.29); "Hear! Calls! Ev-
erywhair!" (108.23). A closer look at Joyce's self-referential preoccupation
with voice and silence, and its culmination in *Finnegans Wake*, supports the
critical trends regarding the three primary entities that are arguably speaking, or being spoken for, through the novel's revolutionary language: an ancient Ireland whose vital and expansive culture was lost to colonial modernity, the soul of the politically and morally independent artist, and woman
as a sexually sentient being. But it also reveals tensions between these
three trajectories of emerging voice that cannot be resolved by interpreting Joyce's innovations as strictly cosmopolitan modernist, postcolonial,
or feminist. I will propose that the complex, multidirectional relationship

between national and transnational identity in a postcolonial context offers us a more comprehensive way of understanding these tensions. Ultimately, we can interpret Joyce's motif of emergent voices, and by extension his own modernism, not as the triumph of a new aesthetic over any one historical condition or ideology, but as an expression of the unresolved contradictions between gender, nation, and human universals that inhere in the effort to represent a developing, marginalized Ireland on the international stage.

Like Derek Walcott, Salman Rushdie, and other writers who sought to represent their colonial homelands to international audiences using contemporary techniques, Joyce knew well that to entertain the notion of a global multicultural community from the perspective of a culture in the throes of decolonization is to risk sacrificing an identity in progress to a cosmopolitan modernity that is insensitive to colonial difference.[1] We can see this paradoxical situation, and its relationship to Joyce's concept of art-as-voice, when Joyce writes and speaks to Italian audiences about nationalist and cultural nationalist developments in his home country. Trying to explain the unjust hanging of a Gaelic-speaking peasant in rural Ireland, Joyce cites the "deaf and dumb" old man as "a symbol of the Irish nation at the bar of public opinion," noting that there is no way "to appeal to the modern conscience of England and other countries . . . [who conceive] of the Irish as highwaymen with distorted faces" (CW 198). Unlike expatriates who are able to speak with confident finality about the sovereign states and historicized cultures from which they have separated—Ezra Pound calling the United States a "half-savage country" and the West a "botched civilization" come to mind (I.5, V.4)—the postcolonial expatriate is more inclined to see his or her national identity as something still in process, something always already influenced by a deep but uneven relationship with the global visions of others. He or she is therefore more inclined to look upon the "native" culture as deeply in need of genuine global/national reciprocity, but likely to get shortchanged of its own development, and of others understanding its complex historical profile, in the process.

Identifying precisely this "colonial difference" in the approach to cosmopolitanism or humanitarian universals, Walter Mignolo challenges readers to imagine a global conversation in which those formerly silenced by imperial world systems are not simply subsumed into a vague ideal of hybrid multiculturalism. Says Mignolo:

While Cosmopolitanism [in the past] was thought out and projected from particular local histories [that were] positioned to devise and enact global designs, other local histories in the planet had to deal with those global designs [and their] abstract universals. . . . For that reason, cosmopolitanism today has to become border thinking, critical and dialogic, from the perspective of those local histories that had to deal all along with [the repercussions of such] global designs. (182)

Mignolo stipulates that in order for this to happen, cosmopolitanism "cannot be reduced to a new form of cultural relativism but must be thought out as new forms of projecting and imagining ethically and politically, from subaltern perspectives" (181). The crucial link between this "critical cosmopolitanism" and the tensions between Joyce's emerging voices lies in the idea of an extraction from colonial experience that is *not* a one-way entrance into an abstract "global design," and especially not an emergence from a given culture into a universe "of cultural relativism."

For Joyce, who is at times quite taken with the idea that an atavistic Irish identity has been repressed, silenced, forgotten, and disfigured (leaving Irish citizens "deaf and dumb . . . at the bar of public opinion"), the revival or waking of Irish culture is often a source of deep and genuine feeling. But it can also be the butt of jokes, an idea inextricable from a patriotism that had become narrow and illiberal in practice (as in Bloom's flatulence-interrupted reading of Robert Emmet's claim that the national cause must continue until Ireland "takes her place among the nations of the earth" [*UL* 11.1284–94]). Rather than different, opposable positions on a single geo-historical entity that can be identified as "Ireland," this shifting attitude reflects the challenge of defining an origin that is always contested—a connotative field whose political, cultural, and historical valences are constantly shifting and realigning, especially when one is called upon to state what it means to "be Irish" in the world at large.

As is structurally implicit in so much of the author's work, Joyce's Ireland can therefore be both a claustrophobic place whose tendency to restrict morality to the context of nation building inspires idealistic visions of its cosmopolitan opposite *and* an undiscovered country, a spatially and temporally capacious realm within which a multitude of individual lives are yet to be understood and expressed. As early as the lyric poetry of *Chamber Music*,

Joyce depicts his artistic soul and literary voice as struggling to awaken out of the first Ireland while simultaneously channeling the suppressed speech of the latter:

> From dewy dreams, my soul, arise,
> From love's deep slumber and from death,. . . .
> While sweetly, gently, secretly,
> The flowery bells of morn are stirred
> And the wise choirs of faery
> Begin (innumerous!) to be heard. (*CP* XV.1–12)

The reference to the artist's "soul" eschewing its social and mortal confines anticipates the many times in *A Portrait* that Stephen tunes out the "accustomed world" of colonial Dublin, "hearing its language for the last time," so as to permit the "call of life to his soul" and liberate his "lust of wandering . . . to set out for the ends of the earth" (184). But the fact that the "innumerous" voices that, in the fasion of *Finnegans Wake*, "begin to be heard" belong to "wise choirs of faery" implies that, ironically, the wellspring of this new expression is a vibrant cultural Ireland of the deep past. This superimposition of the spiritual awakening of the individual cosmopolitan artist and the vocal stirrings of the collective native culture anticipates the "recurring note of weariness and pain" in the "choirs of endless generations of [Dublin] children" (177) that haunts Stephen just prior to his "soaring" epiphany about the "imperishable" nature of art (183). Indeed, throughout Stephen's artistic awakening in part IV of *Portrait*, which is set on Ireland's coastal border and full of figurative linkages between incipient art and voices, waking and listening, Stephen's desire is not simply to steal away from a "weary [and] subject[ed]" Ireland while it lies silent and asleep, but somehow to counteract or avenge the containment from world society, the sequestration from international culture, that has led to its muted and passive state (181).

Stephen's threshold of expatriation and new expression is undeniably cosmopolitan, but its subtext is that he is "[d]isheartened" (181) by the shameful quiet of the "seventh city of Christendom" lying "prone in a haze," as "patient of subjection" as it was in the seventeenth century. Although it is on one level a lyrical expression of art's triumph over material conditions, this well-known scene is also laced with indicators of the paradoxical sources, or double locations, of the Irish artist's modernism. Consider, for example, Stephen's need to decipher voices within and without:

Disheartened, he raised his eyes towards the slowdrifting clouds. . . . a host of nomads on the march, voyaging high over Ireland, westward bound. The Europe they had come from lay out there beyond the Irish Sea, Europe of strange tongues . . . of entrenched and marshaled races. . . . He heard a confused music within him as of memories and names which he was almost conscious of but could not capture . . . ; then the music seemed to recede [into] one longdrawn calling note, piercing like a star the dusk of silence. Again! Again! Again! A Voice from beyond the world was calling. . . . This was the call of life to his soul not the dull gross voice of the world of duties and despair. (181–84)

Stephen's "confused music" recalls the "thought tormented music" of the interplay between unresolved nationhood and cosmopolitan longing that troubles Gabriel Conroy in "The Dead." For Stephen as for Gabriel, the implication is that on the threshold of departure from the incompletely comprehended national life, one senses its ghostly lacunae more acutely. Granted, for Stephen, the "dull gross voice[s]" (*P* 184) on the surface of late-colonial Dublin have so sedated the soul that it can only yearn for an ideal opposite: a "Voice from beyond the world" (*P* 184), an echo of the "other world" into which Gabriel supposes one should "pass boldly" (*D* 223). But those same morally strident voices have also silenced a deep and diverse Irish history and society. Thus, when he is on the verge of transcending the national question, Stephen is "almost conscious" of the "memories and names" of those who have comprised his native society, just as Gabriel is "conscious of, but [can] not comprehend" their ghostly presence (223). Stephen is often deeply affected by this subaltern population that still yearns to be heard, to be "summoned from sleep" (*P* 153), to be called to life, to speak or be spoken for. Here, this is reflected by the nomadic clouds, passing westward over Ireland, which seem to embody his wish to align cosmopolitan flight with an unearthing of the repressed vitality of the Gaeltacht—to have Ireland share the "entrenched" European nations' experience of a symbiotic relationship between national and international identity.

The wish to engage Ireland's as yet unrecognized, still occluded national culture in an international dialogue is also of course encapsulated in Stephen's paradoxical exile. He eschews his Irish background to free his creative spirit, but this gesture simultaneously reveals the incompleteness of that background: "the uncreated conscience of [his] race." Hardly triumphant in its detachment, this famous proclamation merely repeats the cycle of separation from and immersion in Dublin society that recurs throughout the novel—a cycle that registers the great difficulty of synchronizing national and international culture in a postcolonial context and that begins again in *Ulysses*, which opens with Stephen back in Dublin after a short, ill-fated, and ironic exile. Throughout *A Portrait*, Stephen's isolation from society can only be temporary, for he is always again compelled to absorb and channel its suppressed speech. For example, when his self-absorbed reveries of spiritual awakening and Catholic vocation threaten to remove him from physical life, his "consciousness of place ... ebb[s] back to him" as "the squalid scene" of Dublin overwhelms his senses: "the common accents, the burning gasjets in the shops, odors of fish and spirits and wet sawdust, moving men and women." Stephen asks an old woman directions to the nearest chapel and is "saddened and soothed by her voice" (152). This again suggests that the sources of his new, modern mode of expression cannot in fact lie "beyond the world" of his native environment, for they are in many ways contained within it. Inside, kneeling beside "bearded workmen with pious faces," he hears "the faint murmur of a voice [trouble] the silence" as one of the men begins his confession (153).

Even when the voices stirring restlessly within Stephen's artistic soul are calling him to seek freedom from cultural particularity and historical circumstance via artistic originality, they are also, ironically, a manifestation of his longing to "wake" local voices, to be the conduit of their suppressed speech: "His blood began to murmur in his veins, murmuring like a sinful city summoned from its sleep to hear its doom. Little flakes of fire fell and powdery ashes fell softly, alighting the houses of men. They stirred, waking from sleep, troubled by the heated air" (153–54). Indeed, across all of Joyce's work, the act of breaking silence—a figure of his own modernist point of departure—points to two deeply related, but still distinct, needs: on the one hand, to rise above national concerns via an art that responds to a socially and morally liberated conscience; on the other, to hear more clearly the suppressed sounds of the misunderstood homeland, to give voice to its "peculiar cases" that "desire to confess something" (*D* 11).

The matter becomes more complex, however, when we consider that emergent or nascent voices in Joyce's work are so often figured or cast as feminine. Indeed, Stephen's desire to give birth to his artistic soul is most intensely expressed, or potentially realized, when it is coupled with the motif of feminine bodies or voices waking from sterile, repressed silence into fertile, fluid speech. Such is the case with his ongoing efforts to speak, through the form of verse, to and for the "temptress of his villanelle" (*P* 242): "Towards dawn he awoke. O what sweet music! His soul was all dewy wet. . . . His mind was waking slowly to a tremulous morning knowledge. . . . O! In the virgin womb of the imagination the word was made flesh" (*P* 235–36). The repetition of the O, Joyce's symbol of feminine sexuality (the womb) as well as the eternal, here underscores the link between women, nascent artistic voice, waking, (nonterritorial) water, and breaking silence that is essential to *Finnegans Wake*. But it also involves a more complex and problematic balancing of the artist's cosmopolitan longing with his unresolved national identity. For what Stephen is arguably doing here is borrowing an entrenched, anticolonial Irish tradition of sensually feminizing the pre-Anglophone nation and transposing it into a sensual feminizing of the act of breaking free from the moral strictures of nationalism. In other words, he is taking the cultural-nationalist trope of the nation as a desired woman whose chastity is endangered, or whose youth has been eclipsed, and modulating it into an image of national transcendence: the erotic awakening of the universal soul out of the "weariness" and "ardent ways" of the insular and formative state (235).

This is by no means a simple gesture, and Joyce is certainly well aware of the problematic linkage between gender and nation in Irish history. Nonetheless, it reveals Joyce's own serious difficulty in overcoming what Margaret Mills Harper has called "the near fatal tendency [in Irish writing] to confuse the erotic with the national" (184). In the lectures on the Irish Renaissance that Joyce delivered in Trieste, Joyce's vexed relationship with this tendency is again evident. Facing the familiar challenge of trying to distance himself from Irish cultural traditions while also explaining and championing those traditions to unaware European audiences, Joyce speaks in gendered and sexually charged metaphors about the need for Ireland's "old national soul" either to awaken or to die out for good. Laced with references to repressed voices, his comments reveal the relationships, as well as the problematic tensions, between his sympathies for women, Ireland, and cosmopolitan conscience: "Ancient Ireland is dead just as ancient Egypt is dead. Its death chant has been sung, and on its gravestone has been placed the seal. The old national soul that spoke during the centuries through the mouths of fabulous seers, wandering minstrels, and Jacobite poets disappeared from the world with the death of James Clarence Mangan. . . . One thing alone seems clear to me. It is well past time for Ireland to have done once and for all with failure. If she is truly capable of reviving, let her awake, or let her cover up her head and lie down decently in her grave forever" (*CW* 169). In many letters to Nora, but especially those of the autumn of 1909 while he is in Dublin, sensing the national significance of his artistic emergence, and she in Trieste, Joyce employs a similarly volatile association between sensual womanhood, awakened artistic conscience, and a redeemed Irish race: "I thought I heard my country calling to me, or her eyes being turned towards me expectantly. . . . Everything that is noble and exalted and deep and true and moving in what I write, comes, I believe, from you. . . . O take me into your soul of souls and then I will become indeed the poet of my race. I feel this, Nora, as I write it" (qtd. in Richard Ellmann 287).

Not surprisingly, many of Stephen's most vexed efforts to command the contradictory sources of his artistic vocation involve the problem of speaking of, for, or to Irish women. Rarely is the forging fire of his young artistic conscience hotter than when, about to depart for Europe, he tries to separate his anger at women as the symbol of nationalism's moral provinciality from his awareness that their suppressed self-awareness is an unjust colonial symptom:

> On all sides distorted reflections of her image started from his memory: the girl in the ragged dress . . . who had called herself his own girl . . . , the kitchengirl in the next house who sang over the clatter of her plates . . . the first bars of *By Killarney's Lakes and Fells*, a girl who had laughed gaily to see him stumble . . . , a girl he had glanced at, attracted by her small ripe mouth. . . . And yet he felt that, however he might revile and mock her image, his anger was also a form of homage. He [had a] feeling that perhaps the secret of her race lay behind those dark eyes upon which her long lashes flung a dark shadow. He had told himself bitterly . . . that she was a figure of the womanhood of her country, a batlike soul *waking to the consciousness of itself* in darkness and secrecy and loneliness. (240; emphasis mine)

Here indeed are gathered all the signatures of Joycean artistic becoming: incipient voice (the song, the "ripe mouth"), the soul waking from sleep, the secrecy of confession, the Irish as an ancient and longsuffering "race," and the surfacing of feminine sensuality. And where these are gathered the tensions between the trajectories of Joycean linguistic revolution are also most visible. At one level, these lines indicate Stephen's strong compulsion to move beyond national preoccupations, to wake the soul's universal conscience from the sleep of a parochial morality; at another, they express a desire to articulate "the secret of her race," to hear the voice of a pre-colonial Irish soul waking up from the historical nightmare of imperial subjugation and nationalistic, cultural isolation.

Importantly, then, Joyce's women can be, and often simultaneously are, the vehicle of both transformations: the embodiment of what is universal (that is, for Joyce, that which is eternal, cyclical, fluid, and resistant to the grounded linearity and oppressive sexual binaries of the father, the nation, and the historian) as well as of what has been lost, unspoken or occluded in the ancient "race" or "old national soul." A further complication is that women, as actual beings, can also be, as they are here for Stephen, the unwitting sirens of nationalism's overdeveloped fixation on corporeal sin, the worst evidence of how cosmopolitanism in its classical sense (a *conscience* that rises above state-sanctioned morality) is being foreclosed. Given this triple and overlapping significance, Joyce's women are in a tremendously volatile position: perceived as a barrier to both artistic-cosmopolitan awakening and national-cultural renaissance, they also become the focal point of the desire to *unite* these objectives, to wake Irish subalternity not just into nationhood, but into a global or universal conscience. One of the most intriguing and troubling connections between woman's voice and Joyce's innovative language is that in order to serve as this focal point, she has no alternative but to experience this waking consciousness as does the artist: in isolation, secrecy, and darkness; that is, in a perverse exile.

It is not surprising that the effort to synthesize the Irish subaltern, the universal, and the feminine produces three of Joyce's most aesthetically charged passages: the endings of "The Dead," *Ulysses*, and *Finnegans Wake*. Each of these works concludes with a fluid lyricism that is new, in comparison to the prose that precedes it. Each also ends with a voice breaking imposed silences (in "The Dead," the voice of Michael Furey, as well as Gretta's utterance of the long withheld memory) and with an effort to recall a vital, sensual Irish memory while at the same time feeling diffused into the universe or world at large. Each also ends with a woman, alone or inaccessible and lying in bed in a liminal state of consciousness between sleep and waking, whose voice is the conduit or catalyst of all of these things.

ALP, whose voice or textual presence is arguably the greatest manifestation of Joyce's artistic originality, is certainly all of these things at once: she is the voice that breaks imposed silence or tries to alert deaf listeners ("Lsp! I am leafy speafing. Lpf!" [619.20]), the voice of atavistic Irishness ("the ancient legacy of the past," the "voi of day gone by" [68.26–27]), the universal or eternal entity, and the feminine. Yet she is also the river "babbling, bubbling, chattering to herself" (194.5), and she delivers her monologue "loonely in me loneness," and fades "a way a lone a last" (627.34, 628.15). This despite the fact that, as water, her body merges Irish locations (Dublin Bay, the Liffey) and global ones (such as the plethora of world rivers named in the washerwomen episode [213–16]) along a single continuum.

One could argue that the great irony of Anna Livia Plurabelle, whose "voice is the voice of Joyce" (Tindall 325), is that her speech is at once a possible culmination, or ultimate realization, of the sought-after formal originality through which Joyce deconstructs historical ideology and the character or event in his works most entangled in the traumatic intimacy of gender and national identity in Ireland. On the one hand, it can be argued that ALP is a quintessential agent of cosmopolitan freedom, a "universal" voice in the sense that Philippe Sollers means when he calls *Finnegans Wake* "an active transnationalism, . . . annulling the maximum number of traces [of nationalist consensus]" until "*nothing remains but differences*" (109). This is because, as poststructuralist interpreters point out, she is linguistic *différance* itself: the fluid river of signification that both compels and frustrates the phallogocentric effort to name, to historicize, to map. Within the male dream, she is repeatedly invoked as the possessor of the desired truth of history, the author of the "untitled mamafesta" (104.4) that presumably contains the truth of the sins of the father, the telos of his historiographic desire. She does not of course write or possess that actual history but instead *is* its inherent contingency, its self-demolishing basis in the wish for totality, the instability of signs that compels patriarchy to construct, to narrate, and to invent historical meaning. As the supplement and deferral of historical writing, ALP is "the mouth that tells not [which] ever attracts the unthinking tongue" (68.32), the reality of *différance* to which storytelling cyclically tries to lend structure.

Looked at from this angle, ALP is the ultimate transnational voice because to listen to her speak is to "hear" about the utter uselessness of particular and partial narratives, to hear in words the arbitrary linguistic current itself, the river Liffey which is at once the rivers of the world, the dark current in which all falsely named and separated objects are joined: "didn't you hear it a deluge of times, ufer and ufer, respund to spond? . . . It's that irrawaddying I've stoke in my aars. It all but husheth the lethest zswound. . . . Hey? What all men. Hot? His tittering daughters of. Whawk? Can't hear with waters of. The chittering waters of. . . . all them liffeying waters of. Night" (214.7–21). As the voices of the washerwomen fade, as the waters make them deaf to the sounds of "all men," we approach "hearing" ALP, the "tittering daughters" and "liffeying waters" of all speech. Carried to its end, however, this means that what she speaks of is the limit of language—the silence of an ultimate relativism—and the process of equivalent repetition which it generates: "Then all that was was fair. Tys Elvenland! Teems of times and happy returns. The seim anew. Ordovico or viricordo. Anna was, Livia is, *Plurabelle's to be*" (215.23–24).

Citing this deconstructive energy, many critics have interpreted ALP as the source of the subversive language of *Finnegans Wake* as a whole, that is, as the driving force of Joyce's entire, liberal project of transforming narrative. As Colin McCabe, a pioneer of this approach, puts it, "The *Wake* is a continuous lapsus. . . . [a perpetuation] of that moment when the subject loses control of his or her discourses [allowing] something else to be heard: 'it' speaks there where 'I' have lost control." For McCabe, the "it" which speaks is difficult to define: it is variously "a 'feminine libido' which threatens to break all boundaries" (146), "the unconscious" (147), and a potential "feminine discourse [that is] the constant excess of any limits prescribed by the male" (150–51). Easier to define is what is being destroyed, which is not only the "simple correspondence between sign and referent" that allows the illusion of "presence" but also "nationalist politics," a particularly insidious manifestation of the former because it offers "a new secure position . . . from which the trauma of difference can be ignored" (144). *Finnegans Wake* is thus the "riot of words" (143) and "reality of difference" (145) that we experience when we are liberated from such false securities. Sheldon Brivic, in *Joyce's Waking Women*, notes that "the *Wake's* deconstructive texture has an affinity with feminism in going against phallocentric authority," and argues, therefore, that "[t]he noncoherence of every page of the *Wake* speaks for Anna Livia Plurabelle" up until the point that she speaks for herself (4–5).[2] Anticolonial and Irish historical interpretations have also tended to align the text's noncoherence with the voice of the other, as in Terry Eagleton's claim that *Finnegans Wake* is an "alternative strategy of outstripping and overturning English linguistic accomplishments, . . . the non-Irish speaking Irish author's way of being unintelligible to the British" (268). Margot Norris, in her analysis of the tangible and intangible aspects of Joyce's musical rendering of rural Irish dialects, concludes by saying that "throughout *Finnegans Wake* what we hear is the voice of the other" (381).

Such approaches have afforded us invaluable understanding of Joyce's work. They also, if indirectly, tend to envision a one-way relationship between the repressed other and linguistic effects in the abstract: as standard English is deconstructed and the voice of the other is thereby articulated or "heard," language is universalized from the perspective of the oppressed, transformed into a nonhierarchical play of lexical difference that is either implicitly unlocated or working toward an ideal of global tolerance. The same might be said for the location of the always intentional Joyce who lurks in such interpretations, a Joyce cerebrally above the fray of the national and patriarchal discourses that he expertly diagnoses and dismantles. Yet the voices of *Finnegans Wake*, along with their author, can also be seen as grounded in a more contentious, ongoing, and unresolved interplay of feminine, national, and transnational concerns.

One key to this more irresolute context is Gayatri Spivak's analysis of the persistent occlusion of subaltern feminine voices in the discourses and texts of anti-imperial nationalism. Unfortunately, Spivak's work on subaltern voice has been so often invoked that its own capacity to signify has been ironically diminished. However, the core theoretical premise of "Can the Subaltern Speak" still maintains a great deal of immediacy with regard to Joyce's thematic and structural preoccupation with feminine voice, especially as that preoccupation plays out in *Finnegans Wake*. Spivak argues that because "the concept-metaphor of woman is pervasively instrumental in the *shifting* . . . of discursive systems," actual subaltern voice "is never fully recoverable, . . . is effaced even as it is disclosed, [and thus remains] irreducibly discursive" (203). The reason this much-cited argument affords a fresh angle on *Finnegans Wake* is that Spivak raises it largely as a counterpoint to poststructuralist tendencies to equate slippage and contingency in language, or the exposure thereof, with an articulation or representation of alterity.

In Irish studies, feminist critics have for decades argued a related point, namely that the longstanding use of "the concept-metaphor" of woman as a figure for Irish national identity—a practice that is maintained even as its types of feminine figures have shifted—makes it difficult for the voices and actions of Irish women to be interpreted as independent of national significance. Images of Irish womanhood have often changed from active to passive, pagan warrior to virginal victim, elusive muse to the austere mother or wife in mourning; but as they shift, and even where their changes signify a break with or loss of tradition, they still tend to symbolize some aggregate idea of Irish nationhood or identity. Together, the arguments of Spivak and Irish postcolonial feminists point to a more labyrinthine, less complicit, relationship between linguistic deconstruction, female voice, and the awakening of Irish or anticolonial consciousness.

Indeed, some of the greatest challenges to reading *Finnegans Wake* as a specifically revolutionary text—that is, a work whose deconstructive practice represents or articulates a specific "other"—lie in how deeply its generative energies and emergent voices are entangled with the formidable, protean legacy of gendered tropes for Irish national and cultural identity. Working against the more abstract levels of the text's feminist and postcolonial agendas, for example, is the fact that ALP's role or position within the work inherits much from two of the most significant, patriarchal traditions in the effort to form an Irish national literature. The first of these is the *aisling* tradition. Aisling, an Irish word that translates loosely to "dream vision," refers in literary contexts to visionary, allegorical poems, translated or adapted from seventeenth and eighteenth century Irish language lyrics, in which spectral women symbolize Ireland's repressed or threatened national soul. The second is the early twentieth-century Irish Renaissance practice of using women's enigmatic mourning and inarticulate rage—especially in depictions of keening—as signifiers for the loss of traditional Ireland and the Irish language to the encroachments of imperial, Anglophone modernity. Both are signature examples not only of the linkage of woman and nation but also of Irish culture's penchant for making female voice and silence, presence and absence, into equally potent signifiers of national identity.

In aisling poetry, as C. L. Innes explains, the poetic speaker "typically envisages Ireland in a dream vision as a beautiful woman pleading for rescue from the invaders, or less frequently, as a harlot collaborating with them," a betrayer signifying the loss of indigenous culture or nationhood (19). Like ALP, whose "untitled mamafesta memorialising the Mosthighest has gone by many names at disjointed times" (104.4–5), this ephemeral female personification of Ireland has taken on many forms: Cathleen ni Houlihan, the Shan Van Vocht, the Poor Old Woman, and Dark Rosaleen are all aisling types, or antitypes. The more overtly political examples of this tradition are undeniably among the targets of *Finnegans Wake*, and there can be little doubt that Joyce intends to satirize them and, through innovation and complexity, to out-think them.

As with many other modes of Irish lyric and musical traditions, however, Joyce also harbors admiration for the tradition, or, at the least, a prideful displeasure that the tradition is internationally unrecognized. He must therefore go to the lengths of self-reflexive parody—critique of his own ambiguous and complex relationship to the aisling tradition—in order to achieve a wholly cynical or "cosmopolitan" disengagement from it. In episode seven of book one, where Shaun puts Shem on trial for the poor job he is doing composing his "letter to last a lifetime" on behalf of ALP, Shaun accuses Shem of being "a poor acheseyeld from Ailing" (148.33). That is, he charges Shem/Joyce with being a poor exile from Ireland, a man with aching eyes from Ireland, and a writer unsuccessfully trying to detach his work from the aisling tradition. Shaun combines these meanings again when he indicts Shem for making every page of *Ulysses* "an aisling vision more gorgeous than the one before" (179.32).

As much as the *Wake* parodies the aisling tradition, it is hard to imagine how its characteristic penchant for exclamations, appeals to hearing, and motifs of resurrection and waking—indeed, much of its polyvocal dream language—could exist as it does, could be the "transnational" aesthetic that Sollers understands it to be, without using the aisling dream vision, the "deepseep daughter . . . bourne up pridely out of medsdreams unclouthed" (336.13), as one of its primary frameworks and repeated motifs. As the ephemeral entity at the deep recesses of the male dreamer's internalized historical nightmare (his "invision of Indoland"), ALP's connection to the tradition is arguably as deep as the structure of the text gets. After all, many of the main conventions of nationalist aisling poetry are also primary keys to the *Wake*: the liminal consciousness of the male, the desired but non-speaking, elusive woman at the depth of the dream, and the resulting repetition or deferral of the desire for hearing her voice and thus bringing about a national re-awakening. James Clarence Mangan's nineteenth-century translation of the Irish language lyric "Dark Rosaleen" is an excellent example:

> To hear your sweet and sad complaints,
> My life, my love, my saint of saints . . .
> My Dark Rosaleen!
> My fond Rosaleen!
> Would give me life and soul anew,
> A second life, a soul anew (126–27)

To be sure, there are also many differences between ALP and her sisters in cultural nationalist verse traditions: for one, she does eventually speak from within this objectified position, and she does so with all of the ironic and deconstructive energy mentioned previously. Yet, her emergence is still embedded, to use Joyce's own metaphor, in the context or structure of the dream. The *différance* of the *Wake*'s arising voice is thus both the key to its emergence and the key to its confinement: "Dream. Ona nonday I sleep. I dreamt of a somday. Of a wonday I shall wake" (481.7–8).

As with Stephen's hope that the "temptress of his villanelle" could become "conscious of his desire . . . , waking from odorous sleep" (*P* 242), the ultimate instance of reviving Irish identity is to have the woman awake *in*decently from her environment of moral provincialism, to claim her rightful role as not only a sensual but also a universal, uncontainable, being. But if she actually does so, if the eternal feminine does in fact subsume the male and his phallic-geographic location of culture into her sensual universe, then the notion that what has awoken is in any significant sense "Irish" would also become irrelevant, subsumed into global relativity. It would indicate something close to the problematic category of the subaltern universal—an ideal superstructure that, for Ireland as for any society in the long throes of decolonization, gravely exceeds the reality of uneven global incorporation at the base.

One way to avoid this is either for the woman to awake and speak alone, to emerge from her veil but somehow still be contained in distinct cultural vestments, or, to have her try to arouse HCE both sexually and consciously but to do so either within his dream or from outside it, "still by [him] in bed" (622.20), which means that her voice remains a factor of, or factored by, his dreaming mind. This is what arguably happens. Rather than actually unifying the Irish past and the timeless universe, that is, "waking," ALP's voice instead sustains an intense vacillation between memory and forgetting, returning to the subject of "home" whenever the couple's identities are on the verge of being joined:

> now it's me who's got to give. . . . And can it be it's nnow fforvell? . . . But you're changing, acoolsha, you're changing from me, I can feel. Or is it me is? I'm getting mixed. . . . I pity your oldself I was used to. . . . I thought you the great in all things, in guilt and in glory. Your but a puny. Home! My people were not their sort out beyond there so far as I can. . . . For all their faults. I am passing out. O bitter ending! (626.32–627.35)

In both its context and its content, ALP's monologue not only sustains but also intensifies the double direction of Joyce's own emerging voice: his desire, on the one hand, to redeem a deeply cultured Ireland from the sleep of its colonial trauma and, on the other, to wake from the national nightmare into a universal conscience. We might say that the "voice of Joyce" works its magic here because it mutually entertains but does not synthesize these two objectives.

This need to vacillate between transcendence and resurrection of national identity is also true of Joyce's debt to domestic Irish literary traditions, especially those involving the close figurative association between woman and nation. For just as ALP's takeover of the narrative dislodges her from the aisling tradition, so too does her delivery of an "incessantlament" (614.20) invoke its successor: the keening woman of the Irish Renaissance. When she speaks, ALP is performing a keen—a lament for the dead in which the female mourner, often a professional hired for the occasion, celebrates the heroic and genteel attributes of the deceased and sometimes, as in the case of wrongful death at the hands of an enemy, calls for him to return to life and finish living.[3] ALP combines both themes: "Rise up now and aruse! . . . And stand up tall! Straight. I want to see you looking fine for me. With your brandnew big green belt and all. . . . You make me think of a wonderdecker I once. Or somebalt thet sailder, the man megallant, with the bangled ears. Or an earl was he, at Lucan?" (619.28–620.8). "It's Phoenix, dear. And the flame is, *hear*!" (621.1).

As with Joyce's use of aisling, the keen is also partly a parody of keening, but there is a significant tension between the genuine and the critical deployment of the trope. As Emer Nolan argues, this duality in "ALP's lament" indicates not ambivalence, but the crucial postcolonial reality of seeing both the nationalistic ideal of the pristine racial or cultural past and "those distinctively modern ideologies of liberation" that presume to cleanse us of such mythologies as equally insufficient:

> ALP's last words undercut any . . . symbolic deployment of womanhood. But none the less, ALP and Ireland—woman and nation—are both victims . . . When ALP-as-river joins the sea, something specific is lost in an oceanic chaos. As with her, so with Ireland. Both have entered the devil's era of modernity, liberated into difference, lost to identity. This is not a simple transition. Joyce both celebrates and mourns it; his readers have so far tended only to join in the celebration. (181)

While I entirely agree that the fraught, perhaps impossible transition from an unresolved Irish identity to the sly sameness of global modernity is something Joyce "both celebrates and mourns," I'm not so sure that ALP's last words have cut *all* ties to symbolic womanhood. In fact, the Joyce who mourns this transition is also the one who is inclined to deepen his homage to the traditional woman-as-nation figure—a tradition that is itself protean—while the Joyce who celebrates it equally needs such a figure, so that he can "mock and revile" what she stands for.

ALP's lament, her "keen [that] made him able" (102.2–5), brings together two of the more prominent motifs in *caoineadh* for the deceased male: telling tales of his heroic past and entreating him to arise and return to his living affairs. This combination is quite suitable for the postcolonial, or "expatriate" postcolonial, dilemma that Joyce confronts. The need to mourn the past by sanctifying it, honoring it, and thereby settling its disputed meaning is also, in a sense, to awaken it, to give it an authoritative voice. At the same time, however, modernity boasts numerous rewards for those who can awake from the national-historical nightmare, who can pull away from their untimely dependence on national mythologies. Voicing these contradictions, ALP is "a darktongues, kunning" (223.28): at one level, she is trying to "wake" HCE out of his nightmare of history, telling him to "rise up, man of the hooths" (619.25) from his domestic mythologies and look to the transnational future: "[y]ou make me think of . . . somebody erse from the Dark Countries. Come and let us! We always said we'd. And go abroad" (620.6–10); "the book of the depth is. Closed. Come! Step out of your shell!" (621.3–4). But, as the "somebody erse" at 620.9 indicates, her lyrical farewell is also shot through with a genuine desire to sanctify what has been lost, to understand the past before it is abandoned: "To hide away the tear, the parted. It's thinking of all. The brave that gave their. The fair that wore. All them that's gunne" (625.30–32). In fact, these lines echo Thomas Moore's plaintive "Oh, ye Dead!": "It is true, it is true, we are shadows cold and wan; / And the fair and the brave whom we lov'd on earth are gone" (162).

As if caught between these two agendas, the seemingly egalitarian deconstruction of all national legends and the sincere wish to honor and rectify a particular, misunderstood history, ALP ends up expressing a longing to revive not actual Ireland, which does not exist, but fictional Ireland, the stories of origin it has told to itself. She promises HCE that "I will tell you all sorts of makeup things. . . . And show you to every simple storyplace we pass," including the restoration of his aisling visions, wherein "I was the pet of everyone then. A Princeable girl. And you were the pantymammy's Vulking Corsergoth. The invision of Indelond" (625.5–6). One of the outcomes of this cunning keen is the idea that "Ireland" itself is an inevitably postponed, perpetually deferred entity. The comprehensive image of Ireland becomes, like ALP, the muse of an unending process of supplementation, a totality that poets and historians have tried but failed to achieve, and will again try and fail to achieve, their words but evanescent leaves upon the fluid surface of their subject. ALP even tries to alert us to this problem: "If I lose my breath for a minute or two don't speak, remember! Once it happened, so it may again. Why I'm all these years within years in soffran, allbeleaved" (625.29–30). Thus it is by retaining many features of both the keening and aisling traditions that Joyce achieves his notoriously affective balance of universal and Irish historical concerns. That is to say, there is a direct correlation between Joyce's only *partial* overturning of the woman-as-nation trope and his unique ability to articulate the double obligation of home and world.

In fact, even in its deconstructive approach to national identity, ALP's mourning song is not as distant from the "domestic" Irish Renaissance as we might suppose, for the contributors to that movement often used the keening woman as a way to unite Irishness and a more universal sense of modernity through negative representation. An important example of this trend lies with John Synge, of whose work Joyce became increasingly fond while living in Trieste and Zurich, where he helped to produce *Riders to the Sea*, with Nora Joyce as Cathleen, in 1918. In the 1901 record of his journey to the Aran islands, Synge describes the "recurring chant of sobs" uttered by the keening women of Aran as an "inarticulate rage" against modernity, a signifier of the more general loss of romantic and rooted traditions in the postorthodox West (294). Synge transfers this idea of the keen as "inarticulate rage" to other passionate gestures of Aran women. When describing a woman evicted from her home due to property laws enforced from the mainland, Synge, who knew Gaelic well and translates it elsewhere, nonetheless renders her diatribe as the mysterious articulation of an Irish race poised incomprehensibly at the threshold of the modern: "In the fury of her speech I seem to . . . feel the passionate spirit [of the islanders] that expresses itself, at odd moments only, with magnificent words and gestures" (294). These "magnificent" feminine articulations thus mark the site of an irresolvable loss, or what Yeats would later describe, in "In Memory of Major Robert Gregory," as the "nightfall upon a race" (133). Indeed, they anticipate Yeats's own use of undecipherable feminine voices to mark utter modernization, in such figures as the genteel Countess Markievicz ("what voice more sweet than hers"), whose "nights in argument until her voice grew shrill" are turned to a stony silence by the violence of 1916 (180).

Transferred to the stage, this motif of inaccessible feminine consciousness, especially in the form of the lamenting woman, creates a nearly metaphysical sense of loss. The best example is at the conclusion of *Riders to the Sea* when, just after a trio of cloaked women perform a keen for the last of three sons whom Maurya has lost to the sea, Maurya's own entranced lament prolongs and perpetuates the enigmatic voices of the mourners:

Maurya (*raising her head and speaking as if she did not see the people around her*). They're all gone now, and there isn't anything more the sea can do to me. . . . and you can hear the surf is in the east, and the surf is in the west, making a great stir with the two noises, and they hitting one on the other. I'll have no call now to be going down and getting Holy water in the dark nights after Samhain, and I won't care what way the sea is when the other women will be keening. (96)

This was a potent idea for the Abbey Theatre: the idea of an Irish identity that can be identified only as an absence or lack. For to imply that Irishness can only be articulated as a crisis in representation is also to evoke, within the same aesthetic of negation, the more universal implications of a world lost to the irrevocable forces of modernity.

Joyce's many differences from Yeats and Synge are well documented. But he is similar to them in that his original aesthetic stems largely from his need to establish or speak for a disfigured Irish identity and culture while simultaneously addressing international audiences, influences, and themes.[4] Hence it is not surprising that his deployments of the unrepresentable, the enigmatic, the stylistically new, and the uncanny—features of his modernist poetics—tend, like theirs, to hint at something within the nation as well as something beyond it. His aesthetic overlapping of national and universal is also, like theirs, heavily invested in symbolic women—an investment that, from the perspective of a globally abstract, ecumenical idealism might even be called "provincial." Indeed, to consider how gender constructs function within his stylistic genesis is to note that that genesis is not always and at every level an egalitarian subversion; that it does in fact retain *some* associations with the more conservative and essentialist strains of the effort to articulate a national or postcolonial identity.

As such, it returns us to one of the central challenges inherent in developing a "critical cosmopolitanism": namely, how to create a transnational mode of belonging and identification that resists a "unified polychromatic culture" or idealistic global multiculturalism by respecting the specifics of minority culture and incipient national sovereignties (Brennan "Cosmopolitanism and Internationalism" 41), but that also champions a translocal ethical discourse. The problem of how to articulate, as Kwame Appiah puts it, a "rooted cosmopolitanism" that "must reconcile a kind of universalism with the legitimacy of at least some forms of [national] partiality" (*Ethics* 223). The plural location of Joyce's emergent voices speaks very much to these contemporary cosmopolitical challenges: the site of a struggle to articulate universal belonging while one's idea of national belonging remains actively unresolved, it is also the site of a vexed feminine agency. Woman waking—vocally and sexually, into consciousness and conscience—comes to represent not the nation, but the paradoxical desire to both remember and forget it.

For better and for worse, then, ALP is indeed the voice of Joyce. "A Woman of the World who only can Tell Naked Truths about a Dear Man and all his Conspirators how they all Tried to Fall him" (107.4–5), her global inclination, like Joyce's, is configured within and relative to the interminable challenges of articulating a fractured national identity. Theirs is a song of haunted cosmopolitanism, an air of capacious longing and profound hesitancy.

CHAPTER 3

◇
◇
◇
◇

Elizabeth Bowen's Tenacious Cosmopolitanism

The weight of being herself fell on her like a clock striking. She saw the clothes she would put on to go home in hanging over a chair. While it is still Before, Afterwards has no power, but afterwards it is the kingdom, the power and the glory. . . . What [my family] can never know will soon never have been. . . . I shall die like Aunt Violet wondering what else there was; from this there is no escape for me after all. She must rely on marriage to carry her somewhere else. Till it did, she stayed bound to a gone moment, like a stopped clock with hands silently pointing at an hour it can not be.

Elizabeth Bowen, *The House in Paris*

Looking down, it seemed to Lois they lived in a forest; space of lawns blotted out in the pressure and dusk of trees. She wondered they were not smothered; . . . Far from here, too, their isolation became apparent. . . . till the far hills, faint and brittle, straining against the inrush of vaster distance, cut the droop of the sky like a glass blade.

Elizabeth Bowen, *The Last September*

Much of what can be considered aesthetically modern in Elizabeth Bowen's fiction lies in the peculiar, polyvalent innuendo of its prose style. Sentences that are ostensibly meant to move the narrative forward by describing a setting, character, or event are also laced with suggestive, oddly weighted words and syntaxes that tease the reader's mind into more abstract, conceptual registers. Intangible concepts that may be latent in the scene—temporal disturbance, spatial distortion, cultural obliteration—are thus projected in a kind of suggestive shadow play. One of the most prominent examples of this evocative style is Bowen's manner of "weighting" or inflecting the narrator's references to time and space. As in the above passages, syntax, word choice, and metaphor almost heavy-handedly imply that time or space are somehow out of joint, anomalous, disjunct; yet, the narrative remains essentially linear or objectively framed, sometimes insistently so. When on the verge of depicting subjective time, à la Virginia Woolf, Bowen jostles back to an objective voice; likewise, just as she approaches what Frederic Jameson calls the "spatial language [of] modernist 'style,'" whereby a character's awareness of "the unrepresentable [social] totality" is rendered in figures of vague, vast, ever-expanding space ("Modernism" 58–59), something solid "strain[s] against" it.

Like so much in Bowen's fiction, this provocative treatment of time and space is difficult to interpret. It seems to exemplify what Susan Osborn describes as the "shot-through queerness" of the author's work: the way that its stylistic quirks, "destabilizing . . . contradictions and ambiguities" suggest ideas that aren't necessarily congruent with the characters' experiences or the "manifest political conflict" within which they take place (189). As much as I sympathize with Osborn, I think that we do stand a chance of evaluating this feature of Bowen's work. One of the ways to gauge its significance is to contrast it with aesthetics of time and space that are more typical of early twentieth-century British modernism and that reflect its inclination to negate or suspend the geographic parameters and accumulated history of the imperial nation-state. As we study this contrast, a crucial difference emerges: Bowen does not depict subjective time and abstract space as fully as her contemporaries, or with as much formal commitment, because she refuses to see these modalities as the opposites of and successors to a prior experience that was defined by historical and geographic rootedness. The nature of this difference, and its larger significance, are also illuminated by the shifting definitions of cosmopolitanism in critical approaches to global democracy.

The Cosmos and Early British Modernism: Spaces of Aftermath

Older ideas about cosmopolitanism, including many that remain central to the intellectual climates of early twentieth-century London, are a corollary to a rational view of statehood and the function of achieved or settled states that developed in the Enlightenment. Immanuel Kant, writing in 1795, disdained "the opposition of states," but deduced that such belligerent opposition was rational, or integral to Natural design, insofar as it was a logical precondition for "a law of equilibrium [between] secure . . . state[s]" (257)—a precursor for a "distant international government for which there is no precedent in world history" that would promote the "universal cosmopolitan condition, which Nature has as her ultimate purpose" (260). Importantly, the best evidence for this natural progression of rule is not objective but subjective: the individual's inclination that something about the present system is at odds with his or her noblest aspirations, a sense of disassociation that Kant describes as a "rising feeling which each [individual in a state] has for the preservation of the [global] whole" (260). As in the *Critique of Judgment*, the subject perceives its universality via a "rising feeling" that the present milieu (in this case, the "established state[]" [257]) cannot accommodate. Because an objective structure does not exist to reify this feeling, it must find temporary expression in metaphorical or abstract figures of a global community, a world unity "without precedent" that might materialize in the "distant" future.

Interpreting modernist style as a vehicle for such an idealistic, nation-state transcendent form of cosmopolitan belonging was a key component in both the production and early critical study of international English language modernism. Many of its creators and interpreters, especially those invested in the idea of an avant-garde "era of artistic migration and internationalism" (Bradbury and McFarlane 13), tended to see inclinations toward an abstract or subjective "universality" in its experimental aesthetic gestures. For example, speaking of the combined effect of experimental form in Ezra Pound, T. S. Eliot, and James Joyce, Hugh Kenner claims, in *The Pound Era*, that "[t]he province of these works, as never before in history, is the entire human race speaking, in time as well as in space" (95). Many early contributors to British modernism, in particular those who stridently defined London as a cosmopolitan rather than a national center, not only depict the disassociation from national histories and geographies as an encounter with—or a rising feeling of being subsumed within—universal time or space, but also make this sharp contrast central to their aesthetic vision. In his "Vorticist Manifesto," for example, Wyndham Lewis champions the "fundamental Artist that . . . has ceased to belong to any milieu or time" (2310), hence he curses the rooted Victorian idea that "London [is] a provincial town" and "Bless[es]" the "vast planetary abstraction of the ocean" (2316–18). In "Hugh Selwyn Mauberly," his "farewell to London," Pound decries a "botched civilization" and ultimately envisions, in its stead, "siftings on siftings in oblivion, / Till change hath broken down / All things save Beauty alone" (lines 91, 243–45).[1]

British modernist treatments of universality, or nonnationalistic modes of human interconnection, are of course not limited to such abstract and absolute proclamations of unbounded space and time. As Rebecca Walkowitz has demonstrated, for example, "modernist style" often resists nationally sanctioned modes of imagining community—for example, Woolf's "evasive" subjectivity as an "alternative to wartime patriotism" (18)—so as to encourage openness to new modes of community, as in Joyce, Joseph Conrad and Virginia Woolf's subjective focus on quotidian, subnational, microcosmic human relationships. Rather than simply promoting an ideal "planetary detachment," these authors assume a more grounded "cosmopolitan . . . stance" by resisting the consensus-building narratives of realism and nationalism and promoting new "communal aspirations, urban patterns of participant observation, and ethnographic self-consciousness" (10).[2]

In order to challenge entrenched perceptions of national community and to open the space for such subversive behaviors, however, many prominent early British modernists, especially those affiliated with and artistically compelled by the English empire, still tend to employ images of sociopolitical disaffiliation or dislocation that evoke Kant's opposition between "established states" and the "ultimate" cosmos. That is to say, certain of their aesthetic maneuvers work to negate something that can only be bestowed, in the first place, by the sovereign, imperial state: the notion of a normative, stable, or "traditional" correspondence between history and geography. I am thinking, in particular, of Woolf, E. M. Forster, and Conrad's occasionally sudden and capacious representations of space and time—gestures that implicitly oppose the oriented consciousness of the past to a new, ideologically liberated or reflexive consciousness in which space and time become vast, dark, immaterial, subjective, uncanny, and uncontained or ungoverned. As Louis muses in Woolf's *The Waves*, "the lighted strip of history is past and out; Kings and Queens; we are gone; our civilization; the Nile; and all life. Our separate drops are dissolved; we are extinct, lost in the abysses of time, in the darkness" (225).

By no means do these writers always or exclusively execute this absolute negation. It is, however, always an option—a card they can play, and perhaps must play, to disengage the inherited weight of established national traditions, state-sanctioned ethics, and imperial cartographies.[3] When Mrs. Moore visits the Marabar Caves in Forster's *A Passage to India*, for example, her sudden estrangement from British—and more broadly western—sociocultural interpellation is figured as the subjective inrush of a universal void, an echo that "undermine[s] her hold on life" by "murmur[ing]" that "[e]verything exists, nothing has value," leaving her "terrified over an area larger than usual," lost in a "universe [that] offered no repose to her soul" (165).

Forster again emphasizes this sequential opposition of national and universal belonging when Fielding, after his effort to prove Aziz's innocence makes him feel "devoid of the fervours of nationality or youth" (210), retreats to the verandah to reflect on the significance of his actions: "he went on to the upper verandah for a moment, where the first object he saw was the Marabar Hills. . . . It was the last moment of the light, and. . . . At the moment [the hills] vanished [from sight] they were everywhere, the cool benediction of the night descended, the stars sparkled, and the whole universe was a hill" (211–12). Ian Baucom has argued that "Englishness [since the mid nineteenth century] has consistently been defined through appeals to the identity-endowing properties of place" and that these "synecdoches of the nation's space . . . have also been apprehended as temporal contests, [sites in which to dispute and] determine the meaning and the authority of the 'English' past" (4). Given the immense weight of this tradition, and in order to introduce, in its stead, the possibility of postimperial encounters and global-cultural self-consciousness, Forster cannot help but opt for the aesthetic impact of a total, if momentary, universalizing of all spaces—the implication that the "places" representing Englishness and English historical consciousness are no longer simply up for debate and revision, but lost entirely, subsumed by the greater reality of the undifferentiated, subjective, synchronic universe.[4] Woolf also has this maneuver at her disposal. As Mrs. Ramsay muses in *To the Lighthouse*, "this self having shed its attachments was free for the strangest adventures. . . . Her horizon seemed to her limitless. There were all the places she had not seen; the Indian plains; she felt herself pushing aside the thick leather curtain of a church in Rome. This core of darkness could go anywhere, for no one saw it" (62).

The Postcolonial Cosmopolitan Difference

It is important to note this particular stylistic predisposition within the emerging modes of cosmopolitan consciousness in British modernism, because it speaks to presumed relationships between lost and gained modes of affiliation, past and present spheres of belonging, national and transnational identities that are either significantly different from cosmopolitanism as thought out and debated from postcolonial and minority perspectives, or significantly different from at least one key component therein. That key component is the need to develop more global scales of thought and feeling beyond the homeland while also accounting for the fact that the homeland is not itself a coherent experience coterminous with a national past. This means recognizing such realities as the feeling that one has *yet to belong* to a stable consensus of nationhood, the volatile association with a postcolonial state whose normative form is disputed and still in process, and the more immediate need for protective association with sovereign states (as in the procurement of new or dual citizenship). For many postcolonial and minority transnational subjects, new communal connections and identities are not so clearly contingent upon the rejection of a previously embodied or "achieved" national and cultural episteme—upon, as Jessica Berman says of the cosmopolitan inclinations of modernist narrative, "a wholesale rejection of the politics linked to realism and consensus . . . implicated in the imagining of the imperial nation-state" (21).

Especially in postcolonial and transnational forums, the term "cosmopolitan" therefore vacillates between positive and pejorative connotation,[5] but it has also, in contrast to earlier uses of the term, helped to identify experiences in which dislocation becomes relocation, in which mobility beyond cultural borders becomes movement between them, and in which departure from and attachment to national states (especially those interrupted, contested, and characterized by subaltern occlusion) are not incompatible, but dynamically and vitally connected, phenomena.[6] At its more figurative level, it identifies forms of travel in which world territory, although frequently or broadly traversed, is never a vague and dim, un-bordered universe, but a continually physical or material, if cartographically layered and historically overlapping, ground.

In a recent study of cosmopolitanism in postcolonial and transnational contexts, Sheldon Pollock and his coeditors call for "a cosmopolitanism grounded in the tenebrous moment of transition," and champion "emergent discourses of cosmopolitanism [that reflect] our need to ground our sense of mutuality in conditions of mutability, and to learn to live tenaciously in terrains of historic and cultural transition" (4–5). Like other advocates of a postcolonial cosmopolitanism, they propose that we take serious account of intermittent and polyvalent, but still concrete, affiliations with nations, states, cultures, and localities in our thinking about global collectives. This means recognizing that for many, if not the majority, of people on earth, movement "beyond" the homeland (whether physical, psychological, ideological, or aesthetic) rarely involves comprehensive or absolute gestures of postnational imagination, but instead remains subnational and dynamic, for it is typically undertaken while one's "nation" is still a disputed concept applied to a disputed territory, and while the naturally diverse and porous culture related to one's national belonging remains falsely contained or ideologically overdetermined. It means being aware, with Pheng Cheah, that it is therefore insufficient to think of a national-cultural framework as a previously existing or formerly accepted situation out of which one critically emerges. Instead, it is "a nontranscendable moving ground extending across the globe" ("Given" 324).

To think of serially interrupted national and cultural processes as "nontranscendable" is not to remain ideologically grounded relative to a particular place (as in fundamentalist forms of nationalism), but to be more grounded to particulars, more aware of material needs and hopes tied to the incomplete nationhood of the past and present "back home," when we think about the relationship between mobility and socioeconomic attachment, detachment or re-attachment.[7] To understand the reality of deferred and mobile attachment in the context of one's homeland is to be enabled to see and understand it elsewhere, and thus to see the world itself as populated by settlers and travelers who are involved in distinct, sometimes multiple, regional economies, cultures, and political processes. But perhaps most importantly, it is to think of civilization as still in the process of being made rather than as a "botched" project—to visualize a world populated, in the majority, by those who are still waiting for, and working for, the convergence of national belonging, equitable statehood, and international exchange.

Elizabeth Bowen: Tenacious Cosmopolitan

I think that we can learn a great deal about Elizabeth Bowen, an eminently mobile writer whose relationship to twentieth-century literary movements—and to modernism in particular—has been notoriously hard to pin down, when we consider her work through the lens of these differences. Bowen's life was quintessentially cosmopolitan in what we might call the "older," middle twentieth-century understanding of the term. She moved between, and used as settings, many of the major cities in the network of international modernism, such as London, Paris, Rome, and New York. Indeed, few things are more characteristic of Bowen than mobile characters, transient lives, and the exaggerated distances and proximities of wartime played out at the level of the personal. Bowen was both invested in this trans-European, transatlantic mobility and aware of its limits: "Given the size of the world, the scenes of my stories are scattered over only a small area: but they *are* scattered" (*MT* 282). But unlike many of her modernist contemporaries and predecessors, she does not treat this restlessness with regard to place as part of a historically "new," ontologically revelatory mode of thought and experience. In Bowen, separations from and attachments to place are equally contingent, typically partial, and always in process.

Especially for her female protagonists, displacement is the norm of the "now," but it has also been the norm of the past. In the London-based novel *The Death of the Heart*, for example, Portia Quayne ends up as "a refugee" who "seemed to belong nowhere, not even [this] temporary little stale [hotel] room" (293), but there is nothing historically new in this displaced condition, for she lived an itinerant "childhood of exile" before coming to stay with her London relations. Rather than citizens of the world who are undergoing, or have recently undergone, an initiatory exile or uprooting, Bowen heroines are usually in process of negotiating belonging relative to one or more adoptive families, past affiliations, or foreign communities, and they are just as likely to cherish separation from as to seek attachments with these societies. As Bowen writes, regarding Portia, "It is not our exalted feelings, it is our sentiments that build the necessary home. The need to attach themselves makes wandering people strike roots in a day: whenever we unconsciously feel, we live" (140).

Indeed, as much as these female characters "enjoy the sensation of being on furlough from [their] own li[ves]" (*HD* 103) or desire "to be enclosed in a nonentity, in some ideal no-place, perfect and clear as a bubble" (*LS* 127), they also yearn "to be in a pattern. . . . to be related" (*LS* 142). Like Karen Michaelis in *The House in Paris*, they are inclined to "hate exile, hate being nowhere, hate being unexplained, hate having no place of [their] own" (*HP*

207). Chronologically and spatially absolute expressions of dislocation, as well as the idea that transnational modernity involves an unprecedented estrangement, are thus not suitable for describing their predicaments. It is not that they *once* belonged somewhere else, and suddenly feel adrift in the globe-as-universe; rather, it is that they always "belong somewhere else" (*HP* 115).

As Bowen writes of her ambiguously Anglo-Irish heroine Stella Rodney, in *The Heat of the Day*, "The times, she had been told in her youth on all sides, were without precedent—but then, so was her own experience: she had not lived before" (24). This sentence encapsulates the most pervasive characteristic of Bowen's focal characters: they do not possess an orientation that precedes their disorientation. They live in the "now" of disruptions and historical crises, but they have not "lived before," in the sense of not having experienced a mode of belonging that was, at some point in the past, stable enough to *be* negated, buried, or "botched" by the sudden and seismic turmoil of modernity. Emotionally and in many cases historically, where they come from is still subject to debate "on all sides," still being processed even as they depart it or while they seek new emotional and communal attachments, as is the case for the transient lovers in *The House in Paris*, *To the North*, and *The Heat of the Day*.

Incomplete or perpetually unsettled, the prior places and experiences in their lives therefore remain material and volatile, liable to dictate or intrude upon the present in objective or concrete ways, not just as facets of consciousness or fragments of memory. In *The Heat of the Day* and *The House in Paris*, where characters travel from the bustling, transient modernity of London and Paris to the "disturbing repose" of Protestant Ireland during the years when Eamon de Valera's Fianna Fáil majority was constructing the nationalistic Republic (*HP* 75), we get a hint of the historical and biographical realities that underlie this difference. In *The Heat of the Day*, Stella must return from "timeless" London to settle the "historic future" (52) of a family estate in Cork—a property that, in its disputed ownership, represents both the ideologically contested enclaves of the Anglo-Irish Ascendancy in the nascent Republic and the extensive history of partition and colonization in Ireland more generally. Having no claim to prior historical and geographic rootedness, Stella's experience of modernity is less about resisting a territorial and traditional milieu of the prior generation than it is about the multiplicity and ongoing partiality of her spatial and temporal belonging.

Living in a rented London flat during the Blitz, Stella relishes the "hypnotic, futureless day-to-day" of her love affair with Robert Kelway (in which "life stories were shed as so much superfluous weight") and enjoys the feeling that wartime London is absorbed—as only Bowen could have put it—by "the 'time being' which war had made the very being of time" (103). But she also feels "the anxieties of the hybrid" (125), principal among which is the difference between shedding a known, settled history and shedding the unsettled, disputed history and property of the Anglo-Irish. That legacy, also Bowen's own, was of a perpetually unsettled, shifting, incongruent relationship between the nation, the state, and the community and culture of home. As has been well documented, Bowen was deeply aware of the Anglo-Irish lack of position—their sense of being stranded between anti-imperial nationalisms increasingly driven by lower-middle class, rural, and Catholic Irish and a British nation whose drift toward capitalist-democratic modernity the Ascendancy had historically defined itself by opposing.[8] Indeed, the Anglo-Irish sense of location, prior to any identifiable modern "moment," was already one of geographic exclusion and historical dispute, as was Ireland's more broadly.

Not surprisingly, Bowen's tendency to depict time and space as disjunct or anomalous, but not globally expansive or fluidly subjective, is deeply evident in her comments on the Ascendancy, whom she describes as "queered—by their . . . divorce from the countryside in whose heart their struggle was carried on" (*CI* 197), and as "notably unhistoric" due to having been "left to operate in what was materially a void" (*BC* 452–55). Stella Rodney's involvement in settling a convoluted family history in Cork that she had, twenty years earlier, taken the opportunity to dismiss as over, is a metonym for the closure-resistant narrative of Irish decolonization in the early 1920s ("having it all dragged up. . . . Everything disarranged" [249]). It also hints that the novel's skeptical view of synchronic, place-bereft modernity has its roots in, or is afforded by, the peculiar combinations of property and disinheritance in Anglo-Irish experience. Crucially, in a wartime environment where the utter loss or rejection of stable pasts can also lead to extreme political ideologies,[9] Stella may feel rootless, but she has never fully experienced rootedness. Consequently, her need for attachment and her capacity for critical detachment are not sequential opposites but almost simultaneous, or superimposed, phenomena. Indeed, one could argue that her need for this simultaneity is more democratic than indecisive.

Trying to compare her sense of prior belonging to the "self-evident position" of the family life Robert had left behind in rural England, Stella remembers "derelict" memorials that recall those erected for Ascendancy gentry in rural Ireland; this "gave some sort of locale, however distant, to her unmarried name," though "she seldom asked herself what her own was now—still less, what position was in itself" (126). The implied questions here are pivotal: how can one dramatically "leave behind" a world whose location has been unstable, subject to point of view, from the beginning? If the former home in question has always been a contested space, then how can one gauge one's detachment from it, or speak in emphatically positive or negative terms about one's new "position" in the present? Although Bowen's world is trans-European and cosmopolitan in an older sense of the term, this combination of mobility and instability of prior position, so central to the lives of her characters, strikes much nearer to the ideas of place and time advanced by postcolonial and non First World émigrés—of those who emerged not out of history, but with it.

To be sure, Bowen's class status and race, which are often reflected in her characters, remove her considerably from the "discrepant cosmopolitan" experiences of forced migration and mobile subaltern existence that scholars of transnational culture, following James Clifford, have posed against the privileged cosmopolitanism of a predominantly pan-European elite. Yet, what she shares with cosmopolitan approaches influenced by postcolonial and transnational perspectives is crucial: the awareness that living and thinking "beyond" the homeland begins with the understanding that "home" is not easily understood in terms of fixed space and linear or sequential time, and that one's "country" signifies incongruent and deferred associations between political sovereignty, shared territory, and historical or cultural identity. Therefore, it is not a candidate for something that one transcends or emerges or graduates from, even as one becomes separated from it.

In *The Last September*, Hugo Montmorency, who has returned to the Naylor's Big House in Cork after a ten-year absence spent largely in England, poignantly sums up this contingent sense of position when another temporary returnee of Ascendancy society, Marda, asks him what he feels will be "the outcome" of the Anglo-Irish war. Hugo predicts "a few more hundred deaths on our side—which is no side—rather scared, rather isolated, not expressing anything except tenacity to something that isn't there—that never was there" (117). It is nearly impossible, from Hugo's point of view, to speak in temporal absolutes (the "aftermath" of war) or spatial absolutes ("the" country, or the degree of contrast in his expatriation and return), much less link these typically modern crises to a sudden sensation of disorientation or homelessness, for home is already a state of exile, a tenuous orientation upon a shifting ground.

Instead of evoking the "abysses of time" that Woolf's characters experience when they are dislodged from what would be their normative historical orientation, Hugo's claim speaks for a society that, although it is on "the dusk of oblivion" (*LS* 143), lacks the collective sense of established position that is necessary to lend immediacy or impact to the concept *of* oblivion. On the verge of extinction, it presents "an affair of prolonged 'hesitations'" in which it is always "time something happened" (226) and in which societal intercourse seems always "doomed to incompletion" (133). As much as *The Last September* is Bowen's remembrance of things irretrievably past, so too does it demonstrate what Bowen called "the imperious hauntedness of a period not understood in its own time" (qtd. in DiBattista 233)—the residual urgency of a society that, contemplating its finality, could not agree upon its beginning, its normative place in time. The final meeting between Lois and Gerald, which Bowen appropriately sets at the edge of the wooded boundary of the demesne, powerfully reiterates this point: "'Where shall we go?' [Lois] asked, while something in her stopped like a clock with foreboding. . . . She wished they had not come down—overruling, possibly, in each other some desire for space—to the plantation where constricted by firs, thought and movement were difficult and upright shadows emphasized his severity. . . . she saw him standing confused, like a foreigner with whom by some failure in her vocabulary all communication was interrupted" (279).

As is often the case for Lois, the thought (or the threat) of making a decisive emotional move is accompanied by the fear that such gestures "finish off people" (252) or "stop, seal, finish one" (83). More than a symptom of youth, this indecision also reflects the Irish, and more broadly postcolonial, problem of how to conclude, leave behind, or "finish" that which has lacked integration from the beginning: "'One can't move, one doesn't know where one is.' . . . 'But, Gerald, where *are* we?' He said: 'Don't worry.' They were both, he knew, entirely lost." (282).[10] The "loss" of a national-cultural milieu depicted in the novel thus reflects the considerably more partial, less absolute, more tenacious sense of dislocation written about by postcolonial expatriates and transnational subjects. Indeed, Sheldon Pollock's definition of contemporary cosmopolitans as those who "learn to live tenaciously [on] terrains of historic and cultural transition," and who, in so doing, suggest that our "mutuality [may lie] in conditions of mutability" (4), resonates deeply in the theme of "tenacity to something that never was there" which pervades Bowen's highly ambiguous tableau. An important result of this lack of finality—as is foreshadowed when Lois Farquar, the semiautobiographical protagonist, ambivalently departs for Paris just before the Big Houses are burned by the IRA—is that the nation/cosmos distinction is broken down, made less absolute or applicable, not only in one's "homeland" but also in one's life after or beyond home.

From a formal or aesthetic standpoint, it is therefore not surprising that Bowen tends not to share in the aforementioned, British modernist tendency to depict disengagement from the national and imperial milieu with images of synchronic vastness or of the inhabited globe as abstract cosmos. Although her characters experience significant feelings of "cancelled time" (*LS* 28), "time lag" (*CI* 4), the "glare of space" and the "unestablishable distance" (*HD* 154) or "slipping and widening [of the] distance" (*LS* 86) between one another, they are also ultimately subject to and influenced by the external, manifest pressures of history and place. In temporal terms, because the linearity or prior coherence of the past is not *yet* understood, the notion of an absolute disruption of what is called "external time" is less relevant, not fully applicable. Linear time and historical frameworks, although obscured from view, are still being constructed: "There had been no beginning. Time, loose textured, had a shining undertone" (*LS* 14); "perpetually one was subject to the sense of there having had to be a beginning somewhere. Like the lost first sheet of a letter or missing first pages of a book, the beginning kept on suggesting what must have been its nature" (*HD* 146); "the eye of time never stops watching you" (*HP* 165).[11]

In spatial terms, because there is no normative, prior place of belonging, the material environment may seem on the verge of dissolving into a universal void or an expanding darkness—departing guests "t[ear] great shreds from the season's texture," Lois's flirtations with a British soldier make "the cracks of the walls . . . [bulge] out visibly" (243), and her run-in with an IRA soldier in a ruined mill makes the cracks in its walls "seem to widen, to . . . peel back from a cleft" (180)—but all that is solid never completely melts into air. Although figuratively fissured, physical structures like the abandoned mills (which were "never quite stripped and whitened to a skeleton's decency: like corpses at their most horrible" [178]) and the Naylor home, which stands with its door "open hospitably" as the flames consume it (303), tend to retain their enigmatic physical presence and to assert themselves, almost willfully, as evidence of the temporal volatility of ideologically contested space.[12] In all of the above examples, too, it is the oddly weighted vocabulary of the prose itself—the peculiar suggestiveness of a style that otherwise remains committed to describing objective, manifest places and events—that conveys these more abstract notions of tenacious spaces and histories.

A further example of Bowen's investment in the closure-resistance of disputed space is Lois and Marda's encounter with the gunman in the abandoned mill, which is rendered in a strangely mixed idiom of elegy and nightmare: initially described as part of "the democracy of ghostliness" (179) that is Ireland's eroded agricultural economy, the mill abruptly becomes an active site in decolonization's violent present—a narrow miss of being shot that "affect[s] [them] like a sense of the future" (182). Thus, in marked contrast to the Marabar Caves scene in *A Passage to India,* which symbolizes the swift and capacious leveling of a formerly instilled milieu, Bowen's description of the mill scene suggests the ways in which an unsettled, incompletely internalized milieu can alternate rapidly between ghostly and material presence, between assimilation into the generality of history and irreducible resilience. To be sure, if we hope to appreciate Bowen's different attitude toward space and time—showing them as disjunctive, but never universally abstracted—we cannot emphasize enough the fact that Ireland for Bowen, and the Anglo-Irish enclaves within the partitioned, fledgling state, were simultaneously a familiar home and a site of disorientation— an "unstrange place [with a] troubling strangeness," as Karen observes of Rushbrooke, Cork, in *The House in Paris* (75).

But it is in Bowen's treatment of houses, and of Ascendancy Big Houses in particular, that we most clearly recognize her awareness of the stubborn, enigmatic materiality of unassimilated and unsettled places. This becomes especially apparent when we compare an exemplary description of a Big House, by Bowen, to an exemplary depiction, by Virginia Woolf, of the contest between physical structures and universal time and space. In *To the Lighthouse,* the cataclysmic effect of the Great War on British consciousness is represented by "a downpouring of immense darkness" that engulfs the Ramsay home, subsuming its entities into a vaguely global, presumably universal time and space:

> Nothing, it seemed, could survive the flood, the profusion of darkness . . . ; there was scarcely anything left of body or mind by which one could say, "This is he" or "This is she." . . . [Nights] lengthen, they darken. Some of them hold aloft clear planets, plates of brightness. The autumn trees, ravaged as they are, take on the flash of cool cathedral caves where gold letters on marble pages describe death in battle and how bones bleach and burn far away in Indian sands. (125–28)

In Bowen, by contrast, a similar profusion of darkness begins to envelop the Big House but never fully absorbs it:

> Only the massed trees . . . of the demesne were dark and exhaled darkness. Down among them, dusk would stream up the paths ahead, lie stagnant on lawns, . . . dulling the borders as by a rain of ashes. Dusk would lie where one looked as though it were in one's eyes, as though the fountain of darkness were in one's own perception. Seen from above, the house in its pit seemed a very reservoir of obscurity; . . . But as they drove down the home-sense quickened; the pony, knowing these hedges, rocketed hopefully in the shafts. The house became a magnet to their dependence. (92–93)

For Bowen, the Big House cannot be swallowed by the mists of synchronic time because it does not yet have a concrete history; too dubious to have first existed positively, it resists the space-conflating onrush of negation and reasserts itself as the half-realized entity it already was: a "reservoir of obscurity."

Deeply resonant here is Hugo Montmorency's paradox of "expressing . . . tenacity" to a contingent origin ("to something that . . . never was there"), for what the description registers is the crucial difference between separation from a home in the throes of decolonization and separation or estrangement from one's place in the achieved nation-state. While the latter involves the severing or suspension of ties to a structure that had previously fixed both self and world in a coherent frame of reference, the former involves a continuation, now mobilized, of a belonging in progress and a feeling of being "torn in herself, dividedly sympathetic" (LS 30)—a journey across borders which begins with the knowledge that "in a secular and contingent world, homes are always provisional" (Said, "Reflections" 185). One stylistic manifestation of this multidirectional perspective is a unique ability to show how disputed places, unresolved history, and the paradoxical act of becoming displaced from these must resist both sides of the abstract binary of national/universal time and space.

Cosmopolitical Bowen

Like many of the "new" (and newly identified) cosmopolitans studied in the current, geographically and culturally particularized literature on the subject, Bowen's understanding of departure or expatriation thus leads not to "an ideal of detachment," as Bruce Robbins puts it, but to "a reality of (re)attachment, multiple attachment, or attachment at a distance" ("Intro-duction" 3). Not just in her fiction, but also in her personal life and her extensive body of nonfiction, Bowen's capacity for multiple attachments and her penchant for international dialogue is informed by her dearly main-tained but unsettled and irreducible Irishness. To be sure, one cannot even remotely delineate an "Irish" from a "post-Irish" period in her literary sub-jects, her political and historical outlook, or her residency (until, arguably, 1960, when she hastily sold Bowen's Court).

Rather than a national mode of thought and feeling that is gradually sub-sumed into a worldview, her Irish outlook is always specifically and elemen-tally present within it: this is because, as she once wrote while reviewing a book on modern Irish history, "nothing in Ireland is ever over" (CI 173). Indeed, Bowen's view of the world at large is always in dialogue with her view of Ireland's potential futures and its still unreconciled past, as is evi-dent in the political commentaries, book reviews, and literary essays that she produced for English, Irish, and American audiences from the late 1920s to the late 1950s. Her nuanced treatment of such subjects as Sinn Féin, Irish neutrality, patriotism, and the need to diffuse stereotyping in English/Irish relations, suggest a deep awareness of the vital interplay between the volatil-ity of the nascent postcolonial state, the constructedness of history, and the incipient promise of both Irish and international democracy.

In her 1928 introduction to *The Last September*, mindful that she was writing at a pivotal moment for the international reputation of the recently formed Irish Free State, Bowen had assured her international audience that the troubles are "already, part of history" (*MT* 124), and that, with the evanescence of the Big Houses, Ireland is also now unified geographically:

> writing *The Last September* [in 1928 in England], 1920 seemed a long time ago. By now . . . peace had settled on Ireland; trees were already branching inside the shells of large burned-out houses; lawns, once flitted over by pleasures, usefully merged into grazing land. (*MT* 124)

Writing to an Irish audience, in a 1940 essay for the Irish literary magazine *The Bell*, she again tries to promote both democratic Irish statehood and international understanding, though here, seeking to disarm a now more entrenched republicanism, she proposes that Ireland would benefit from resurrecting "the idea from which these houses sprang"—that is, revisiting their potential to promote democratic social intercourse on both an intranational and international level—and making it "an alive part in the alive Ireland of today" (*MT* 29). In a 1941 essay in the British periodical *The New Statesman*, Bowen again revisits the unsettled history of the Ascendancy as a means to advocate democratic dialogue both within Ireland and between Ireland and Europe. While defending the neutral Irish state by deflating rumors of its Axis sympathies and entreating the English to see the new Irish state as "a people young in political life, not yet adult in citizenship, . . . and in no sense fit or ready to enter war" (*MT* 31), she also proposes that Ireland is aware of and wishes to avoid the "abnormal isolation" of excessive nationalism and the "sequestration from Europe [which] is . . . the principal ill of her neutrality" (32–33).[13]

Key to her negotiation is a historical reimagining of the Big House[14]—not a foreign enclave spatially disrupting the settled state but a place that potentially embodied ideals of cosmopolitan exchange that were always already disrupted by their ties to colonialism. As if to graft this potential Ascendancy to Ireland's vital historical body, Bowen proposes that the present-day "country" knows this intercultural exchange to be necessary: "accustomed . . . to being much visited . . . by people of cultural sympathies and enquiring mind, *the country* does not like segregation" (32; my italics). In a similar vein, she states that Ireland as a whole has always been culturally aware that "claustrophobia is the threat to every civilized mind" (32). Bowen is thus looking back to eighteenth-century cosmopolitan ideals, but she is also, in a much more contemporary, cosmopolitical sense, arguing that imperialism always manages to foreclose the cultural pluralities it might have introduced, and that specific potential functions of the postcolonial state—such as its ability to promote "citizenship" and "society" by breaking down "barrier[s] between city and country Ireland" (29)—are necessary to reintroduce this lost potential.

Bowen's reflections on James Joyce, following his death in 1941, demonstrate a similar desire to complicate the historical and geographic absolutes that—especially during World War II and the nascence of the Republic of Ireland—tended to characterize debates about nationality and allegiance. In a 1942 review of Herbert Gorman's biography of Joyce, written for England's *New Statesman*, Bowen disclaims that "[i]n days when there is a bad name for detachment, it is hard to assess the detached man," then proceeds to deny that Joyce was simply "an aesthete piqued with his own country, choosing to live abroad" (*MT* 154); instead, she proposes that what "made [his writing] possible" was a difficult, painful, and *partial* separation. According to Bowen, both Dublin and Catholicism were, for Joyce, a milieu "from which a deep nature does not without crisis secede, and from which a lonely nature dreads to detach itself" (*MT* 155).

More extensive in its portrayal of the half-removed Joyce is the much less frequently cited, considerably longer reflection on the author that she penned in 1941 for Ireland's cosmopolitan-themed periodical *The Bell*.[15] One of the first, if not the first, posthumous defenses of Joyce directed to an Irish audience by an Irish writer, Bowen's reflection on why "the death of James Joyce was felt by few in his own land as a personal tragedy" seeks to deconstruct the oppositions of cultural tradition and aesthetic experiment, patriotism and cosmopolitanism, Irishness and exile, that had dominated mainstream assessments of Joyce. "It is surroundings that tie us closely to people, that are the earth of friendship," Bowen concedes,

And that physical, associative tie with his countrymen Joyce broke when he went to live abroad. Yet he was before all an Irishman. All the cerebral complexity of his later art went to reproduce the physical impressions that he had received in Ireland. ("James Joyce" 40)

Commenting on the vital relationship between the universal appeal and local, visceral groundedness of Stephen Dedalus, she asserts that

Across the quadrangles of old English universities, through the streets of London, New York, Paris have walked many self-seen Stephens. . . . But to be truly Stephen one must be a born Catholic and Irish city-bred man. "Crying aloud in the rain on the top of the Howth tram"—Stephen is undetachable from his place. (48)

Bowen even goes so far as to argue that *Finnegans Wake* exhibits a "fundamental Irishness" that "has defeated, and . . . antagonized, the critics." But where she is most ahead of her time is in her profoundly more cosmopolitical recognition that to make such a triumphant declaration is also to raise the question of what "Irishness" is: "The English can never know us—and are we ready to know ourselves? To challenge our view of ourselves . . . is more academic than we realize" (41).

Bowen also used the lessons of complex, multiple, and unresolved attachment that she learned through her relationship with her homeland (as well as her fraught extractions from it) as a lens through which to view "the" human predicament more broadly—a way to consider "humanity" not as a detached abstraction but as everywhere affected by similarly complex attachments and particular, dynamic affiliations. Bowen essentially made this argument in a 1950 article for the *New York Times Book Review*. Writing to an American audience that, like her English and Irish audiences, was in the throes of what she saw as an excessive but understandable phase of patriotism ("Never has loyalty, on the face of it, been ranked higher than it is today"), Bowen criticizes "restrictive loyalties" (6) but goes on to make a considerably more nuanced point: "[H]uman values are [the writer's] concern," she argues, but "they are neither abstractions nor standing points; . . . in their nature not fixed but shifting" because they are subject to "the endlessness of human variation and dissonance, the doublings and twisting of mankind under the grip of circumstance" (60). The writer's "ideal," she therefore concludes, "is to be at once disabused [of] and susceptible to [loyalties], and for ever mobile" (61). Bowen, it seems, had become increasingly aware of the need for almost simultaneous attachment and detachment, loyalty and disloyalty to place, the inevitability and painful partiality of departure.

During and after World War II, when her reputation as an English novelist was justly on the rise, given her uncanny visions of wartime London, and later when she was moving between countries, cities, and audiences, Bowen was also returning, with equal feeling and skepticism, to the irresolute subjects of her Irish past: to the "anxious history" (*BC* 452) of her family estate in Cork, in *Bowen's Court* (1942); to her childhood in Dublin, in *Seven Winters* (1942); and again to the Big House, in the midst of the Anglo-Irish war, in *A World of Love* (1955), a novel whose theme is the disruptive return of the misunderstood, unprocessed past. Yet the intensity with which she could superimpose the need of attachment and the inevitable inconclusiveness of belonging was, as Victoria Glendenning has memorably observed, most poignantly evident in the conclusion to *A Time in Rome*, completed in 1960. Writes Glendenning:

> The last two sentences of the book, after describing the pain of departure, come as a slight shock. What she wrote, and what she had the panache to leave written, is the controlled, undirected cry of the displaced person: "My darling, my darling, my darling. Here we have no abiding city." (245)

Indeed, a major key to Bowen's work, her sense of time and space, her view of people and of how or where they connect, lies not just in the idea that her "original" home remains psychically vital in its irresolution, but in the quintessentially Bowen idea that homes of any kind, and in any place, remain contingent, volatile, and vital—as dearly needed as they are forbidding, as resistant to completion as they are to negation.

CHAPTER 4

◇
◇
◇
◇

Crossings Still

Irish Interludes in Bowen's European Novels

Nothing in Ireland is ever over.
Elizabeth Bowen, *Collected Impressions*

What's unfinished haunts one.
Elizabeth Bowen, *The Heat of the Day*

Thus far, I have sought to identify a distinct, alternative mode of cosmopolitanism within the themes and aesthetics of Irish expatriate modernism. This "Irish cosmopolitanism" stems from the overdetermination of national identity during Ireland's long decolonization, the related postponement and obscuring of Irish international and transnational identity, and the resulting need (or ability) to interlace one's still-forming Irish identity with one's often capacious global perspective. Its aesthetic of orientation is not merely double, or happening on two scales, but doubly transformative. Resisting the closure of Irish backgrounds even as it looks beyond them, it also defies historically absolute and geographically abstract images of modern dislocation by depicting extranational experiences that remain suffused with questions of unresolved origin. Bowen's most self-consciously modern and cosmopolitan novels, *The House in Paris* (1935) and *The Heat of the Day* (1948), dramatize this dynamic interplay of orientations in compelling ways.

On one hand, these two narratives focus on the disruption of historical time, the phenomena of subjective and psychological time, and the uncertainty of identities and allegiances in metropolitan European societies (London and Paris) engulfed in modernity. On the other, they are shot through by the contrary notion that historical time and traditional social orders are merely interrupted and are still moving toward coherence. Bombs drop, parents and lovers are killed in war, social mores and familial expectations are radically upset, yet events are often described as moving toward the future with objective force, according to the "overruling coldness [with which] things guided themselves" (*HP* 191). In both narratives, modern urban transience seems to dictate that "everything is on its way to somewhere else." Yet this peripatetic condition also exists, as the narrator intrusively reminds us in *The Heat of the Day*, because "unceasingly something is at work" (*HD* 218).

This double-vision of historical time draws, at least in part, from Bowen's own effort to live wartime, cosmopolitan modernity while still assessing her connections to an Irish history increasingly defined by nationalist movements and the contested role of the Protestant Ascendancy—an effort that allowed her to scrutinize the time-consciousness of modernity from different spaces or different cultural-geographic perspectives. We often speak of exilic and diasporic writers as having the ability, or need, to think at a critical distance from both their native and their adopted countries. Bowen, who lived in London and traveled frequently on the modernist axis to Paris, Rome, and New York from the late 1920s into the 1960s, established a critical distance not simply from her adopted "country" of England, but more specifically from her adopted, Anglo-European cosmopolitan milieu. Having come from what she called "a race of hybrids" (*CI* 4), she was able to participate in a European culture of diplomatic displacement while also looking skeptically upon it, recognizing the ways in which its ideas about history, change, and worldliness were locally produced.

This dual vision is introduced structurally into each novel via an interlude that, about midway through the narrative, removes the heroine from London or Paris and takes her to the comparable stillness of an Ascendancy estate in southern Ireland.[1] At first glance, these crossings appear to be quests for rootedness and stillness that use the relative calm of the Irish Big House to signify a social order of the prewar past that is now seen, in the midst of modernity's upheavals and eroded orthodoxies, as a source of stability or intrinsic meaning. As Barbara Brothers observes of Stella's journey to Cork, during the London air raids, in *The Heat of the Day*, "While T. S. Eliot's experience of the wasteland led him to the established church to find a timeless order . . . , Bowen's experience of it led her to the Anglo-Irish tradition of a circumscribed family life within the history of a social order when preserved that transcended the individual's experience of time" (131).

Other readers see Bowen's Irish interludes as more structurally and thematically complex. Marian Kelly, for example, interprets the dissonant Irish flashback of *The House in Paris* as a vague episode that "punch[es] a hole in the plot" and "disrupt[s] the forward motion of the text, forming a kind of black hole within it" (1). This structural disruption reflects the novel's thematic "examination of both the pleasures and the problems created by nostalgia" (1). I agree with Kelly, who does not include the *Heat of the Day*'s Irish interlude, which achieves a similar effect without a temporal flashback. But I would add that, taken as a pair, the two subplots also work to critique the ways in which mainstream cosmopolitanism, by relying upon reductive and static notions of national affiliation, produced a dangerously unpragmatic view of transnational identity. This critique, as it plays out in each novel, highlights the generative tension of Bowen's modernism: the need to scrutinize both the intoxicating fantasies of national tradition or origin and the perilous eroticism of philosophies of statelessness.

Each of the Irish subplots involves an adult woman who is trying to maintain self-possession as she decides between love interests and who, in the midst of this predicament, journeys to an Ascendancy Big House in Cork that is part of her family history. Within Bowen's oeuvre, it is important to note that these Irish episodes are thus quasi sequels to the much younger Lois Farquar's ambiguous departure for France, in *The Last September*, just after her home has been burned by the IRA in the Anglo-Irish War. Lois's story had stopped abruptly, and ambiguously, with her departure for Europe after her family's home was burned in the troubles (in September 1920); in these novels of the 1930s and 1940s, the Irish interludes involve older women returning to sites that are similar to, and are imbued with the same "anxious history" (*BC* 452) as Lois's Danielstown, although now in the aftermath of revolution. As such, the interludes are projections of Bowen's tendency to return to Irish places and concerns (as Neil Corcoran has shown), to revisit their unfinished stories in the midst of her international existence, as well as narrative analogues for the desire to reopen the case of Protestant history in the south as the Free State evolves into the Republic. Even more, they reflect Bowen's refusal to adopt a single and inflexible stance, in the international community, on the increasingly republican and sovereign Irish state.

Before leaving London during the autumn of the German Blitz in 1940, Stella tells her lover Robert that she was last in Cork "twenty-one years [ago]" (179), which means that she, like Lois, left Ireland during the Anglo-Irish war, just as the tide of nationalist sentiment turned forcefully against Protestant landowners, in part as reprisal for their complicity with English occupation and Catholic suppression. Robert, who discourages her from "digging up the past" and preaches that "there are no countries any more, nothing but names" (301), answers her "vaguely": "What a lot of water . . . has flowed under the bridges since then, or hasn't it? Floods enough have washed most bridges away" (179). Somewhat like Haines in *Ulysses*, who tells Stephen "it seems History is to blame" for England's treatment of Ireland, Robert here serves as Bowen's reminder that those who come from an established history are more likely to be in a position to declare history over. In *The House in Paris*, Karen visits her Aunt Violet, who is married to a Protestant "whose home was burned in the troubles" and who now "hasn't even a place" (74). Sailing into Cobh harbor, and its insular enclave of Protestant homes, Karen observes the "nineteenth century calm hanging over the colony," which "stood in that flat clear light in which you think of the past and did not look like a country subject to racking change" (72). Thus, the interludes are not a return to a stable entity left behind, but a return to the unresolved history represented by the final image of *The Last September*: the Naylor's big house, burned in "a design of order and panic," with its "door st[anding] open hospitably upon a furnace" (303).

One can certainly understand Brothers's reading of the Irish scenes as an Eliot-esque search for stillness—a point others have made as well[2]—for, at least initially, Bowen does set them up as a drastic temporal and spatial contrast to the unsettling modernity of the European metropolis. The perplexed heroines leave London "wanting to rescue something" (*HP* 69), or seeking "everything [they] had lost the secret of being" (*HD* 193), and they do, upon reaching Ireland, discover a reflection-inducing stillness. Karen finds the rooms of the estate at Rushbrook to be "at a sacred standstill," notes that "ticking clocks d[o] little to time," and later feels that her "time in Ireland [was] like one long day spent in waiting" (*HP* 77, 82, 102). Similarly for Stella, life at Mount Morris "seem[s] to be outside time" and "outside war," resulting in the sense that "[one's] place in time had been lost" (*HD* 180, 185, 196).

But each protagonist's journey also involves the discovery of a more convoluted family history and raises more complex questions of ownership, allegiance, and identity, than was expected. In *The Heat of the Day*, Stella never discovers the truth of what her recently deceased Cousin Francis had been doing in London (he may have helped British intelligence to identify the Nazi counterspy Robert, which would square with the totalitarian sympathies in certain strains of diehard republicanism and the rejection of these sympathies by those, like Francis, who still sought alliances with English sovereignty).[3] She also never finds out what his exact intentions were in bequeathing his estate to her son Roderick, or how exactly she is to feel about being reconnected with her Anglo-Irish legacy. In *The House in Paris*, Karen discovers that her Aunt Violet is dying, finds herself strangely drawn to the cause of Ireland's "anti-treaty" republicans, and is unable to discern what she ought to do about her impending, dispassionate marriage to Ray. She returns to England on the Cork/Holyhead ferry wondering "How much had happened? Everything or nothing?" (92). Unsure of "What [she] hope[d] to find," she feels "hungry, empty instead of sad" (92). At the emotional and personal level, the nervous evanescence of Ascendancy Ireland has afforded both women a space for reflection, but it has not offered up any transcendent or deeply rooted truths.

In the previous chapter, I proposed that two ostensibly conflicting drives are operating at once in the minds of Bowen's focal characters: the drive to belong or to become rooted and the drive to be free of attachments and histories. Bowen's Londoners, Parisian expatriates, and European travelers are arguably unique among European modernism's cosmopolitans in the degree to which they simultaneously desire to escape and to locate their social moorings. *The House in Paris* and *The Heat of the Day* play out this dual motivation in significant ways, but rather than providing a cure or hiatus for this condition, the Irish intermissions instead reinforce it. In so doing, they suggest that this double longing has evolved from, or is itself paradoxically "rooted" in, an unsettled colonial affiliation.

For as Bowen, perhaps even more than Yeats, saw it, to be Anglo-Irish in midcentury is to be equally sensitive to two contending historical viewpoints. One is that anti-imperial revolution and republicanism are, at least in spirit, ultimately an assertion of human right and a Hegelian, cultural-collective will—an organic development to which the outdated colonial class, in the broadest view, is right to capitulate. The other is that the nationalist agenda, and its violent, ideologically inflexible contrivance of a Gaelic-Catholic state, amounts to an extirpation of certain aspects of Big House society that are worth saving, not least of which are its traditions of cosmopolitan thought and diplomatic approaches to the national question. Because they are permeated with this irresolute double consciousness, the Cork interludes cannot function as a site of ex-urban rootedness or transcendent order; but they can and do perform a more significant function, which is to deconstruct the binary that would align Ireland with nation-centric rootedness and metropolitan Europe with cosmopolitan disaffection and historical omniscience.

The Cork interlude in *The Heat of the Day* is in fact riddled with contrasting sentiments about history and belonging. It focuses around the question of an Ascendancy estate, Mount Morris, that Stella's son Roderick stands to inherit after he serves in the British army during the war. As much as Stella sees the Big House, from the perspective of London's wartime modernity, as a "ghostly" place of "unearthly disassociation from everything" (182, 196), she also senses "the arrested energy of the [home's] nature," the Yeatsian "strength . . . in the rising tree trunks rooted gripping the slope" surrounding the demesne. She detects the "unfinishable hours" of its once social atmosphere (194), and the "unfinished symphony of love" interrupted by "all the wars," that is, the world wars as well as the armed conflicts between England and Ireland and then within Ireland (197). Increasingly affected by the notion that this is a narrative still being written—"the story was [not] at an end—at a pause it was, but perhaps a pause for the turning point?"—Stella comes to see the property as a "historic future," as does Roderick when he travels there (194, 353).

Stella, like Bowen, is not certain where she belongs in relation to the past, especially given its traditionally patriarchal (and, for Ascendancy property, patrilineal) authorship, but it is *because* of this uncertainty that she realizes her story cannot be cast aside, that it cannot be, as it had been among London's moderns, "shed like so much superfluous weight." It cannot be shed, as Robert wishes, because unlike his, which is frozen in the museum-like preserved rooms and the numerous photographs of his past at the Kelway home in the London countryside, her story has never been so conclusively written in the first place: "She, like [Robert], had come loose from her moorings; but while what she had left behind her had dissolved behind her, what he had left behind him was not to be denied" (125). Thus she is compelled to look twice at, to re-vision, the governing ideas of national and historical loss or aftermath in English modernity. She is beginning to realize that her future may lie not just in revisiting, but also rewriting, the "dissolved" past she is being wooed into abandoning. As Stella walks through the rooms at Mount Morris, Bowen's narrator tells us that "[o]ne could only suppose that the apparently forgotten beginning of any story was unforgettable," and indeed, in the novel itself, the narrative is beginning to turn against the notion of temporal stasis and displacement, to punch a hole in the "vacuum as to future [and] vacuum as to past" that had defined the London scenes (103).

Stella's return from Ireland does in fact make something significant happen—the demise of Robert, who confesses his work as a Nazi spy. The connection between the two events lies in the fact that Stella's overall or "final" reaction to inheriting the Big House, and her sense of connectedness to the counterfactual national history it represents, is liminal, not decisive. What she gains or "inherits" from the Cork interlude, in other words, is that neither a nostalgic nor an apocalyptic reading of history holds true. Speaking of the home and its furnishings, but also indirectly of history, she notes that because "the fatal connection between the past and future [was] broken [by] her generation," the inherited property need not be a return to that past: "old things [could] be pushed into a new position; those which could not comply, which could not be made to pick up the theme of the new song, would go" (195). She understands the pitfalls of "unload[ing] the past" on the new generation (177)—just as Bowen, regarding the new Republic of Ireland in 1949, insisted that "we cannot afford to have ghosts on this clearing scene" (BC 459)—but she also "never would agree that Roderick had been victimized: he had been fitted into a destiny; better, it seemed to her, than freedom in nothing" (194). Roderick's carrying on of the Big House tradition but in his own fashion ("This powerhouse of nothingness, hive of lives in abeyance, seemed to Roderick no more peculiar than any other abode" [226]), not only posits a postwar future but also open-endedly inserts Ireland, and the possibility of a new Protestant generation involved in inter-sovereign relationships between Eire and England, into that future.[4]

This insistence on the importance to the *future* of an unsettled relationship to the past is crucial, and in it lies the key to Bowen's Irish critique of mainstream modernist oppositions of national and postnational thinking and belonging. Positioned between these two options—just as Stella is initially pinned between the imperial allegiance of Harrison and the fully disaffected, posthistorical totalitarianism of Robert—Bowen draws from her awareness of Ireland's anxious position between nation-as-identity and nation-as-parochial-regression and elaborates it into a cross-examination of modern political absolutes in general. Reading the Ascendancy estate neither as an esoteric, racial order nor an outdated and invalid tradition, she in turn, when back in London, reads the tense political moment as calling for neither totalitarianism nor an imperialist brand of panoptic internationalism. For although Stella draws no firm ideological convictions from her trip to Ireland, she does now find the courage to confront Robert on his spying for Germany, which "undo[es] everything from the beginning" and breaks the historical seal of their "hypnotic, futureless" love affair (304, 109). She also ultimately resists Harrison, the spy-detective who represents the empire's all-seeing, all-equating eye. To extrapolate this position, one might say that "indecision," deemed a colonial neurosis, is in fact no different than what an established, internationally reciprocal state would be allowed to hail as its democracy.

Maude Ellmann refers to Stella's double refusal as a move from "practicing neutrality involuntarily" to proving that "no island can remain immune to history, or to horror" (152). Stella's action is exactly that, for it not only denies historical and geographic exclusivity to *both* islands but also challenges nationalistic and modern absolutes of time and space in the process. Back in London, Stella is full of a resistant indecision that she is accused of "br[inging] back from Ireland . . . like the flu" (208). Acting out of this indecision—not accusing Robert of spying, but refusing to dismiss the possibility—ruptures Robert and Stella's tacit agreement about what Graham Greene called "the enormous equal past" (163). Andrew Bennett and Nicholas Royle observe that even as the novel illustrates the "inextricable knitting together of the individual and the national, the personal and the political," it also "works towards an affirmation of the undecidability of identity" (92, 93). I would further specify that the novel, in so doing, is engaging in a form of democratic and critical cosmopolitanism, revising international modernity from a vantage point sensitive to the more continuous, interruptive nature of a postcolonial history. That is to say, it tempers absolutist ideas about the individual's relationship to nation and history not just for the abstract or purely subversive sake of "undecidability," but from a specific colonial perspective that understands national affiliation and historical particularity as indissoluble contingencies. Bowen's point is that we must weigh equally the need and the limits of these particular affiliations as opposed to seeing them as former orthodoxies, now on the brink of annihilation, whose aftermath calls for extreme ideologies.

This challenge to absolute historical and national positions is also evident, with more subtlety and perhaps greater craft, in *The House in Paris*. Within its English, Irish, and Continental landscape, the novel presents two worlds, or two international modes: one is manifest and secure, the other potential and erratic, always struggling to come to light as a totality. The first, manifest world is the social realm ordered by the ubiquitous eyes of Mme Fisher and Mrs. Michaelis, whose "worldliness beg[an] so deep down that it seem[ed] to be the heart" (174). From their inland, domestic centers in Paris and London, each of these matriarchs is renowned for seeing, knowing and controlling the lives of others, across substantial distances if need be. The narrow world of feminine possibility they authorize is "like ice beginning to move south.... [a] cold zone [that] crept forward everywhere" (89). The other world—opaque, tentative, and fragmented—is comprised across a succession of islands, channel crossings, and coastal peripheries.

This insular and peripheral world is characterized by socially destabilizing events, interstitial national affiliations, and hybrid identities: Leopold is suspended in transit between his adoptive parents in the Italian port city of Spezia and his mother Karen, in England; Max and Karen have their clandestine rendezvous in the coastal towns of Boulogne and Hythe, on either side of the English Channel; and Karen's relations in Ireland, the Bents, live on Rushbrook, an island in Cobh harbor whose "nineteenth-century calm . . . makes the rest of Ireland a frantic or lonely dream" (75). Crossing from Cork to Holyhead, Karen has an auspicious conversation with an anonymous Irish woman who has "crossed eleven times" (96). Rife with innuendo, their discussion links Karen's Englishness and impending marriage with being "settled" and the woman's Irishness and single status with being "reckless and mad and bad" (94–96). But these distinctions prove to be mostly performative—"a mixture of showing off and suspicion, nearly as bad as sex" (94)—and they are blurred when Karen is later the one to take a sexual risk. Bowen signals this blurring of presumed national-racial distinctions when Karen repeats one of the Irish woman's phrases—"your poison's not mine"—to Naomi, and, after sleeping with Max, to herself (95, 168). Narration and dialogue also frequently suggest that this tentative, watery world is on the verge of engulfing the stable one, such as when Leopold evasively tells Henrietta that his greatest desire is "crossing the sea" (59), when Karen thinks of marriage as "stead[ying] a ship in a rough sea" (67), or when, regarding Hythe, Karen muses that being there with Max "made an island of the town," which "stayed like nowhere, near nowhere, cut off from everywhere else" (162).

These islands and crossings—and the tentative, in-between worlds they embody—have both an Irish historical significance and a more philosophical, minority-cosmopolitan significance. As for the former, they can be seen as reiterations of both Anglo-Irishness—that notoriously insular and, by the 1930s, nearly eclipsed category of cultural identity—and the uncertain international position of the young Irish state in general. That is to say, the novel's frequent scenes of isolation within an international, social landscape echo the tensions surrounding Irish identity within the dominant cosmopolitan milieu of the late 1920s and 1930s. Throughout this period, even though she rightly confessed to having little authority in speaking for Catholic Ireland, Bowen increasingly found herself speaking on behalf of the entire country and, not unlike Joyce, defending its international relevance. For example, she had recently taken occasion, during her review of a book on Irish history, to criticize English and Anglo-Irish "ignorance of Irish history": "Her entity as a country [and] . . . [h]er native—as opposed to the Anglo-Irish—culture w[ere], before the height of the Gaelic movement, ignored. In fact, Ireland was not objectified. [Only now does] Ireland [appear] on the European map" (CI 173–74). For Bowen, this diplomatic role was analogous to being suspended in the midst of a sea crossing. Indeed, in ways reminiscent of Joyce's symbolic use of the Kingstown/Holyhead ferry in "Nestor," Bowen's description of the Cork/Holyhead ferry, on which "everyone [was] bound for nowhere. . . . [as] [t]he ship plowed ahead steadily through the dark," strongly implies this concern for being occluded or unrecognized within an international, traveling milieu (95, 98).

Bowen more directly connects the novel's insular and peripheral settings to the challenges of an international Irish identity by setting its retrospective middle section, "The Past," in Ireland when she need not make the reach to do so. The gesture seems to be a deliberate effort to link the abstract idea of "the past" and Ireland symbolically, as if to imply that a significant portion of history is suspended there, as difficult to abandon as it is to carry meaningfully across the sea. Moreover, the section entitled "The Past" *begins* in Ireland, on "an April morning ten years ago" (67), in a setting that suggests not only insularity but also national irresolution. The modernist effect of the abrupt, unexplained jump of historical and geographic setting is thus associated with the disconnect, or de-synchronization, of Ireland and Europe. By selecting a date ten years prior to the novel's present, Bowen is referencing the first tentative year or two of the Irish Free State, just following the cessation of the Civil War in May 1923. Her choice of the island of Rushbrook—where Karen's uncle Bill, "who had not even a place [after] his house, Montebello, had been burnt in the troubles[,] . . . clung to the edges of his own soil" (75–76)—is also significant. As members of the transplanted Ascendancy recently compensated for their losses by the new pro-Treaty government (under Cumann na nGaedheal, which, in the novel's present, has just been unseated by the less internationally cooperative Fianna Fáil), the Bents are also signifiers of the uncertain global-democratic position of the island of Ireland itself.

In the context of the novel's present, an early 1930s Anglo-French social alliance whose politics, though not overt, lie in defending a vague ideal of democratic internationalism against nationalist socialism and ethnocentric fascism, the Irish Free State is suspiciously shifting away from a more discreet independence, with sworn allegiance to the English crown, and becoming a fully sovereign yet more insular republic. Internationally, this had raised concern over the degree to which the emerging state, as an outgrowth of cultural and political nationalism, was influenced by Continental fascism. The general election of 1932 had led to the rise of Fianna Fáil, a political party that, due to its cultural-nationalist ties, mass mobilization, and promotion of a centralized state economy, "had some similarities with [European] mass fascist movements, yet operated on democratic rather than totalitarian lines" (Girvin 134). The 1933 elections solidified the party's rise to prominence. An international Irish identity was therefore a subtle, tense, and nuanced matter, as Bowen's own quasi-espionage reports on neutral Ireland to the British Ministry of Information would soon make abundantly clear. Bowen's indecision regarding the Ascendancy (who "got their position and drew their power from a situation that shows an inherent wrong" [*BC* 452]) had also recently been redoubled when she inherited her family's estate, Bowen's Court, in 1930. To say the least, the idea of Anglo-Irishness, especially as it appeared to members of English and French society given to global-democratic views, was more than ever a matter of insularity and strange tenacity.

This concern is reflected in the Michaelis family's English-cosmopolitan opinion of Aunt Violet's decision to move from Florence to Cork:

> "Abroad" was inside their compass. But the idea of Aunt Violet in Ireland made them uncomfortable; it seemed insecure and pointless, as though she had chosen to settle on a raft. (75)

The tension between international society and an insecure nationality is underscored by Bowen's decision to associate the Irish subplot with the busy harbor of Cobh, which the Bents, who feel "the harbour is good company" (87), watch routinely each day. Cobh, called Queenstown until 1921 and not in Irish control until Eamon de Valera's government regained the four "Treaty Ports" in 1938, quite literally embodies the young state's vexed connection to interstate commerce and relations. Bowen in fact begins her "Notes on Eire" for the British Ministry of Information, in 1940, by explaining why Churchill's recent disparagement of Irish control of the ports had reignited anti-British sentiment, arguing that both countries would ultimately benefit from the ports remaining in Eire's control ("Notes" 11–12).

In the main, though, rather than commenting directly on these political contexts, *The House in Paris* extrapolates from them a more philosophical, subaltern-cosmopolitan concern for states of indecision and historical irresolution. Arguably, it challenges us to see these uncertain, interstitial states as democratic and influential, rather than simply tragic and passive, modes of being in the world. The story of the Italian-English-French-Jewish Leopold, whose future depends upon an origin he had not known was his, embodies this concern in a fundamental way. When Leopold responds to Henrietta's query about the place he would most like to visit, he pinpoints the distinction between the uprooted traveler and the traveler not yet sure of his origin: "where can you go if nobody knows you're born?" (55). To put this question—quintessentially Bowen in its connotative saturation—another way, how does one register destinations without a sense of beginning, or seek general without particular being?

Indeed, the combination of mobility and placed autonomy is what the well-traveled child Leopold, whom "journeys [do not] upset" (6), so viscerally yearns for: not a static home in which to be grounded, but a place to be *from*, an origin to render his movements meaningful. This desire for a retroactive origin is arguably the crux of Bowen's more flexible modernist temporality, one in which historical time is not cataclysmic (a traditional or mythic "then" partitioned from a modern "now") but overlapping and continuous (a past still happening, still being determined, and thus knifing into and influencing "now"). As the narrator, scrambling for verb tenses in an effort to frame Leopold's not-yet-factual backstory, observes, "nothing then could impair what had not been. So everything remained possible" (54).

Importantly, this tension between the present and a still "possible" past also has a spatial component, one that returns us to the idea of the novel's insurgent, unorthodox-cosmopolitan counternarrative. As we have seen, the transgressions and disruptions of the novel's past—events that the dominant social narrative engineered by Mme Fisher and Mrs. Michaelis tries to suppress or gentrify—have transpired primarily on islands, coasts, and sea-crossings that Bowen depicts as foreign or hybrid spaces. One of the more remarkable features of *The House in Paris* is its awareness that if these peripheral events and places could be strung together in their own narrative, they would form a second dimension of reality, an alternate vision or version of things. There is always an abiding threat, registered both thematically and formally, that such a counternarrative will, like a political rebellion, unite its fringe elements to interrupt and transform the status-quo narrative. If her affair produces a child, Karen thinks, "[t]he streets would stay torn up, the trams could not begin again" (169).

Seeds of this self-aware, dual narrative are sewn during the Irish scenes, when Karen surprisingly aligns her desire for Max with Ireland's "diehard," antitreaty republican revolution and, perhaps, leftist rebellions in general: "I wish the revolution would come soon; I should like to start fresh while I am still young, with everything that I had to depend on gone" (86). Karen's figurative association of her affair with prosovereignty Irish nationalism amounts to more than just a vague politicizing of a personal crisis. After all, the paternally Jewish Max is himself a transgressive figure, a suspect, stateless border-crosser whom the more traditional cosmopolitan societies in both Paris and London will only superficially accept. "I don't think he is as confident as he seems," Mrs. Michaelis opines: "The question of background: curious, isn't it? . . . And there is always that touch—Jewish perhaps—of womanishness about him . . . no one they knew in Paris had heard of him" (124–25). Max and Leopold (Max's offspring, and thus the lynchpin in the counternarrative) are indeed mobile outsiders, travelers whose lack of sovereign "background" renders them vulnerable, leaving them unable, as Mrs. Michaelis chides of Max, to "'mix' when [they] ha[ve] to" (124). As Neil Corcoran has observed, Leopold thus shares not only a name but also a thematic role with Joyce's Leopold Bloom (Corcoran 97).

It is not merely incidental that Max and Karen conceive Leopold while Ray has "sail[ed] to the east . . . on a mission so delicate that it must not appear to be a mission at all" (68). For their affair, "a [meeting] of refugees, glad to find themselves anywhere" (119), is literally of a world alternate to the one that Ray's imperial-corporate mission, sanctioned and genteel, represents. Hence, Bowen associates the time-bending "conception" of Leopold—"the idea of you, Leopold, [that] began to present with [Karen]" (165)—with different, more alienated modes of travel. The two-part romantic rendezvous that produces Leopold takes place in Boulogne and Hythe, coastal enclaves whose foreignness and insularity Bowen sharply augments. As Karen observes of Hythe, just after Leopold is physically conceived, "The stretch of forlorn marsh and sad sea-line made the snug town an island, a ship content to go nowhere . . . Karen, walking by Max, felt more isolated with him, more cut off from her own country than if they had been in Peru. You feel most foreign when you no longer belong where you did" (172).

Significantly, these musings about the dislocating foreignness of an ostensibly familiar ground echo Karen's feeling about Rushbrook, in Cobh. It is as if that former island has "repeated," to borrow a surprisingly apt phrase from Antonio Benitez-Rojo. Although the Caribbean and Irish contexts differ substantively, and although the "world" of the novel is primarily European, the idea of reorienting that "world" based on a dynamic starting point—an "instability . . . that 'repeats' itself, unfolding and bifurcating until it reaches all the seas and lands of the earth" (Benitez-Rojo 3)—does legitimately illuminate how the alternative transnational narrative of *The House in Paris* operates, or threatens to operate.

The novel does, after all, drop frequent hints about an island counternarrative whose instability "begins" in or is associated with the Irish subplot—a different story, born of accepted transgressions, that would originate in a dissenting view of worldliness. One of these hints is Bowen's intriguing use of the motif of poisoning, such as the repeated phrase "your poison's not mine." These words are originally uttered by the flamboyant, anonymous

Irish woman during her conversation with Karen on the ferry from Cobh to Holyhead. She uses it to imply that sexual liberty, not marriage for social stature, is her "poison" of choice. However, it is Karen who later repeats the phrase, twice, in reference to her affair with Max. Her decision to be with Max indeed "poisons" the dominant international and social narrative, just as Stella's journey to Mount Morris during Irish neutrality threatens to "undo everything from the beginning" in her relationship with Robert Kelway (*HD* 304).

Karen's decision to indulge her passion for Max also comes at the precise moment that she learns of Aunt Violet's death in a Dublin hospital, an event that she later tells Max "seemed to crack my home" (147). This phrase is particularly indicative of the interruptive power of the marginalized past, given that Karen is standing in her mother's well-appointed Chester Terrace home when she hears the news. Bowen implies that the entire, imperial-genteel worldview of Karen's upper class is "cracked" open by Jewish and Irish counternarratives that are resilient not because of their singular "other-ness," but because of their complexity of feeling. Aunt Violet signals a dis-ruptive carryover or re-surfacing of the Irish/insular subplot in other ways, for it is she, Karen thinks, who seemed to portend and desire Karen's affair with Max, in spite of Karen's mother: "What made Aunt Violet look at me like that? She saw Ray was my mother: did she want this for me? I saw her wondering what disaster could be like" (168). As a traveler who had moved from Florence to Ireland, Violet also links, or potentially links, Ireland and the continent in a narrative of murkier, more occulted motives—a story of "whatever in marriage stays unmapped and dark" (133). Moreover her name, Violet Bent, suggests its own discrepant permutations: in English, "violent," and in French, "*violer*," "to violate."

Indeed, it is with a kind of violence that the alternative transnational nar-rative begins to manifest itself aesthetically in the novel. Bowen is arguably nowhere more modern, or nowhere is her stylistically dissonant brand of modernism better displayed, than in the middle pages of part two, chapter 9, where the narrator describes the conception of Leopold. Here, as Karen looks about the Hythe hotel room after intercourse with Max, the prose be-comes dramatically disruptive, fitful, and discordant. Verb tense and point of view each shift numerous times as the narrator and character ponder whether time and space could have been altered by this act of willful "disas-ter" (168): "Is the outgoing current not strong enough to let you back? Were you not far out, is there no far out, or is there no current there? I am let back, safe, too safe; no one will ever know. . . . I shall die like Aunt Violet wondering what else there was; from this there is no escape for me after all. She must rely on marriage to carry her somewhere else. Till it did, she stayed bound to a gone moment, like a stopped clock with hands silently pointing at an hour it cannot be" (166).

In this suspended moment in Karen's mind, which is shot through with ellipses, dashes, and abrupt questions about time and memory that knife in from different narrative points of view, it is as if the counternarrative is "poisoning" and bending the primary narrative. During one series of abrupt memories, Bowen clearly links the "poison" of the Irish woman on the ferry with Aunt Violet and Leopold: "[The child] would be disaster. . . . They would have to see me as someone poisoned. . . . If a thing does act on you, it can only be poison, some foreign thing. 'Your poison's not mine,' she said . . . What made Aunt Violet look at me like that? . . . I saw her wondering what disaster would be like" (168). Bowen even implies that the words and time of the governing narrative have stopped, or will have been stopped, with Leopold's conception: "The street would stay torn up, the trams could not begin again. . . . How silent it is! Surely it must be time for a clock to strike? You would never think there was the street out there" (167).

The would-be child is in fact described as a narrative transformation, an event that would order the disparate elements of the peripheral, "foreign" past and thus transform the future:

> If a child were going to be born, there would still be something that had to be. . . . He would be the mark our hands did not leave on the grass, he would be the tamarisks [at Hythe] we only half saw. . . . Paris, then Twickenham, the boat train at Victoria, Boulogne . . . if he ran through those like a wire they would not fall apart. The boat going up the estuary [in Cork], the silent mountains, the harbour the day I knew Aunt Violet would die—those would not have been for nothing. He would have been there then and then and then. (167–68)

Leopold is born, and to some extent he does "r[u]n . . . like a wire" connecting the peripheral and central settings, coasts and inlands, pasts and presents, of the novel. But, in the telling, these remain disjunct, out of harmony, reflecting a violation rather than their own, new order. Despite this, and despite Max's tragic end, it is not so easy to say that the status-quo social narrative simply wins.

As in *The Heat of the Day*—which ends with the birth of a son named after Stella and Louie's dead husbands, Roderick's taking ownership of Mount Morris in "the hour of the never-before" (352), the end of World War II, and Louie hoping her new son will "perhaps remember" as they watch swans flying westward from England (372)—the conclusion to *The House in Paris* is a study in contrasts, a combination of forward and backward glances, exiles and attachments.

In *The Heat of the Day*, Stella condemns Robert's fascism—"it is not so vastly simple as all that," she tells him, staring "at the mathematical spaces between the [stars]" (303)—without committing to Harrison's imperial allegiance. She allows the newspaper account of Robert's death to leave his motives, and her role, vague. Meanwhile, new futures are established, both in Ireland and England, independent of the fathers and husbands who died in the two world wars but under their names. In *The House in Paris*, Ray meets Leopold at Mme Fisher's and tentatively plans to bring him into his life with Karen ("till things get fixed up—if they ever do get fixed up" between them and Leopold's adoptive Italian family [251]), thus at least partially actualizing the hypothetical counternarrative quoted above. The overriding implication, in both novels, is that history has been altered, not ended—the story partly taken over, swerved from its expected course. Life "goes on," even formidably so, but without being wed to a specific doctrine: "Life, it was to be seen, selected its own methods of going on" (*HD* 366). This is all the more relevant when considered in the context of the immense pressures of teleological worldviews in Europe's midcentury.

These implications are strikingly evident in the final scene of *The House in Paris*, which takes place amidst the rush of Gare de Lyon station, where Ray has somewhat impulsively come to retrieve Leopold. The scene is laced with mixed attitudes toward modern dislocation:

> Where are we going now? The station is sounding, resounding, full of steam caught on light and arches of dark air: a temple to the intention to go somewhere. Sustained sound in the shell of stone and steel, racket and running, impatience and purpose, make the soul stand still like a refugee, clutching all it has got, asking: "I am where?" . . . The tramp inside Ray's clothes wanted to lie down here, put his cheek in his rolled coat, let trains keep on crashing out to Spain, Switzerland, Italy, let Paris wash like the sea at the foot of the ramp. . . . But the sto-

len boy is too delicate. Standing there on thin legs, he keeps his eyes on your face. Where are we going? Where are we going now? (267)

Early in the novel, disappointed at the likelihood of having no future with Max, Karen had accepted that she "would have to look for Max in Ray" (133). These descriptions of "the refugee in" Ray seem to do just that, turning Ray's typically refined, professional travel into a more abject journeying. They also make an island of the train station, at whose sides "Paris wash[es] like the sea," and from whose shores trains "crash out" to their distant destinations. It thus implies a bending or blending together of mobile worldliness and alienated displacement; aptly, it also merges the novel's symbols for dominant and discrepant cosmopolitanisms: the city and the sea.

In classic Bowen fashion, the passage also intersperses the desire for directional certainty and position with the sublime allure of rootlessness, at one level expressing a wish to make modern, mechanical travel into one's territory while at another expressing an almost instinctive need to know the direction, to locate the future, as embodied in the child's wish to know "where are we going now?" The resulting state of mind, although ambiguous, is perhaps most remarkable for the more static or total displacements in modernism that it is not: it is not, for example, the irrevocable, existential "walk home in the rain" that ends *A Farewell to Arms*, for Ray has shown up to get Leopold, the living embodiment of a past only tangentially his, and will leave with him. But neither does it echo a Yeatsian anxiety over the inability to make meaningful movements outside the "great-rooted blossomer" of tradition; for even though Ray and Leopold do not and cannot elect the life of full-on wanderers, their future direction and objective remain hauntingly obscure. We last see them "wait[ing] . . . for their taxi to come," set to return into the Paris night, perhaps to Karen, perhaps not (269).

In his study *Modernism, Ireland, and the Erotics of Memory*, Nicholas Andrew Miller makes an observation about the need for a "continuous renegotiation" of the past in Irish writing that is profoundly apropos of Bowen's resistance to historical and national resolution:

The belief in a progressive historicism, in which the past is paradoxically known and revered precisely so as to be left behind, commits Irish culture to a myopic [and lethal] determinism. . . . Rather than [this] perpetual . . . divide across which the present obsessively confronts a dead past, ... [Irish modernism seeks] not to get the story straight, but to return to it continuously through narrative acts.... Such acts enable a process of memory work that, while always at some level invested in laying the past to rest, is also the very mechanism that ... giv[es] the past its opportunity to "occur," suddenly, eruptively, and interruptively in the present. (186–88)

Miller does not mention Bowen in his analysis, for it is based on Joyce and Yeats, but what he says here about the Irish modernist compulsion to maintain a dynamic, "interruptive" engagement with the past certainly applies to what Bowen is doing in these two Irish-European novels.

Far from a symbol of order or stillness, then, Ireland's role in Bowen's European narratives is to help illustrate that the modern dilemma of partitioned, space-engulfing time—what Stephen Spender called "an immense landscape with, on one side of a central divide, the order of the past, on the other, the chaos of the present" (x)—is based on a false premise. The exclusive choice between retracing the past, with the purported detachment of psychology or anthropology, or claiming that there is "nothing so positive as the abandoned past" (HD 125), is based on assumptions about the past as object, or as a fixed entity, that are disproven by the unfolding of a postcolonial present. For in that unfolding, the past—and the other places, presumably "outside time," in which it was experienced—show themselves to be inconclusive and still happening. The Cork interludes and their active, subversive reverberations throughout each narrative might therefore be taken as an analogue for Irish cosmopolitanism in its entirety, for they suggest the positive inevitability of revisiting these past questions and associations—physically, in memory, in subject matter—not simply as a vital part of one's life elsewhere, but also as a vital part of one's ever-evolving worldview. For Bowen, as for Beckett and Joyce, the result is a restless literary aesthetic that levels out false distinctions between the drives of attachment and detachment, rootedness and cosmopolitanism, culturally specific interpellation and universal affiliation, and instead speaks to the ways in which both kinds of drives, both types of psychic orientation, can and must operate simultaneously.

CHAPTER 5

"Haunt[ing] the Waterfront"

Place and Displacement in *Echo's Bones* and *Les Nouvelles*

Strictly speaking I believe I've never been anywhere. But that day I must have come back.

Samuel Beckett, "The End"

No single aspect of Samuel Beckett's modernism is more emblematic of the whole than its minimal, cartographically ambiguous settings. In these chapters, I want to consider the possibility that these vague spaces are neither universal, as Beckett criticism has traditionally maintained, nor singularly and manifestly Irish, as recent historical interpretations suggest, but transitional, situated in the overlap of incomplete and ongoing processes of national and global identification. To do so, I will read Beckett's transformation from named to unnamed places against the grain of the traditional national-to-cosmopolitan narrative, skeptically revising but not abandoning that narrative's ideas about the relationship between Irish contexts, nonterritorial poetics, and global humanitarianism. While lending new support to the emerging postcolonial argument that an original sense of cultural estrangement relative to Ireland lingers actively throughout Beckett's work, this reading will hopefully also lead us to a farther-reaching conclusion; namely, that it is the paradoxical process of thinking and moving *beyond* this estranged origin that generates Beckett's unique aesthetic of place.

A suitable way to begin is by examining the relationship between location and dislocation in four works from the key, transitional period in Beckett's career during which the author moved from being an "Irish" writer of lesser importance to an "international" writer and a major figure of modernism: the 1935 series of poems *Echo's Bones*, written in English and set in Ireland and Europe, and the three *Nouvelles* "The Expelled," "The Calmative," and "The End," Beckett's first French narratives, written in 1946.[1] All four of these short works focus on dislocation as a concrete socio-geographic phenomenon as well as a more abstract, philosophical concern. Taken together, they also reflect the travels (journeys between Europe and Ireland in the 1930s and 1940s, flight to Roussillon as a refugee of the French occupation, residence in Paris in 1946) and stylistic transformations (from specific settings, English language, and excessive intellectualism to vague settings, French language, and the impossibility of knowledge) that are usually understood in terms of the increasing cosmopolitanism of Beckett's life and art. Indeed, these texts embody the extended "moment" in which his aesthetic is transformed. They also help complicate the typical understanding of the cultural geographies of that transformation.

Locating Nowhere

Scholarly interpretation of Beckett's shift to ambiguous settings has developed along two primary trajectories. The more traditional of these holds that Beckett's "remorseless stripping away of [contextual] superfluities" (Alvarez 123) parallels his pursuit of fundamental human crises such as Cartesian duality or the contingency of language, as well as his increasing focus on the "unintelligible universe" (Webb 15), or "universe beyond redemption" (Hamilton and Hamilton 196), that is western, postwar modernity. As Colin Duckworth notes, Beckett's irreducibly vague landscapes help the author "[paint] a picture . . . of man in solitude imprisoned within the time and space of a silent and unresponsive universe" (104). Implicit, and sometimes explicit, in this approach is the idea that the modern and universal dilemmas Beckett depicts do not develop from, or at least do not draw their philosophical depth from, his relationship with Ireland. This is, in part, because the dominant idea of the "universe" within modernist discourse required the opposing concepts of rootedness and tradition—the known or knowable cultural space out of which the modern subject had been irreversibly thrown—and because Ireland could be easily used as an example of this familiar, known space. The fact that many of the settings in Beckett's earlier works were concretely Irish helped to align the philosophical and political implications of this opposition. Because Ireland meant location, rootedness, the territorial tribalism of civil war, and the familiarity that breeds contempt, the postwar cultural climates of Europe could all the more strongly signify dislocation, transience, and the ability to witness humanity's equal and pervasive undoing—its utter displacement from tradition and abandonment in the universe.

Beckett's aesthetic of placelessness thus became emblematic of an older cosmopolitan ideal which held that any reclamation of human dignity lay in our capacity to reject the known boundaries of particular nations and histories and to empathize instead with the mutual dislocation of humanity at large—"a human condition bedevilled by suffering [in a] world without end" (Hamilton and Hamilton 196). Lawrence Harvey, in his seminal study of Beckett's poetry, invokes this narrative when he calls *Echo's Bones* a "cosmic" poem that gradually transforms the "identifiable landscape" of Dublin into "Beckett's universe" (136) and that, in so doing, posits inexorable subjectivity as the "universal plight" of mankind (136). Citing a stanza in which the speaker turns from the polluted Liffey to gaze across an expanse of suburban fields—"a travesty of champaign to the mountains" ("Enueg I," line 25)—Harvey lauds Beckett's "poetic utilization and metamorphosis of an identifiable landscape" as emblematic of the link between European milieus and cosmopolitan aesthetics: "the image clearly expands and becomes . . . a metaphor for human existence. One would hardly think that the green Irish fields, patchy though they may be as they stretch out to the south, could furnish appropriate matter for the funereal vision. Yet with a scornful jibe (and a metaphor suggesting his own artistic metamorphoses) the poet reduces them, by a comparison to more favored relatives, to 'a travesty of champaign'" (128).

The assumption here is that Ireland, even for the outsider, is an all too familiar place, a territory that is everywhere defined by a provincial and rooted nonmodernity. With Ireland thus reduced to a symbol of antimodernity and located being, it is easier to accept the elision whereby French landscapes, the "more favored relatives" of Irish ones, can represent both a great tradition of cultural particularity and, via their witness to war's horror, a universal dislocation from history. That the "patchiness" and greenness of south Dublin's fields are assumed to be their most salient feature—even after Ireland's long, violent history of land dispute and partition—speaks volumes about the extent to which Irish landscapes are being placed outside modernity and used as emblems of orientation and rootedness.

The second and more recent trajectory examines place and displacement in much thicker cultural and historical contexts, especially with regard to Irish decolonization and the middle-class, Protestant perspectives from which Beckett experienced it. In the early 1990s, John Harrington and David Lloyd argued that it was not Beckett's use or dismissal of Irish settings but his concern for dislocation itself—his restless "dialectic of home and away" (Harrington) or, more emphatically, his "aesthetics of non-identity" (Lloyd)—that resonated most deeply with Ireland's colonial history. Harrington posited that "[i]n all [of Beckett's] work, Ireland [is] abstracted but never replaced by anyplace else," and noted that the "syndrome . . . of attraction and repulsion" to home that Beckett's characters experience is a pervasive motif in Irish literature (5). For Lloyd, Beckett's resistance to identification, and his refusal to socially orient his subjects, constituted a "resistan[ce] to the unifying drive of the ethical state" (*Anomalous* 9). His depictions of the disjuncture of subject and environment were, at least in part, the product of an Irish postcolonial intellect resisting both the hegemony of imperialism and the reactionary cultural essentialism of bourgeois nationalism. Alex Davis extends this approach when he argues, of *Echo's Bones*, that "the modernist 'homelessness' or 'displacement' experienced by the speakers [is] not reducible to existential 'throwness,'" for it is "conditioned by, and constitutes a reaction from, the Irish Free State" (144).[2]

I think that we can put these two interpretations of Beckettian dislocation, the Irish historical and the universal, into dialogue. Specifically, I would like to consider how Beckett's sense of disorientation within Ireland—and the irresolution with regard to Irish identity that his works convey—invite us not to overturn, but to redefine, his cosmopolitan significance. Once one recognizes that the lack of native belonging and the subversion of statist integration are major components of Beckett's poetics of dislocation (as postcolonial readings help reveal), one is also then compelled to reconsider the nature and meaning of the ways in which his work reaches beyond Irish contexts. Perhaps the defining transition in Beckett's modernist emergence is not the move from a familiar, historical ground to a worldly, philosophical space of uncertainty, but the far subtler move from a culturally particular lack of integration into a more pervasive experience and understanding of the same.

I would offer that—rather than a rootedness in history jettisoned in favor of Europe's cosmopolitan modernity, yet also more than a cultural dislocation within the colonial homeland—the source or generative locus of Beckett's aesthetic of disorientation is Ireland's ambiguous border itself. That is to say, his unique expression of homelessness is neither Irish nor universal in nature, but an expression of the vague boundaries between colony and world and of the interminably multidirectional move between a minority origin and an ecumenical perspective. This possibility emerges more distinctly when we look at how the works that mark the emergence of his mature style repeatedly stage the problem of departing or abstracting a native, but unfamiliar, place.

Echo's Bones: Radical, Local Displacement

The thirteen poems published as *Echo's Bones*, which Beckett felt represented his best work in the genre, offer some of the author's most tangible engagements with Dublin, but they also draw upon his early travels in Europe and contain some of his most formidable images of universal vastness, territorial negation, and subjective space. The second and longest poem in the series, "Enueg I," is particularly remarkable for its abrupt vacillation between close-range encounters with Dublin's socioeconomic disenfranchisement and images of vastness and subjective spatial annulment:

> at Parnell Bridge a dying barge
> carrying a cargo of nails and timber
> rocks itself softly in the foaming cloister of the lock;
> on the far bank a gang of down and outs would seem to be mending a
>   beam.
> Then for miles only wind
> and the weals creeping alongside on the water
> and the world opening up to the south
> across a travesty of champaign to the mountains
> and the stillborn evening turning a filthy green
> manuring the night fungus
> and the mind annulled
> wrecked in wind. ("Enueg I," lines 18–29)

These lines amount to more than a deployment of modernist fragmentation against nationalist ideals of order, for they also express disunity as a sited emotional predicament. The estrangement, in other words, is not introduced into the setting via disruptive aesthetics but drawn from it, an expression of the speaker's frustrated inability to connect with, or to draw connections between, the people and places in his immediate environment. This ultralocal source of the poem's social and environmental dissonance is again evident when the speaker recalls trying to engage a child who had been turned out of a gated playing field:

> I stopped and climbed the bank to see the game.
> A child fidgeting at the gate called up:
> "Would we be let in Mister?"
> "Certainly" I said "you would."
> But, afraid, he set off down the road.
> "Well" I called after him "why wouldn't you go in?"
> "Oh" he said, knowingly,
> "I was in that field before and I got put out."
> So on,
> derelict,
> as from a bush of gorse on fire in the mountain after dark,
> or, in Sumatra, the jungle hymen,
> the still flagrant rafflesia. (lines 37–49)

The aborted gesture of empathy, and the dissonant juxtaposition of industrial density and open fields, are not just a subversive assault on nationalist and bourgeois consensus—what Patricia Coughlan, in her assessment of the poem, calls a "willful scattering of the lineaments of the phenomenal world into disorder" (190)—for they also reflect the actual socioeconomic fragmentation and environmental imbalances of 1930s Dublin. Like those I quoted previously, these lines evoke the uneven development, social dichotomy, and struggles over land and property that were signatures of late colonial and Free State Dublin.[3] Moreover, they reflect the simultaneous empathy and estrangement that Beckett frequently claims to have felt as he witnessed, and recognized his own participation in, these dichotomies.

Indeed, Beckett often referred to "the unhappiness around me" as one of his most "obsessional" memories of life in Dublin (qtd. in Gordon 7; qtd. in Knowlson xxi). The speaker's dejected "so on, / derelict," as he walks away, anticipates numerous scenes of stifled compassion for native exiles or local homeless persons in Beckett's later work, from the bedraggled vagabonds of the *Nouvelles* (1946) to the stooped and hooded peasant woman of "Not

I" (1972) and the "old beggar woman . . . fumbling at a big garden gate" in "Company" (1980). Like the speaker's other attempted exits and separations in the poem, it also implies an effort to break with, or to move "on" from, this alienating native situation. This is jarringly emphasized by the poem's sudden reference to the Indonesian jungle. I will consider this second, extranational, dimension of Beckettian displacement shortly.

In their efforts to correct Eurocentric locations of modernity, Luke Gibbons, Terry Eagleton, David Lloyd, and Joe Cleary have each argued that life in nineteenth- and twentieth-century Ireland was typically not defined by absorption in the monoliths of nationalist ideology or "the torpor of tradition" (Gibbons 6), but by the daily challenge of identifying oneself, or setting one's normative values, relative to a society beset by cultural and historical dispute, shifting political divisions, and complex class affiliations. Protestants and Catholics, men and women, upper and lower classes of course witnessed markedly different aspects of this division. However, a great number of people in each of these groups have also shared substantively in the experience of a country defined by "disintegration and fragmentation" (Gibbons 6), "the episodes and fragments of a history still in progress" (Lloyd, *Anomalous* 11), and "a history of claim and counter claim" that resulted in "an exemplary nursery of exilic consciousness" for both immigrants and emigrants (Cleary, "Introduction" 2, 7). Although general, this distinction is important, for it reminds us that Beckett's Ireland was absolutely not, at ground level, characterized by its "knowness" and familiarity, but, as in many instances of colonial modernity, by an inherent and pervasive sense of internal estrangement.

As Sean Kennedy has argued, Beckett's poetics of dislocation is not merely a resistance to nation-statist hegemony, for it also expresses his genuine and unresolved feelings of unbelonging—his "hauntological" memories of disconnection and fraught attachment within his family and Ireland more broadly ("Require a Subject?" 16–18). Speaking of Beckett's early French narrative "The End," whose narrator is lost in an unnamed urban environment that heavily implies the culturally divided Dublin of the Free State, Kennedy notes that the narrator's bewilderment not only "resist[s] the strictures of social location" under nationalism (102) but also expresses Beckett's own deeply seated and unresolved feelings of unbelonging. More than an antistatist "refusal of integration at any level" (Lloyd, *Anomalous* 55), in other words, the text's obscuring of place also conveys a genuine

"disorientation . . . linked to Beckett's memories of the revolutionary period . . . and specifically to certain changes in the spatialized *mentalité* of
Ireland's Protestant minorities during the Irish revolution" (98).

As opposed to First World concepts of modernity, in which the dislocations of the present dramatically supplant a previous phase of stability or
tradition, social and cultural bewilderment in the colonial idiom may thus
be a point of origin in itself, a phenomenon that takes place before, not after,
one has experienced the homeland as a sovereign consensus. The feeling of
radical disorientation in Beckett's poetry, of being cut off from the land and
from other individuals, reflects this broader experience of colonial modernity, as well as the version of it that Beckett, a member of one of Ireland's
least assimilated Protestant sub-classes, encountered personally. In *Echo's
Bones*, this native disunity is most palpable when the speaker's psychic alienation mirrors the unsettling proximity of urban disenfranchisement, spacious suburban property, and vast natural landscapes:

> Exeo in a spasm
> . . . .
> and lapse down blankly under the scream of the hoarding
> round the bright stiff banner of the hoarding
> into a black west
> throttled with clouds.
> Above the mansions the algum trees
> the mountains
> my skull sullenly
> clot of anger
> skewered aloft strangled in the cang of the wind ("Enueg I" lines 1–14)

Leaving What's Partial: The Paradox of Colonial Expatriation

This problem of radical dislocation in the "unfamiliar native land" one oc-
cupies is, however, only half of the Beckettian crisis of location (*Unnamable* 314). For it is also compounded by the paradox of *leaving* this unsettled
place and of what it means to move "beyond" the unresolved origin. An
international poem written when Beckett was "caught between the two im-
possibilities of domestication and exile" (Harvey 67), *Echo's Bones* includes
scenes in Kassel, London, and Paris. In addition to this actual or physical

movement outside of Ireland, the poems also contain frequent gestures of cosmic spatial annulment, capacious references to the "earth" and "world," and nearly hermetic internalizations of the physical environment. In these ways, the poems do reflect the European-international modernist idea that synchronic and subjective time and space subsume particular historical and geographic phenomena and that international travel, urban modernity, and cross-cultural encounter make us feel this negative equalization of time and space more acutely.

In the first excerpt I quoted from "Enueg I," for example, the local expressions of displacement expand rapidly across space into "the world opening up" as well as, subjectively, into "the mind annulled." In "Dortmunder," set in Kassel, the speaker's late-night excursions are into "the magic of the Homer dusk," and he is "Habakkuk, mard of all sinners" (1, 12). A unifying theme of the poems is the insurmountable disjuncture between "earth" and "skull" and "sky"—the disconnect between environment, mind, and metaphysical cause or entity. These more synchronic and ontological expressions of estrangement do not, however, supersede or replace the Irish contexts of the speaker's disorientation; rather, they emerge while his questions about native or original orientation are still being asked, and still being felt.

Indeed, one of the striking features of the poems is the manner in which they intersperse memories of social alienation and frustrated belonging in Ireland—sometimes reaching back far into youth—with images of universal or earth-wide brokenness. "Serena II," written when Beckett had been traveling between London and Dublin, contains the following example:

> All these phantoms shuddering out of focus
> It is useless to close the eyes
> All the chords of the earth broken like a woman pianist's
> . . . .
> The fairy-tales of Meath ended
> So say your prayers now and go to bed
> Your prayers before the lamps start to sing behind the larches
> Here at these knees of stone
> Then to bye-bye on the bones ("Serena II" 43–53)

This is the first instance of a scenario that will recur frequently in Beckett's later work and quite soon in the *Nouvelles* of 1946: the memory of trying to imagine the lives of the stonecutters and laborers in the neighboring hillsides as their lamps are lit at night ("Except the stars, the first lights I ever knew," says the narrator of "The Expelled" [22]). As elsewhere in Beckett's work, but especially when here combined with the memory of Celtic fairy tales at bedtime and a cairn of stones atop a hill, it strongly conveys the feeling of being simultaneously close to and cut off from a cultural sense of place. More than a loss of familiar ground, then, the "clonic" and broken earth that the poem envisions implies a reiteration or perpetual rediscovery of that initial, domestic irresolution.

When one's sense of home has been confused from the start, the prospect of leaving home is sure to throw that confusion into sharper relief, frustrating one's efforts to see it whole and apart. This paradox is a powerful undercurrent of *Echo's Bones*, whose verses return, in a near-obsessive fashion, to the coastline itself, fixing on the act or moment of departing Dublin as if to suggest that the site of departure is an inexorable space in its own right. In "Serena II," for example, the speaker recalls standing above Kingstown harbor with county Meath visible in the northwest distance and the busy harbor below:

she took me up on to a watershed
whence like the rubrics of a childhood
behold Meath shining through a chink in the hills
posses of larches there is no going back on
a rout of tracks and streams fleeing to the sea
kindergartens of steeples and then the harbour
like a woman making to cover her breasts
and left me
with whatever trust of panic we went out
with so much shall we return ("Serena II" lines 27–36)

This is another first instance of a scene Beckett will render many times over, though without naming the setting, in his upcoming French narratives: the focal character alone in the hills of South Dublin, near the sea, contending with memories of walking with his father or mother amidst what he described to Thomas MacGreevy as "the calm secret hostility" of the fields around Foxrock (*Letters* vol. 1, 136). Indeed, as late as "Company" (1980) Beckett returns to the memory of "your hiding place on the hillside. . . . Straining out from your nest in the gorse with your eyes across the water till they ache" (17). Here as there, the coastal scene superimposes the inclination toward home and away, the trajectories of "[going] out" and "return," as if the firm resolve of exile has mingled with a poignant awareness of home as something incomplete, a "rubric" that never fully materialized. Such sentiments abound in a 1948 letter to Georges Duthuit wherein Beckett conflates the aging Henri Matisse and his own deceased father: "I had a dream about Matisse—he was saying, in Dublin slang, that he was exhausted ('I'm bet'). My father, in his final coma, kept saying Fight, fight, fight. Yes, I have wonderful memories, which can only grow in volume. I am going to have lunch, then go for a walk on the long green slopes from where, on a clear day, when I was a child, I used to see the mountains of Wales. . . . Romantic landscape, but dry old stick of a traveler" (*Letters* vol. 2, 87).

Like the multidirectional epiphanies of Stephen Dedalus as he stands along this same coastline, the lines from "Serena II" proclaim a terminal expatriation—"there is no going back"—even as they hint at a larger, traumatic history of Irish dislocation that dwarfs the individual departure and undercuts any presumption to delimit national time and space. The "rout of tracks . . . fleeing to the sea" denote the roads and rail lines around the imperial port and docks; but at a more subtle and spectral level, they suggest the still-visible trails carved into hillsides by famine refugees in the 1840s. The general tone of flight and abandonment also hints at this traumatic emigration—one that Beckett deeply sympathized with but also felt disconnected from. It is thus a poem of departure, to be sure, but a departure that revives and carries with it an unresolved sense of origin. So too is the penultimate short verse of the collection. Although geographically abstract, it seems to leave us in the midst of a coastal departure, or series of departures, that can never be finalized: "redeem the surrogate goodbyes / the sheet astream in your hand / who have no more for the land / and the glass unmisted above your eyes" ("Da Tagte Es" lines 1–4). Rather than signifying a terminal separation from Ireland that, as Harvey maintains, "forecasts the poet's eventual migration to the continent," *Echo's Bones* speaks profoundly to the indelibility of an irreconcilable origin. Indeed, this would be a viable definition of the Beckett "universe": not a synchronic, transhistorical space, but an original dislocation, a modality of the yet-to-belong, that extends or is repeated indefinitely.

Neither Nation nor World: The Challenges
of Minority Cosmopolitanism

What hangs in the balance of this more continuous interpretation of displacement in Beckett is not so much his degree of Irishness as whether a canonical or a minority paradigm of cosmopolitanism is more appropriate for understanding his parallel movement from concrete to ambiguous social geographies and from Ireland to Europe. That is to say, it is the *kind* of world, and world subject, Beckett speaks to that is at stake. I would argue that postcolonial and minority approaches to cosmopolitanism offer the more suitable framework, for it is only in these approaches that experiences of unachieved and unresolved nation-state belonging are used as a basis from which to project ecumenical modes of thought and feeling. In doing so, they tend to consider the globe or universe as an equally unachieved abstraction, and to see the human subject, in its most plausible generalization, as subsisting between the two.

Distinguishing diasporic intellectual traditions from Enlightenment notions of travel and knowledge, Jessica Dubow has argued that while the latter are "structured . . . by [the concept] of nostos [which was] coincident with the establishment of the boundary . . . of the sovereign state," the former are based in "an originary condition of the open and incomplete" (216). The travels of *Echo's Bones*—the various physical and psychological movements "beyond" Ireland that it stages—are not, as we have seen, movements from known to unknown ground, from rootedness to universal bewilderment, but extensions and internalizations of "an originary condition of the open and incomplete." Although they are extranational, they are also subnational or prenational, insofar as they take place prior to any experience of the homeland as a historical and geographic consensus. The type of mobile perspective or consciousness they reflect is therefore closer to the diasporic than to the supranational; or, at the very least, closer to the minority worldview that Julia Kristeva calls "a cosmopolitanism of those who have been flayed," a worldview based in the "recogni[tion] that one becomes a foreigner in another country because one is already a foreigner from within" (14).

Indeed, Beckett's abiding interest in the paradox of becoming detached from an unachieved origin points to one of the central challenges in critical approaches to globalization and minority or anticolonial cosmopolitanism. That challenge, in its most basic sense, is to particularize the spaces, and articulate the identities, that subsist dynamically between nation and world, between a particularity defined by historical and racial or ethnic difference and a universal human condition based in ontological and ethical sameness. While iterations of postcolonial counterhegemony risk fixation upon the problems of national identity and/or racial difference, iterations of cosmopolitan multiculturalism risk re-inscribing spatially undifferentiated notions of culture that equate hybrid mobility with the flows of capital in the metropolitan First World but overlook the heterogeneity of specific processes of national and racial identification.

As Rachel Lee notes in her analysis of vague settings in Asian-American fiction, when particular experiences of dislocation are elided with modern or postmodern concepts of deracinated or irreducibly plural cultural space, whatever is unique to a minority displacement is canceled out and is thus prohibited from influencing the dominant global imaginary. If we do not "clarify the sited character of transnational identities" by recognizing settings that "[although] geographically unnamed, [are] not altogether placeless" (152), says Lee, we "disassociate the psychological effects of 'dislocation' from the material conditions of being dislocated" (152). The ironic result is that psychic and literal dislocation "no longer pertain to the refugee [but,] under the discourse of the 'universal' subject, . . . to the modern subject, [which] the refugee only [becomes] with his/her emigration to the First World" (153).

Beckett is not a refugee in the same sense as many of the Asian-Americans to whom Lee refers. However, when we subject his settings to this same binary (if named, they are Irish; if unnamed, they represent something universal) we similarly co-opt, within dominant constructs of modernity and universalism, a form of dislocation that is always at some level culturally specific. Challenging this misreading has less to do with applying Beckett's biography or categorizing him as a minority author than with working to redefine the ways in which we think about diversity in a global context. For in a world dominated by the "ongoing conflict between globalization and its internationalism, on one side, and resurgent nationalism and patriotism, on the other" (Darwhadker 5), the key to thinking in broad terms about the human condition lies in resisting standard "formulations [that] pit ethnic particularity in opposition to universalism" (Koshy 595). This means breaking down stubborn oppositions between the knowable finitude of particular origins and the ever-expanding, malleable space of modern or postmodern transculturation; it means, as Susan Koshy has recently argued, that we envision "a cosmopolitanism in which the partial belonging of the minority illuminates . . . the provisionality of human 'residence on earth' [Neruda]" (Koshy 597).

In his definition of "vernacular cosmopolitanism," Homi Bhabha posits that the minority trajectory of global citizenship is not about embracing or rejecting a fixed heritage but rather maintaining a dynamic affiliation with the ongoing construction of a sense of origin. He calls this a "continua of identification [with] the process of being subjected to, or the subject of, a particular historicity or system of cultural difference and discrimination" (197). Rather than claiming or abandoning one's colonial or minority inheritance, one "emphasiz[es] [its meaning] through an insistent repetition of starting again [and] re-visioning," such that it is continually "'*recounted*' or reconstituted as a historical sign in a continua of transformation" (198). This kinetic and interminable process of re-identifying one's derivation resists both the static idea of a primary identity and "the abstract idea . . . of the universal similitude of all humanity" (199). For when the place of one's initial belonging is always yet to be established, so too must the notion of an "ethical universal [be transformed] into an 'unsatisfied' futurity" (202).

The traces of Ireland, and of Irish dislocation, that persist in Beckett's work even as he moves to vague settings can be seen as the "insistent repetition" of an unresolved Irish belonging, or the "starting again [and] re-visioning" of the nonnational (or not nationally integrated) Irish experiences that suffuse his personal continua of transformation. In *Waiting for Godot*, Lucky's speech arguably embodies this re-visioning. It is, after all, a speech of insistent repetitions, "unfinished" fragments, and returns: "I resume the skull fading fading fading and concurrently simultaneously what is more for reasons unknown in spite of the tennis on on the beard the flames the tears the stones so blue so calm alas alas on on the skull the skull the skull the skull in Connemara in spite of the tennis the labors abandoned left unfinished graver still abode of stones in a word I resume alas alas abandoned unfinished the skull the skull in Connemara" (30). The concrete but dislocated, repeated image of the skull has both regional and universal connotations. It suggests rural Ireland and the insufficiently mourned or explained suffering of the famine, while at the same time, "concurrently, simultaneously," it suggests Hamlet's more abstractly philosophical concern for the fleeting nature of human consciousness. The repetition of nonintegrated places, spaces, and objects (including the tennis lawn, Elizabeth Bowen's eminent symbol of Anglo-Irish disconnection) meanwhile reflects the need to reiterate what has not yet been understood, to begin it again, to resist fully equating it with other finished stories. Appropriately, Lucky's diatribe ends with the word "unfinished" (29). Seen in this light, whatever is potentially global about Beckett hinges not on Ireland "disappearing" but, as *Echo's Bones* predicts, on its inability to appear as a coherent site in the first place—a troubled relationship to a troubled nation that is neither negated nor resolved, but rather extended along a continuum as a distinct layer or register in more capacious evocations of displacement.

Crucially, this extension of the unresolved origin, and its aesthetic correlative of local Irish registers that subsist within vague geographies, do not in turn correlate to a restriction of philosophical thought. On the contrary, they signify a vital, decolonial repositioning of the philosophical subject: the self or cogito, removed from the traditional trajectory of rational progression and gradual abstraction, is placed instead in a state of perpetual transition, an overlapping of particular and universal affiliation in which the reconciliation of past injustice and the attainment of universal absolution remain equally remote, if not equally absurd propositions. Perhaps none of Beckett's works speak more strongly to this interstitial positioning of the philosophical subject than do the first works he published in French: the 1946 minitrilogy of *Nouvelles*—"The Expelled," "The Calmative," and "The End."

Each of these fictional monologues is narrated by an unnamed vagabond who is compelled to tell tales of his former existence in order to stave off the silence of death. It is implied that he does so just after his "death by drowning" in a small boat that he had set adrift on "the choppy waters of the bay" ("Calmative" 29; "End" 71). The subject of his compulsive, posthumous narration is his itinerant existence in the perplexing city of his birth and his apparent returns to that city after having departed it. Whether he has actually departed and/or returned to his native city cannot be verified because, having always felt "out of order" when there, he can't recall its proper limits ("Calmative" 32). He bid many "strange farewells" to its denizens, or so he recalls, yet he can't verify that the other places he then visited were in fact other ("Calmative" 32). As the narrator of "The Calmative" puts it, "there was never any city but the one. . . . I only know the city of my childhood, I must have seen the other, but unbelieving" ("Calmative" 28). The narrator of "The Expelled" claims always to have lived in the same confusing place but ends up with a very similar uncertainty about whether he's ever crossed a border: "I did not know the town very well, scene of my birth and of my first steps in this world, and then of all the others" ("Expelled" 13). The narrator of "The End" also remarks upon the difficulty of distinguishing the borders of a contingent origin: "I never look back when leaving. . . . And yet I sometimes did. But even without looking back it seems to me I should have seen something when leaving. But there it is" (53–54). Within the world of these narratives, placement and displacement do not follow a discernible spatial or temporal sequence. Their radical or essential state of confusion refer not to a phase of orientation and belonging that is now gone or destroyed, but to the paradoxical condition of being uprooted or separated from a place that already was disorienting.

Although the narrator does not name the bewildering city of his birth, numerous details of the topography, dialect, and culture strongly imply the environs of greater Dublin in the 1920s and 1930s while its coastal scenes imply the seaside Protestant suburbs of south Dublin, and nearby hills from Kingstown harbor down to Killiney. All of the stories play out a "statodynamic" motif of moving away and back along routes extending from the city in the west, to the hilly suburbs, shoreline, harbor, and bay in the east ("Calmative" 43). Each story also contains references to Beckett's childhood memories of burning gorse bushes in the hills, watching the lights in the harbor, walking in the hills with his father, and, in general, feeling disconnected from the local community. In her guide to Beckett for the Twayne's series, Linda Ben-Zvi accepts this theme of native exile, within an unnamed Dublin, as a matter of course: "The speaker is again an outcast with no fixed address, again in Dublin (unnamed) 'the city of my childhood'" (78). In "The End," the narrator ultimately takes up residence in a shack on "the cliffs . . . [where] the wind howled and the sea pounded on the shore," thus anticipating the more vague, suburban and coastal settings of the French trilogy, which also evoke the seaside vistas on the outskirts of southeast Dublin (58). But more important than their actual or intended setting is the manner in which these texts repeatedly stage the problem of *leaving* this location. Indeed, the *Nouvelles* are veritable odes to the paradox of moving on from an ambiguous origin, of confirming that one is ever elsewhere.

As I proposed in chapter 1, the coastal border of Ireland, particularly in greater Dublin and well into the twentieth century, represents the repeated frustration and denial of Ireland's involvement in a reciprocal internationalism. Rather than a threshold between demos and cosmos, it can therefore become a site at which the incompleteness of history, and the lack of a national or initial orientation, become all the more evident. Importantly, it is on this vexing seaside border—either at the Kingstown pier or on nearby beaches—that Beckett had his crucial epiphany about what became his mature, minimalist style, and it is also on this site that the *Nouvelles* hinge. Each story ends at or en route to the city's harbor on the bay, where the narrator, prior to commencing his narratives, put out to sea and drowned. It is thus in the midst of an unfinished crossing—indeed, a crossing barely begun— that he commences his series of narratives: "my mind . . . always flung back to where there was nothing" ("Calmative" 44). It would be fitting, then, to consider Beckett's aesthetic transformation in terms of crossing and return, of a never-completed movement between, rather than in terms of European arrival. For if the ambiguous space between Ireland and elsewhere is the generative locus of these narratives, the site of their achieved retrospective voice, then this vague space is arguably also the generative locus of the new, pared-down, unknowing mode of Beckett's Francophone art that is begun in the *Nouvelles*.

The stories themselves strongly suggest this possibility. Each one ends with an emotionally concrete example of the narrator's unresolved hope of belonging in his native community. This failed connection to the local community then abruptly dissolves into images that imply a more ontological bereftness. In "The Expelled," for example, a benevolent cab driver, one of "the common people" (21), takes it upon himself to aid the homeless narrator after the latter has been turned out of, or has "extricated [him]self from," a series of provisional and mean accommodations. The cab driver, who elects this duty instead of joining his family and community at a funeral, takes the narrator to visit a series of addresses, none of which pan out. He then offers his own home to the vagabond, who rejects the offer in favor of spending the night in the stable. The kindness of the cab driver leaves an indelible impression on the narrator's otherwise failing memory: "We did our best, both of us, to understand, to explain. . . . He had preferred me to a funeral, this was a fact which would endure forever" (21). As he describes their interaction, Beckett makes references to one of his own most enduring, place-oriented memories of Dublin—watching the lamps lit at dusk in the homes throughout the hillsides around Foxrock: "He was lighting the lamps. . . . if I except the stars, the first lights I ever knew"(22). Elsewhere in Beckett, the image of looking out at the lamps—often mirrored, as it is here, by a cosmic image of sky and stars—strongly evokes Becket's youthful sensitivity to, and feeling of utter disconnection from, his local community. Here it is merged into the more intimate scenario of the two men lighting the lamps on the cab: "I asked him if I might light the second lamp. . . . [I] lit and closed [it] at once, so that the wick might burn steady and bright in its snug little house, sheltered from the wind. . . . We saw nothing, by the light of these lamps . . . but others saw them from afar, two yellow glows sailing slowly through the air" (22).

This potential but unrealized belonging, which implies Beckett's Protestant disconnection and the more general social divisions of Free State Dublin, lingers palpably as the narrator abruptly leaves for the coast, then returns, then leaves again (He "[goes] back" to leave a banknote, then "return[s] to the yard to take it back" and heads again toward the shoreline). The story then shifts to a more spatially abstract register but remains haunted by this unresolved domestic orientation:

> Dawn was just breaking. I did not know where I was. I made towards the rising sun, towards where I thought it should rise, the quicker to come into the light. I would have liked a sea horizon, or a desert one. When I am abroad in the morning, I go to meet the sun, and in the evening when I am abroad, I follow it, till I am down among the dead. I don't know why I told this story. I could have just as well told another. Perhaps some other time I'll be able to tell another. Living souls, you will see how alike they are. (25)

The shift into topographical indifference, linguistic futility in the abstract, and the sameness of all "living souls" is rapid, but it clearly does not signify the move from a *familiar* home turf into the disorienting modern world. Rather, it derives from and expresses the unlocatable, vague boundary of otherness, both in general and in regard to the unresolved question of Irish belonging. Like the narratives themselves, which begin and end in exile while also always deferring a potential native residence, this concluding passage thoroughly complicates the starting point of expatriation. The narrator's movements expand into an eternal "going abroad," the landscape becomes inconsequential ("a sea horizon or a desert one"), and all "living souls" reveal their likeness, while he is still en route to the island's terminus.

The irony of separating from an unknown origin is even more pronounced in the closing scenes of "The Calmative." Having come "across the city . . . to the sea, [by] follow[ing] the river to its mouth," the narrator stops at the harbor, stares out at the lights "flashing from the coast, the islands, the headlands," and prepares to "slip unnoticed aboard a freighter outward bound and get far away" (30–31). Just as he decides "I'll never come back here," he is approached by "a young boy . . . barefoot in rags," an impoverished "[h]aunter of the waterfront" who, like the cab driver in "the Expelled," reaches out to him in kindness. They briefly exchange pleasantries and touch hands, but the potential connection fades quickly into miscommunication and regret as the narrator confesses he "ha[s] nothing"—neither money nor words—to share with the child. The narrator then rushes back into the "vaguely familiar" town (37), as if to confirm that "I was still of this world, of that world too, in a way" (37). While contact with the child proves he is still a living being, still part of the physical world, the boy's dismissal of him equally suggests that he is dead, or that his objectivity is unverifiable. This liminal status is confirmed as he runs about the deserted streets, narrowly missing substantive social encounters, and ending up lost and disoriented. He even tries the local dialect but fails absurdly: "Excuse me your honour, the Shepherds' Gate for the love of God! . . . The right time for mercy's sake! I might as well not have existed" (39).

On one level, the story is clearly playing out the more abstract philosophical crisis of incommunicable subjectivity and unverifiable objectivity. On another, however, its cycles of incomplete departure and unsuccessful return are dramatizing the impossibility of negating a place one has yet to understand. That these two levels of meaning—the philosophical and historical—are complimentary and interactive is increasingly clear as the narrative nears its conclusion. The narrator again makes near-contact with a child, this time a girl wearing "a kind of bonnet and clasped in her hand a book, of common prayer perhaps" who "vanishe[s] down the staircase without having yielded me her little smile" (44). As in "The Expelled," this single encounter is followed by the narrator's poignant awareness of the simultaneous proximity and remoteness of his community. As he wanders the streets in a "blinding void," he recognizes "in spite of shutters, blinds, and muslins, that many of the rooms were lit" and "that the houses were full people" (44–45). At one residence, he "thought of ringing at the door and asking for shelter and protection til morning" (45) but could not bring himself to do so. The scene again suggests the simultaneous hope and impossibility of belonging, a suspension between an equally unascertainable origin and terminus.

In the narrator's last effort to orient himself, and to select a direction, we are reminded of the Irish cultural and geographic significance of this suspended state: "I said, the sea is east, it's west I must go, to the left of north. But in vain I raised my eyes without hope to the sky" (45–46). Against the grain of the traditional, Eurocentric narrative of Beckett's cosmopolitanism and modernism, the last gesture of movement before all is engulfed by the universal image of the indifferent sky is a resolution to travel west, which is not only away from the coast and Europe but also toward the mythologized locus of Irish cultural and historical identity. Indeed, where else but in the partitioned Irish state, which resulted in the Republic's heartland of County Donegal lying to the west of the United Kingdom's "Northern Ireland," is the west so literally and comically "to the left of north"? There are echoes here of Gabriel Conroy's ironic decision, at the end of Joyce's "The Dead," to "set out on his journey westward" even as he stands immobilized, gazing into the snow "falling faintly through the universe" (225). For Beckett's perplexed subject, any actual journey to the west is even more absurd and improbable, but what's significant is not the actual move. What's significant is the manner in which Beckett, like Joyce, transposes the bidirectional consciousness implicit in leaving Ireland, the irresolvable simultaneity of the desire to depart and return, into a universal image of bewilderment. This gesture introduces the possibility that the generative moment or locus of his modernism—the place at which internalization, dislocation, and semiotic contingency are most acutely felt—is the ambiguous threshold of colonial departure itself.

As Alejandro Vallega notes, to "[reinterpret] the history of Western philosophy from the experience of the excluded," or to rethink it from "the underside of modernity," requires taking the subject out of the West's default trajectory of development and historical accumulation, which moves spatially from established to universal milieu and temporally into an irreversible futurity, and repositioning it in the more overlapping, nonsequential space and time of trajectories that originate in colonial conditions. The resulting framework is "not predicated on the futurity of [human] thought but on a poly-temporal exposure in which what is traditionally considered past may very well be a parallel temporal-spatial existence or an outright encroachment and interruption in the present and its futurity" (18–19). I would argue that the unresolved native disorientation in the *Nouvelles*, especially as it is intensified at the conclusion of each story and the prospect of leaving home, reflects this "poly-temporal," poly-spatial exposure more than it does traditional notions of the irreversible sameness and synchronicity of cosmopolitan-modernist space and time.

The conclusion of "The End" substantiates this hypothesis in an especially poignant manner. As in the two previous *Nouvelles*, the narrator recalls having moved toward the coast with designs on departing his city and the physical world. Upon the threshold of departure, he is struck by memories of a former, unfulfilled wish to belong in the community he is leaving. As he sets his small vessel adrift into the "choppy waters of the bay," he looks out at the lights in the hillsides. This time the distant lights, and the frustrated belonging they represent, are clearly tied to Beckett's personal experience: "It was evening, I was with my father on a height, he held my hand. I would have liked him to draw me close with a gesture of protective love, but his mind was on other things. He also taught me the names of the mountains" (71). The luminous symbols of domestic alienation are then mirrored by the lights of the buoys in the bay, and, as if universally, by the distant stars: "all aglow with distant fires, on sea, on land and in the sky, I drifted with the currents and the tides" (72). Depicting the narrator's final moments above water, Beckett then concludes the story, and the minitrilogy of *Nouvelles*, with an intense convergence of confinement and expansion, local and universal landscape: "The sea, the sky, the mountains and the islands closed in with a mighty systole, then scattered to the uttermost confines of space" (72).

To be sure, this is an internalization and spatial projection of a modern moment of departure, but the type of departure it is expressing, and projecting outward, is that which I have sought to illuminate throughout this book: a separation from an unreconciled origin, an expatriation from a homeland that was never familiar. The story ends on the insurmountably spacious image of the extinction of an individual consciousness, and its memories of home, into the "uttermost confines of space." But the experience that this vast image refers to, and projects outward, is the displacement of the yet-to-belong. The implosion and scattering to "uttermost . . . space" of the last vistas of the shoreline, like Beckett's own recognition at Dún Laoghaire harbor of his calling to a new and more abstract poetics, quite powerfully suggests that the threshold between Ireland and other lands is *itself* a site of something expansive and fundamentally human. Indeed, originating as it does from the disputed border between colony and world, the story's closing image of contraction and cosmic expansion is a fitting symbol of the forces conspiring to create Irish cosmopolitan modernism. For what it represents, as Joyce and Bowen would surely understand, is a consciousness that could no more be absorbed in a national than a global abstract—an interstitial subjectivity that negates no former absolute as it diffuses, but rather resonates infinitely the vague moment of colonial departure, the always plural trajectory of minority voyage.

CHAPTER 6

Beckett, Setting, and Cosmopolitical Philosophy

> If anything radically distinguishes the imagination of anti-imperialism, it is the primacy of the geographical.
>
> Edward Said, *Culture and Imperialism*

> The island, that's all the earth I know.
>
> Samuel Beckett, *The Unnamable*

Samuel Beckett's trilogy of novels *Molloy, Malone Dies,* and *The Unnamable,* completed in the late 1940s, marks both the full realization of Beckett's celebrated turn to abstract minimalism and a defining moment for international modernism. In these narratives, for the first time in full, Beckett strips away all identifiable setting so as to isolate a seemingly universal human condition: the "tedious, and perhaps futile" effort to know ourselves in language, to comprehend objectively and to express our subjective existence (214). According to biographers, this new, pared-down style stemmed at least partly from a revelation that Beckett had during a return to Ireland after he had been living as a refugee from occupied Paris in World War II. While visiting his ailing mother near his home in Foxrock, Beckett had been worrying over the feverish composition of his recent novel *Watt,* which chronicled a domestic servant's futile effort to comprehend the banal details of his employment in the Protestant suburbs of south Dublin. As he later explained to James Knowlson, he realized that *Watt*'s hyperbolic treatment of epistemological conundrums—also common to *Murphy*—reflected a Joyce-inspired obsession for "knowing more, [being] in control of one's material." His "own way," however, would now lie "in impoverishment, in lack of knowledge, and in taking away, in subtracting rather than adding" (qtd. in Knowlson 319).[1]

The exact site and intensity of this epiphany may be debatable, but there is little doubt that it transpired on the Dublin coast and that after it, from 1945 onward, Beckett developed a new, revolutionary mode of writing. As S. E. Gontarski puts it, Beckett now employed a revision process whereby he would, in successive drafts, deliberately strip away "world[s] more familiar and recognizable" so as to move "towards simplicity, toward the essential, toward the universal" (3–4). As I have tried to show, the relationship between Beckett's irreducibly vague or abstract settings and concepts of universality has traditionally hinged on an opposition of concepts—"Ireland, nationalism, familiarity, physical territory" versus "expatriation, cosmopolitanism, disorientation, abstract space"—that Beckett's life and work in the 1930s and 1940s actually serve to deconstruct. My aim in so doing has not been simply to reclaim the Irish contexts of the French writer but to propose that we need more politically nuanced theories of global citizenship in order to extrapolate the transcultural significance of his spatial aesthetic.

In what follows, I hope to expand this argument by showing that the narrators of Beckett's *Trilogy* are disoriented not because they are alienated from a formerly stable and coherent milieu but because they are traversing a region that they have never been able to comprehend as a geo-social abstraction. Their ontological and intrinsically human crises of self-knowledge thus arise *while* their attempt to orient themselves within their disputed local environment is still taking place. Similarly, both Beckett's mature style and his international frame of reference develop while his relationship to Ireland and Irish identity is still in process. This is important because it obliges us to consider a philosophical subject that is at once universal and *not* disengaged from historical processes—one that, even in its most fundamental aspect, is continually seeking or fashioning its place of origin.

In the twenty-first century, global consciousness increasingly denotes not a vague egalitarian ideal, but a practice or habit of understanding, at specific local levels, the relationship between identity, community, mobility, and territory. Read from this perspective, the confused perambulations of Beckett's Molloy are likely to strike a different chord than they did in the mid-to-late twentieth century. Today's international readers may be more apt to notice how rooted, or grounded, Beckett's vagrant narrator is as he plods across the "obscure . . . country" of his "end of the island," identifying its distinct topography of "tender pastures," bogs, "undulating land" and "deserted road[s]," but feeling disoriented because he can't "fix [its] landmarks in [his] mind," and because he can't comprehend it according to any fixed cartography:

> Though I fail to see, never having left my region, what right I have to speak of its characteristics. No, I never escaped, and even the limits of my region were unknown to me. . . . For regions do not suddenly end, as far as I know, but gradually merge into one another. . . . I may well have left mine many times, thinking I was still within it. But I preferred to abide by my simple feeling and its voice that said, Molloy, your region is vast, you have never left it and you never shall. And wheresoever you wander, within its distant limits, things will always be the same, precisely. . . . And the cycle continues, joltingly, of flight and bivouac, in an Egypt without bounds, without infant, without mother. (65–66)

Molloy's sense of location is characterized by an uncanny conflation of exile and rootedness, travel and confinement, displacement and familiar space. Patrick Bixby has argued that the eponymous novel thus enacts "an unwriting of the nation space," whereby an island subject to imperial, ideological mapping and partition is transformed into "a deterritorialized [space] that is open and retraceable" (181). I would offer that Molloy's reflections also unwrite or rewrite global space. Specifically, they revise the ideal of world citizenship through the eyes of the perennially homeless of the nonsovereign world—those who, despite being attached to their native land, have nonetheless always been displaced within it, and who are thus likely to experience separation from home not as an estrangement but as an extension, or broadening out, of an alienation that already exists. Indeed, the passage implies that the "universe" is not an abstract space into which people are thrown as they become displaced from well-known regional contexts but an unresolved extension of home, continuing obscurely beyond its borders. Hence, it speaks not to a post-statehood earth inhabited by exiles of "familiar" ground, but a vast realm of deferred, yet-to-be-realized habitations—a boundless Egypt that remains everywhere under the influence of enslavement and colonial dominion as much as it remains everywhere spiritually undelivered.

To demonstrate that this hypothetical, cosmopolitical reading of Beckett is valid, I first want to clarify how different—or how similar, but in subtle ways, how crucially different—it would be from the dominant cosmopolitan interpretation of Beckett we came to know during the latter half of the twentieth century. After all, many of the most influential twentieth-century interpretations of Beckett have claimed that his settings are abstract and meant to stand for physical or external reality in toto, while the more or less interchangeable narrators and protagonists stand for the human subject, trapped in consciousness, isolated from this terrain by thought itself. That these interpretations neglected Irish and colonial contexts has been well demonstrated. My concern, and my rationale for pausing here to scrutinize their logic, has more to do with their tacit reliance on narratives of geopolitical progress that seek to fix national and state belonging in time, mistakenly relegating such affiliations to the philosophical and intellectual predawn of global humanitarianism and universal empathy.

For many twentieth-century readers, Beckett's stark backdrops either suggested, as James Knowlson and John Pilling have so well argued, the confines of the skull, the mind itself, or signified the objective world that human subjectivity—the Cartesian cogito—is inherently separated from yet paradoxically drawn to comprehend.[2] In either interpretation, a basic assumption is the inexorable disjuncture of objective reality and the (unverifiable) philosophical subject, the stark and featureless environment of the "Cartesian separation . . . from the world" (Davies 47), the most basic, and most geographically independent, of modern human conditions.

Key to this line of thinking is the argument that the progressive removal of named places in Beckett's novels, from the social contexts of England and Ireland in Murphy and Watt to the bare room of The Unnamable, parallels Beckett's increasing effort to explore a condition that, although beset by deeply physical encounters, is territorially independent in every other conceivable way (that is, not concerned with distinct national, local, cultural, or political contexts). As J. D. O'Hara puts it, as "the Beckett hero regresses from the social context of [the English and Irish novels] Murphy and . . . Watt, through [the French narratives of] Molloy, Moran, Malone and Mahood to the . . . Unnamable, [Beckett is] peeling toward that possible impossible philosopher's man, the self at once expressed and potential, objective and subjective" (15). The assumption that any geographic contours or contexts less general than "the external or objective world" are irrelevant to Beckett's philosophical themes is important, for it abets the notion of his work's "universal" appeal or transcultural humanistic significance. As Deirdre Bair puts it, Beckett's "first-person monologue became stripped of the externalities of place, plot and time [so as to] make his life universal, to represent the lives of all men" (299).

The notion that separation or estrangement, in its various forms, is not an anomaly but a sine qua non of modern humanity, and that progressive removal of identifiable and meaningful setting is its aesthetic corollary, has also drawn from and contributed to the idea of Beckett's work as the culmination of "international modernism." When framed as an international movement, modernism's aesthetic innovations were, among other things, often interpreted as promoting a cosmopolitan mindset, a compassionate statelessness all the more meaningful because it was being raised defiantly out of the fresh traumas of nationalism.[3] Given the operative opposition between "national" and "universal" in this approach, it is easy to see how Beckett's vitriolic comments about Ireland in his early work, his departure from Ireland for Paris (and from English for French), and European opinion of Ireland as culturally retrograde due to sectarianism and nationalism contributed greatly to the idea of the universal reach, and intent, reflected in his minimalism. In many readings of Beckett, these three concepts—estrangement or alienation from the objective world, the compassionate cosmopolitanism or universality evoked by his bereft characters, and Beckett's eschewing of Ireland or Irish culture—form a dynamic, centripetal constellation. Ruby Cohn, one of the first to describe Beckett and Joyce as "Irish Cosmopolitans," argued that identifiable Irish geographies gradually dissolve from Beckett's novels because their ultimate objective is to depict an ontological darkness that is at once the human cosmos. "[Even] in [his] Irish dominated novel [Watt]," writes Cohn, "Beckett's cosmopolitan concerns may be read. . . . For [the novel] is about a quest for transcendence that is by definition supranational. . . . In successive works, Beckett strips away people, space, and time" until his characters exist in a darkness that "is the cosmos" (388–90).[4]

The universal, existential interpretation of Beckett is of course not the only major framework that has influenced how we interpret space and place in his works. Many critics, for example, have explored the ways in which Beckett's settings, especially in the plays, imply theatrical space and contribute to the theme of the performative, acted nature of human existence. The universal, humanist approach has also been complicated by recent historical and postcolonial approaches. But when it comes to determining or framing Beckett's undeniably extranational meaning and his broad, international appeal, this influential paradigm still holds considerable sway. In their introduction to the recent *Grove Companion to Samuel Beckett*, for example, C. J. Ackerley and S. E. Gontarski note that when Ireland "disappears" from Beckett's work it becomes "an aura, . . . a specter with its subject gone," a vague geographical contour that haunts an immaterial and purely "psychological landscape" (xv). Although they insist that the "intellectual landscape" of Beckett's modernism is distinct precisely because it is not connected to a "physical" territory (which Ireland represents), they nonetheless align it effortlessly with the specific territory of Europe. A reductive distinction between visceral, national Irish culture and cerebral, unterritorial European culture facilitates the maneuver: "Despite his Irish roots and recent attempts of countrymen to recolonize him, Beckett was a consummate European, more comfortable in the intellectual milieu of Europe than that of his native 'prosodoturfy'" (xv).

Recent efforts to redefine cosmopolitanism from postcolonial and minority-transnational perspectives can help us erode this stubborn opposition between the physical, noncerebral, colonial ground of Beckett's Ireland and the philosophical, psychological landscape of his European modernism. For most contributors to the postcolonial reassessment of cosmopolitanism, a key problem with the older, "supranational" ideal is that its concept of universality is based upon, as Walter Mignolo puts it, a "*temporal* conceptualization of world history [at the expense of a] *spatial* conceptualization of world histories and relations" (189). In other words, it sees the recognition of universal reality as something that happens in the aftermath or estrangement from a historical and cultural milieu that was, at some earlier time, coherent or sufficient, but that has become *no longer* tenable. In so doing, it invariably aligns the psychological, intellectual, and aesthetic spaces of exile, expatriation, and cosmopolitanism with a Western, dominant idea of modernity as a vague or abstract cultural space. It also fails to consider what the "beyond" of a national conscience might mean to those still forming such a conscience—those who reside in and travel beyond territories that are still in the process of achieving a democratic, independent statehood.

The temporal and progressive contextualization of the nation/cosmos distinction is strengthened by the argument, in some critical discourses of modernism, that aesthetic gestures which advocate internalization, the contingency of social contexts and ideologies, or the synchronicity of human experiences reflect a decisive break not simply from the past, but from the past as embodied in a place, from history as "known" territory. "The hallmark of modernism," writes Astradur Eysteinsson, is "a negation of prevalent traditions, a process of becoming critically aware of the . . . writer's immediate background and environment, that is, the history out of which he or she emerges" (52–53). Ricardo Quinones, in *Mapping Literary Modernism*, similarly maintains that "The dominant experience at the modernist point of departure is one of . . . a persistent will and a prevalent code all coming to an end. . . . of a suddenly revealed cosmic emptiness behind human experience, . . . and even of the dissolution of the known, ordinary, solid world" (4). Deeply implicit here is the idea of a simultaneously aesthetic and physical "emergence" or "departure" from a *known* environment: a divorce from an episteme that had, at one time, made sense of the world—which had, prior to the modern "moment," explained one's existence as "solid," accepted, "ordinary."[5] I raise this point again because the linkage between aftermath, or living at the end of history, and the poignant discovery of something universal in "human experience" is nothing less than endemic in Beckett criticism. For Eric Levy, Beckett's later fiction suggests that "[t]he real Fall occurred not in Eden but in our century. After the accumulation of too much history, we have lost the innocence required to believe in any more explanations. The only certainties left are the falseness of all interpretive structures and the radical unintelligibility of human experience without them" (10). Only after our separation from interpretive paradigms we *once* believed in, the argument goes, may we be initiated into a universally human community whose members share the experience of becoming similarly displaced, similarly cast out of some prior place of belonging that we once understood, or formerly objectified, via interpretive historical structures.

Theodor Adorno, whose readings of Beckett provide no end of valuable insights into the author's critique of modernity, also provides some of the best examples of this geographically and historically vague, but spatially and temporally absolute, interpretation of universality in Beckett's aesthetic. In response to Georg Lukács's argument that Beckett's isolated subjects are decadent symptoms of capitalist alienation, Adorno, speaking of the trilogy in particular, makes the crucial point that "solitude, taken to its logical conclusion, turns into its own negation" and thus "reveals itself to be the hidden consciousness of all human beings" (230). For Adorno, Beckett's ambiguous but physically concrete settings are the key to a negative poetics that objectifies our mutual alienation as modern subjects: "the world's hour has struck, and it resounds in [the Beckett narrator's] monologues" (231). But as these quotations already clarify, Adorno's spatial and temporal semantics are abstracted from Eurocentric, established nation-state historicity: the language, again, of an irrevocable separation from a formerly coherent world, of the need to disengage the subject from a manifest orthodoxy or "solid" socioeconomic context in order for that subject to perceive its universality or secular mutuality. Beckett epitomizes, says Adorno, modernity's "annihilat[ion] [of] the meaning that culture once was" (241), and in doing so shows us "Ur-humans [that] are the last humans" (226).

Critiquing these arguments from a contemporary global perspective does not, I would argue, mean denying that there can be such a thing as humanity in the abstract, or deconstructed selfhood as a geographically neutral phenomenon. It means being deeply skeptical about the assumption that a genuine perception or experience of these phenomena must be the conceptual opposite of and the temporal successor to a previously internalized or "achieved" national and cultural episteme. That is to say, it means refuting the assumption that a national geography, history, and culture amount to a *prior* coherence or a "given" modality (Cheah, "Given Culture" 324), and that a critical alienation, or anxious estrangement, from this preexisting state is what places the subject on the threshold of transcendent, transnational being. In place of this model, we can substitute a more nuanced one that understands that our complex and sometimes multiple attachments to cultural, ethnic, or national communities and our sensitivity to shared human conditions must be particularized, intervening, embodied processes; a cosmopolitanism that refuses to limit our local, native belonging to a fixed material domain and that equally refuses to generalize our global belonging. As Bruce Robbins puts it, an "actually existing cosmopolitanism" that is "not merely an abstract ideal," "[but a] socially and geographically situated" or "located and embodied" reality ("Introduction I" 2).

Although there is no singular definition of what "new" cosmopolitanism is, nearly all contributors to the discussion would agree that it begins with understanding how our engagements with particular national or cultural life and our responsibilities to common or global humanity can be collaborative without either form of belonging becoming reductive or static. Indeed, recent debates about global democratic futures often hinge on the point that oppositional models of nation and universe, or concrete national past and abstract global present, fail miserably to describe what it means to "emerge from" a history defined by decolonization, neocolonialism, partitioned states, and contested historiography and language. In such cases, "home" or the homeland can be every bit as elusive as the human subject, thus an extraction from its unsettled ground cannot be simply understood as a gesture of departure from the known into the unknown, the interpellated to the uncanny. It is more likely to be what Molloy experiences in the aforementioned passage: the mobilization, across new territories, of an already existing, interrelated ambiguity of the place and the self.

To reflect on these challenges to older cosmopolitan models is to realize that there are far less oppositional and absolute ways of thinking about Beckett's transition from identifiable Irish settings in his early fiction to the vague or abstract settings of the trilogy. After all, much of the later Beckett is arguably not about life in the aftermath of something prior that has been lost or eroded, but about the experience of waiting for a coherence to arrive, to be realized, in the first place. Especially in *Molloy, Malone Dies*, and *The Unnamable*, there is no "formerly known" place, no prior world that used to make sense. Instead, dating to the earliest days any aging narrator can recall, there is only repetitive motion across, and cyclically renewed and frustrated efforts to set narratives within, a tangible, real, and affective ground that has *never been* comprehensible: "Are there other places set aside for us and this one where I am, with Malone, merely their narthex? . . . No no, we have all been here forever, we shall all be here forever, I know it" (293). In these works, the disorientation that we undergo with the narrators does not arise in the aftermath of a ruptured episteme or temporal threshold; instead, it cyclically returns *while* we are "on the point of vanishing" (195), "on the threshold of being no more" (194), or "on the brink of a better earth" (83). Transformations, such as they are, occur as we plod toward an end that is perpetually deferred: "And on the threshold of being no more I succeed in being another" (194).

The trilogy chronicles the perpetual and failed effort to *achieve* orientation; more accurately, it depicts narrators whose knowledge of self is inseparable from comprehension of their specific local environment, and for whom such confluent knowledge is always *yet* to occur. In *Malone Dies*, when the primary narrator confronts the silence between the exhaustion of one of his stories—all of which are set in the seaside landscape surrounding his hospital room—and the beginning of another, he fixates on the problem of narrating his own local origins. But, as with his numerous stories about "[t]he peasants" (196) who reside in that locality, the challenge is that he cannot find a suitable point from which to begin. The point of origin that eludes him is not an abstract or purely ontological one; rather, as is often the case with reminiscence in Beckett, it is a potential but unrealized integration with a specific community and place:

> One day [my mother and I] were walking along the road, up a hill of extraordinary steepness, near home I imagine, my memory is full of steep hills, I get them confused. . . . I can still see the spot opposite Tyler's gate. A market gardener, he had only one eye and wore side whiskers. . . . You could see the sea, the islands, the headlands, the isthmuses, the coast stretching away to north and south and the crooked moles of the harbor. (268)

While these memories suggest vivid, almost tactile connections to a particular landscape and its inhabitants, they also suggest that the inability to internalize an externally manifest correlation between self, others, and shared land is as old as the memories.

In his letters to Thomas MacGreevy, Beckett notes that walking in the "calm secret hostility" of the south Dublin hills was an intensely nostalgic experience (*Letters* vol. 1, 136) and implies that one of the memories it evoked was his frustrated childhood wish to feel integrated with his family and local community. After a customary walk "from Rathfarnham to Enniskerry" in August 1931, he wrote to MacGreevy that he could not "compose poems walking," like Arthur Rimbaud, because "for me, walking . . . is a carrefour of memories, memories of childhood mostly, moulin à larmes" (*Letters* vol. 1, 93).[6] As in the *Malone Dies* passage, the problem of linking place and self is not, here, a new condition suffered in the wake of a prior, and now lost, sense of belonging, but an *original*, historically extensive condition. All subsequent narratives, no matter their setting, are a repetition of this initial, irreconcilable aporia: "There I am back at my old aporetics" (181). "[A]ll things considered I would be hard set to say for certain where exactly they are, in relation to where exactly I am" (219). Hence the local, and its disorientations, not only exist before any national coherence but also extend beyond national boundaries as recurrent, recollected phenomena.

"[T]o go on means going from here" (302), as the narrator of *The Unnamable* ultimately summarizes the problem, but like Molloy, "he [does] not know quite where he [is], except that he [is] in a plain, and the mountains not far, nor the sea" (240); therefore, although attachment to place remains and although that place, including its inhabitants, is continually and physically present, the Beckett narrator is always "start[ing] again from nowhere," admitting "a certain confusion in the exordia . . . no matter who I am, no matter where I am" (302). In other words, if there is a connection between a basic human perplexity and a sense of detachment from a manifest environment or "historical background," it stems from a form of alienation that is quite different from the one presupposed by the older cosmopolitan model. Beckett's narrators claim never to have left "here"—"having always been here, I am here still" (302)—yet they have *always* been estranged from "here," or have been "here" and "there" simultaneously, because here is, and always has been, a place one cannot speak of with certainty. Ironically, then, the relentless "here" of the trilogy is a "confused plain" (286) that defies the kind of absolute spatial and temporal pronouncements which are necessary for constructing the metanarratives of modernity, loss, or estrangement that we are compelled to employ in our understanding of Beckett.

Just as the passages I have cited above exemplify the trilogy's implicit critique of historical or geographic aftermath, they also introduce a second, deeply related, feature of the work that demands a more nuanced theory of cosmopolitanism: its use of settings that, to whatever extent they are "Irish," are very *locally* so. Although it is rarely considered relevant to serious philosophical understanding of the novels, the trilogy evokes not just a vaguely Irish countryside but the suburban, coastal landscapes along the Kingstown and Dalkey line (including Foxrock, Coliemore harbor, Dún Laoghaire and its imperial port and docks, Glencullen Road, Sandymount). This is, of course, the Ireland of Beckett's youth and his return visits, the site of his crucial revelation that ambiguous minimalism and "lack of knowledge" would be his guiding aesthetic principles (Knowlson 319), the setting of *Watt* and *All That Fall,* and the ground for memories, but possibly also the present, in works with otherwise obscure settings such as *Waiting for Godot* and *Krapp's Last Tape.*[7]

It is also a local context profoundly conducive to the notion that disorientation and estrangement can be consubstantial with rootedness or provinciality and an excellent example of why the "national" pasts of decolonization cannot be reduced to a known ground, or historical "background," that in turn becomes the opposite of a "universal" reality. Although Beckett treats it more ambiguously than James Joyce, this is the same coastline upon which *Ulysses* opens. Replete with Martello towers, exclusive, predominantly Protestant communities, and other landmarks representing the long and uneven history of colonization, it is for Joyce an appropriate backdrop against which to develop themes of usurpation and failed internationalism. At the heart of this region is the harbor at Kingstown/Dún Laoghaire, which Stephen Dedalus calls a "disappointed bridge" in *Ulysses* (2.39) and which inspired Eavan Boland "to record [the] contradictions" of Dublin, its "gradual / capitulations to the last invader" (*Collected* 246). That Kingstown Pier was the site of the epiphany that helped produce Beckett's mature aesthetic, and that this key discovery therefore occurred not only in the midst of a French-Irish crossing but also at a site embodying the contradictions of Irish internationalism, is more apropos of the conditions that produce the mature Beckett than critics have supposed.

For as Beckett himself certainly knew, this region, which returns frequently in the author's fiction, is a microcosm of an Ireland that, between the death of Charles Stewart Parnell and the republic of Eamon de Valera, was too characterized by "the episodes and fragments of a history still in progress" to be thought of in any historically or geographically comprehensive, much less apocalyptic, fashion (Lloyd, *Anomalous* 11). It represents not only the partition of the island but also the numerous economic, social, and political enclaves within its two primary subdivisions. Thus, it embodies the "dislocating intersections between local and global processes" that produced the "uneven development of the island," and that are key to contextualizing Ireland globally (Cleary 121–23). For Beckett, "Ireland" at a local level was defined by these dislocating incongruities in other ways as well, comprised as it was of movement between different kinds of Protestant enclaves (Foxrock, 1906–1919; Portora Royal School in Enniskillen, Northern Ireland, 1920–1923; Trinity College, Dublin, 1923–1927 and 1930) during the escalation of republicanism, decolonization, and civil war. The relatively sequestered life of these enclaves offered their own silent testament to the disunited, irreducible territory within which they were situated and ample opportunity to observe the great distances that ideological partition creates, or augments, between individuals and communities and between communities themselves.

This disjuncture was especially evident during the Easter Rising and subsequent Anglo-Irish War, for in the insular, upper middle-class suburbs along the Kingstown and Dalkey line, the response to the conflicts around their perimeter tended toward "a nervous silence and . . . withdrawal," wherein the "[o]utrage would be condemned and events commented on behind closed doors, but often not even in front of one's servants" (Cronin 36–37). Along with seeing political and class conflicts repeatedly met with anxious silence, Beckett was haunted by memories of watching the fires in Dublin following the Easter Rising from atop one of the many high hills in the region ("near home I imagine, my memory is full of steep hills" [268]), where his father had taken him to join other local residents who watched the proceedings with "a certain amount of jocularity" (Cronin 36). What must have made these juxtaposed scenes so unforgettably troubling to Beckett, at least in part, was the way in which they demonstrated the immense disparity between a visceral event and the language available for speaking of it, an act of outrage and an integrated, internalized map on which to locate it.

The region also contained poor and working-class neighborhoods whose inhabitants crossed community borders for employment and was traversed by impoverished itinerants. Thus to the sentient observer, it embodied a broader reality of alienation, not only of individuals, religions, and classes from one another but also of daily experience from any politically professed rubric of national integration or cultural solidarity, whether it be of a unionist or republican mold.[8] In *Malone Dies*, the narrator tries to compose stories about the "labours of the peasants" that reflect "the inadequacy of the exchanges between rural and urban areas" (194–96). The exhaustion of narrative that results, although it could be experienced or applied elsewhere, thus retains, and requires for its full understanding, a local significance: "In his country, the problem—no, I can't do it. The peasants. His visits to. No, I can't. Assembled in the farmyard they watched him depart, on stumbling, wavering feet, as though they scarcely felt the ground" (196).[9] Significantly, the disconnect here is not only between the narrator and the peasant subjects but also between that would-be tandem and the (thus absurd) concept of "his country."

In Beckett's radio play *All That Fall*, written five years after *Molloy* was published and less ambiguously set in and around Foxrock, a speech by Mrs. Rooney strongly implies that the effort to integrate self, region, and nation from a hilltop vantage point in this area results in a crisis of orientation that is, at the same time, a crisis of subjectivity:

Now we are the laughing stock of the twenty-six counties. Or is it thirty six? . . . The entire scene, the hills, the plain, the racecourse with its miles and miles of white rails and three red stands, the pretty little wayside station, even you yourselves, yes, I mean it, and over all the clouding blue, I see it all, I stand here and see it all with eyes . . . through eyes . . . oh if you had my eyes . . . you would understand . . . the things they have seen. (*All That Fall* 24–25; first ellipses mine)

As with the narrator's confused recollections and failed narratives of the region in *Malone Dies*, these lines merge the frustrated desire to connect with the people who inhabit one's visible region with the problem of self-comprehension. In Mrs. Rooney's claim that if her companions could have her eyes they might "understand . . . the things they have seen," the pronoun "they" could refer to her eyes or to the inhabitants whose lives she is trying to discern as she gazes across the horizon.

Importantly, some of the trilogy's most profound reflections on the contingencies and paradoxes of narrative as a means of self-knowledge (that is, as a means of locating the philosophical subject) are consubstantial with the narrator's effort to orient himself within a divided community. In *Malone Dies*, several passages suggest, as much as any in Beckett, that this would-be community, this insistently material but unclassifiable landscape, is the local region of the author's youth:

When I stop, as just now, the noises begin again, strangely loud, those whose turn it is. So that I seem to have again the hearing of my boyhood. . . . There was nothing, not even the sand on the paths, that did not utter its cry. . . . The sound I liked best had nothing noble about it. It was the barking of dogs, at night, in the clusters of hovels up in the hills, where the stone cutters lived, like generations of stone-cutters before them. . . . From the hills another joy came down, I mean the brief scattered lights that sprang up on their slopes at nightfall, merging in blurs scarcely brighter than the sky. (206)

Several equally poignant moments in *Malone Dies* involve the narrator's effort to imagine the "scattered lights" of his seaside environs as part of a larger human network, such as when, in a similar moment of frustrated reflection, he recalls standing "in tears before the islands and peninsulas where night lit the little brief yellow lights of man" (226). Dalkey, Foxrock, Dún Laoghaire, and environs, internally partitioned and adjacent to a sea coast that symbolizes a troubled and thwarted internationalism—the inability to posit a *beginning* here, to imagine it as a formerly achieved habitation, haunts the narrator every bit as much as his more famous inability "to make an end."

Perhaps, then, Beckett is not so much "stripping away" his Irish settings as much as he is rendering their already existing obscurity from within. Or, more specifically, he is conflating the notion of humanity's common ground with the genuine vertigo of an attempt to perceive late colonial space—an effort to orient oneself in a country whose "most typical experience may be that of occupying multiple locations, literally and figuratively" (Lloyd, "After History" 3). Particularly compelling in this regard is the fact that some of the most disoriented, yet physically interactive, moments in the trilogy involve experiences of policing and surveillance. In all three novels, the "unavoidable police" (33) or "innumerable authorities" (132) are an inscrutable, hovering presence that is integral to the narrator's disrupted sense of place and uncertain sense of self. As Molloy says, concerning his arrest by a constable:

> I felt the faces turning to look after us . . . faces of men, of women, and of children. . . . Listen, I said. Get on, he said. I wasn't allowed to listen to [their] music. It might have drawn a crowd. . . . Was there one among them to put himself in my place, to feel how removed I was then from him I seemed to be, and in that remove what strain, as of hawsers about to snap? . . . I had perhaps gone too far in saying that my mother lived near the shambles, it could equally well have been the cattle-market, near which she lived. Never mind, said the sergeant, it's the same district." (20–22)

Again, the philosophical problem of the "strained" slippage between subjectivity and objectivity ("how removed I was then from him I seemed to be") is not so much examined in detachment from, as it is enmeshed in disconcerting ambiguity with, the problem of place—here, the problem of orienting kin and community relative to the boundaries of a "district."

If one were to insist on a fixed Irish historical reading, these scenes could be interpreted as a reference to the climate of surveillance and suspicion during and after the civil war between "diehard" republicans and supporters of the newly declared Free State (from 1922 to 1923). But more important than our ability to fix the location is the fact that Molloy's arrest, his would-be moment of interpellation, results neither in the identification and placement of the subject nor in the negation of some former identification. That is to say, it confirms that the ambiguities of place and self are inseparable—a condition that stems not from the loss of a known ground, but from the inability to comprehend the present habitus *as* given: "it could equally well have been the cattle-market, near which she lived. Never mind, said the sergeant, it's the same district" (20–22).[10] The narrator and characters are as distant from the abstract idea of "Ireland," of "the nation," from *within* their region as they would be by traveling outside of it.

When Molloy returns to the woman against whom he had committed the crime (accidentally killing her aged and incontinent dog with his bike), she explains that he had actually spared her the expense of putting the dog to sleep, "an expense which I am ill able to afford, having no other means of support than the pension of my dear departed, fallen in defense of a country that called itself his and from which in his lifetime he never derived the smallest benefit, but only insults and vexations" (33). The betrayed promise of pensions and government aid to those who served in or aided the cause of Irish independence from 1916 to 1921, as well as the general failure of nationalistic idealism to address widespread economic disenfranchisement, is a frequent element of plot and theme in Irish literature of the 1920s and 1930s, most notably in the plays of Sean O'Casey. It is also one of many examples in Irish history of a basic truth observed in both postcolonial and transnational studies: that nationalism, as a derivative discourse of imperialism, often conspires with its parent ideology to intervene disruptively not only in the formation of individual identities but also in the potential affiliations, kinships, and communities that one might help to create at the local level. Operating together, the two systems can make one's home into unsettled ground—ground that, whether inhabited or departed (and it is often both), whether loved or despised (and it is often both), remains conceptually and emotionally distant, fissured, protean.

It is imprecise to say that the Beckett landscape is abstract; more accurately, it is rendered with a unique mixture of concreteness and ambiguity, familiarity and disorientation, such that it retains both the ditches and mud of a visceral, particular ground and the obscure aspect of unfamiliar territory: "And I even crawled on my back, plunging my crutches blindly behind me into the thickets, and with the black boughs for sky to my closing eyes. . . . I fancied I saw, faintly outlined against the horizon, the towers and steeples of a town, which of course I could not assume was mine, on such slight evidence" (91). What Beckett's narratives epitomize in such instances, what their effort to commune with "dark forms crowding in a dark place" (23) might suggest for our age, is not the bare essence of life with all national and societal contexts stripped away, but the reality of living on an undeniably material, politically overdetermined ground and not being able to *find* a viable abstraction with which to comprehend it—a condition that is neither limited to a specific place nor historically disengaged. The narrators of the trilogy gain space for critical reflexivity not by separation from a familiar national episteme, but in the midst of traversing a region, "a chaos of gnarled roots, boulders, and baked mud" (204), that they cannot connect with a national abstract. Thus, their challenge to verifiable subjectivity arises at the same time as a vacillation between detachment and attachment to place, a departure that does not occur suddenly or completely, but that is at every moment continuing to happen.

The point, then, is not to claim these as "Irish" texts, at least not in any geographically and nationally confined sense. The fixed nation-state is, after all, the form of abstracting and orienting human experience that is most conspicuously absent from these narratives. "Town," "district," and "region," as well as "earth" and "universe," are, by comparison, in ample supply, as is the adjective "Irish." The point is to show that what may be their unique feature—ontological inquiry that remains consubstantial with an effort to comprehend material space ("Where now? Who now? When now?" begins the narrator of the *Unnamable* [291])—suggests something provocatively similar to some of the basic propositions in contemporary approaches to cosmopolitanism: that inquiries into our human "condition" are no more primary or fundamental than inquiries about our identity and belonging relative to place; that these two inquiries are similarly contingent and in perpetual dialogue; and that this dialogue is mobile.

Here I would emphasize that for many, if not the actual majority, of traveling subjects on our planet, transnational thinking and feeling does not begin "supranationally," by rejecting something as abstract as "one's country," but subnationally, often through the challenge of developing one's sense of self, community, and broader world during a time when, and in a place where, all three of these concepts are subsumed by the conflicting ideologies left in the wake of imperialism. Although it is unarguable that Beckett's novels convey experiences of unknowing that are uncannily relevant to people in multiple locations, a genuinely global recognition of what those ideas are as well as *why* they may apply so widely hinges on our awareness that they arise not in the wake of a destroyed or discarded society but amidst the interruptions and disjuncture of a society still in process. That they arrive not as essences rescued from the fragments of what Ezra Pound called "a botched civilization" (64) nor as archetypes of a synchronic world history that, for T. S. Eliot in "Little Gidding," reverberates "Now and in England" (50), but as an understanding reached en route to a civilization or shared habitation that is *yet* to be, and may never be. As Judith Butler puts it, "the universal which is yet to be achieved and which in order to *resist domestication* may never be fully or finally achievable" (qtd. in Bhabha, "Vernacular" 201). Crucially, this would mean that Beckett's abstract human subject is not held back, but defined, by its incomplete historical emergence—that the "ur human" we uncannily recognize in his bereft characters is a being perennially shuffling between origin and world, native habitus and universe, unable to realize either. Apt indeed, then, is the aforementioned fact that the stylistic transitions that generated Beckett's fully achieved modernism were conceived on the Dublin coast, at or near the "contradict[ory]" port, the "disappointed bridge," of Dún Laoghaire (Boland, *Collected* 246; Joyce, *Ulysses* 2.39).

In the closing moments of *Malone Dies*, the narrator makes a final attempt to stabilize the narrative versions of himself that he has created and to "speak only of [himself]" in the present. But the effort to close his story, to achieve detachment and conclusion, is foiled by the confused aspect of the coastal landscape as he tries to envision it from a distance:

> Lemuel watches the mountains rising behind the steeples beyond the harbor, no they are no more
>
> No, they are no more than hills, they raise themselves gently, faintly blue, out of the disappearance of the confused plain. It was there somewhere he was born, . . . Their slopes are covered with ling and furze [and] the hammers of the stone-cutters ring all day like bells.

The island. A last effort. The islet. The shore facing the open sea is jagged with creeks. One could live there, perhaps happy, if life were a possible thing. (286)

Here, the attempt to comprehend the external environment or to liberate the mind from the epistemological demands of orientation—a dominant of Beckett's early work that culminates not just in *Watt*, we might recall, but in Watt's humble failure to ascertain the essence or logic of a servant's life in a protestant enclave of Dublin—is not only inextricable from but also no different than the individual's inability to claim himself as a coherent subject. In Molloy's claim that he cannot speak of the characteristics of the region he cannot confirm having left, as well as in the *Malone Dies* narrator's effort to locate his characters on the "confused plain," internal and external space are not just similarly indeterminate but mutually analogical. The move into the uncharted country of the contingent philosophical subject, that is to say, occurs not at the *expense* of a solid world that has dissolved and dwindled, but in tandem with an effort to comprehend one's immediate environment that is still taking place.

To understand this deferral of attachment to a broader community in the context of one's homeland is to be prepared to see and understand it elsewhere, and to be more likely to see the world itself as engaged with particular historical and political processes that are difficult to abstract, banish to a premodern past, or confine geographically. In an "Egypt without bounds," "regions do not suddenly end, . . . but gradually merge into one another," as Molloy muses (65). In the governing metaphor of cosmopolitics, it is to be a grounded traveler, to be "connected to the earth—but not to 'a' place on it [whose essence we presume is as] simple and self-evident as the surroundings we see when we open our eyes" (Robbins 3). To be, as the narrator of the *Unnamable* has it, a "great traveler," "unpredictable in direction," "crawling on my belly or rolling on the ground" (327).

This vision of travelers who, due to their own unresolved attachment to home, resist both the nationalistic and imperialistic impulse to cartographically abstract other geo-social collectives reminds me of a passage from *The Unnamable* that is often cited, though typically not in its full context. The passage comes at the beginning of one of the many soon-to-be-abandoned stories that the narrator feels compelled to tell. It is uttered in comical frustration, as if "to keep them quiet" who would demand, even this late in the game, a good old fashioned Irish tale: "To tell the truth—no, first the story. The island, I'm on the island, I've never left the island, God help me. I was under the impression I spent my life in spirals round the earth. Wrong, it's on the island I wind my endless ways. The island, that's all the earth I know" (326–27). What is most compelling about this passage is not its offer of another satirical jab at cultural nationalism, nor its extra hint that the narrator resides in the coastal Dublin hills, but its suggestion that "the Island," this cognitively frustrating place that the Beckett characters can neither successfully interpret nor successfully confirm that they have left, is "all the earth [they] know." Like many others in the trilogy, that statement conflates the unreconciled homeland with the world at large. It speaks to a separation which, although it may have physically happened, cannot be confirmed conceptually or fixed in time because that which would become the "known" terrain, the departed place that would become visible to the smug émigré in either nostalgic or spiteful retrospect, is a terrain perpetually and powerfully resistant to essential identification, irreconcilable with a fixed temporal or spatial matrix.

It is from this mutable origin, this inability to point to a prior and stable habitation "among my compatriots, contemporaries, coreligionists and companions in distress" (326) that the Beckett terrain emerges. Neither Irish nor universal, it is irreducibly situated between these two abstractions. Rather than opposing an ephemeral, airy universe to the tangible ground of nationally circumscribed life, it proposes that the universe is the continuation of an obscure ground, the mobilization of an inscrutable rootedness. As the voice of *The Unnamable* inquires:

> But what's all this about . . . staying where you are, dying, living, being born, unable to go forward or back, not knowing where you came from, or where you are, or where you're going, or that it's possible to be elsewhere, to be otherwise, . . . you can't, you're there, you don't know who, you don't know where, the thing stays where it is, nothing changes, within it, outside it, apparently, apparently." (370)

Thus although these narratives may well hint uncannily at a fundamental human problem, there is a substantial chance that they do so because they deeply understand a condition that has been far more prevalently experienced on our inexorable earth than Eurocentric western modernity. That condition is the vexed compulsion to construct narratives (whether subjective or objective, about staying or going) in relation to ideologically contested, colonized, or subject homelands—"to produce," as the narrator of *The Unnamable* puts it, "ostensibly independent testimony in support of [one's] historical existence" in "that unfamiliar native land of mine" (319, 314).

Epilogue

"On"

In the end you will utter again.
Samuel Beckett, "Company"

In *Postnationalist Ireland*, Richard Kearney refers to Joyce and Beckett as "cosmopolitan exiles" who "possessed no motherland" (115). In this book, I have postulated that the statelessness of the modern Irish writer abroad is less a condition of postterritorial, terminal homelessness than a condition of perpetual movement between the unresolved homeland and the broader world, an itinerancy that can find a home neither in national nor in global abstractions. This condition has far-reaching implications, for its generative paradox—the need to criticize the limitations of statist or national affiliation even as one desires a culturally specific, placed origin—extends well beyond Irish expatriate modernism.

In a theoretical context, it extends into a critique of wholesale, postnational ideals in modernity that continue to inflect and limit our notions of global citizenship and responsibilities. Irish expatriate modernism cannot be reduced to an advocacy for any specific form of political sovereignty. However, its various refusals to abandon the salience of nationality and a sited, recognized cultural origin do speak to a different *form* of "the global": a world not flat but uneven; a world in which the "nation's spectrality"—the "persistence of the nation-form as the most viable political vehicle for freedom" even amidst neocolonial states that have so far failed to actualize egalitarian freedom—is every bit as pervasive as the phenomena of mobility, interconnectedness, and cultural hybridity (Cheah, *Spectral* 346–47). In a literary-historical context, this alternative worldview suggests an important similarity between Irish expatriate modernism and more recent postcolonial- and minority-cosmopolitan literatures. In closing, I will consider these two hypotheses in more detail.

The distinguishing feature of the "Irish cosmopolitan" modernism I have sought to identify is that its often powerful poetics of dislocation are also suffused with a potentiality of cultural location, an ever-present reaching out toward a native or primary habitus that is yet to be. Its inquiries into nonterritorial humanity, universal subjects, or international communities are thus not conducted relative to a normative or prior position of national being and identity. The result is a dual and interdependent process of identification, an engagement in extranational imaginings conducted at the same time as the idea of belonging to a homeland or socio-geographic origin. This dual process engenders a range of creative expressions, from envisioning the condition of the yet-to-belong as endemic in the world, to the superimposition of Irish localities and cosmic worlds (as in *Finnegans Wake*), to the simultaneity of attachment and detachment drives (whether or not the setting is Irish), to the inexorable irony of constructing Ireland and Irishness so as to achieve transculturation.

In terms of theoretical contexts and approaches, I have suggested that these expressions are deeply connected with, but also push beyond, postcolonial readings that see Irish modernism primarily as a subversion of imperial and nation-statist constructs of history and identity. Because it desequentializes native and global belonging—or rather because it gives voice to the already-existing lack of sequence in the colonial experience of these modes of being—Irish expatriate modernism not only resists constructs of national community but also registers the desire for such constructs, especially as that desire materializes within and relative to internationalism. Precisely because of this mobile irresolution regarding placed identity, international Irish modernism also deeply challenges constructions of the global. That is to say, its aesthetic targets are not just ideologies of the nation and colony but teleological models of the human universe up to and including metropolitan, late-capitalist ideals of a "flat world" and premature claims for a new era of nonterritorial, egalitarian multiculturalism.

For to carry the irresolute dual-consciousness of colonial belonging outward and abroad is to challenge readers to seek less teleological and idealistic, more historically continuous models of the human experience outside of states, and of the human subject itself. In this regard, the works of Joyce, Bowen, and Beckett invite us not to abandon or contradict but to improve the philosophy of ecumenical humanitarianism by recognizing the continuing role of national feeling and ethnic belonging in any global imaginary. They invite us to extrapolate that the most shared condition on the planet may well be the sheer commonness of the cultural borderland and its unending expansion as a state of mind: the utterly quotidian act of existing between the unachieved homeland and the global abstract; of inhabiting Gabriel Conroy's position between a "journey westward" and "the universe"; of entire lives lived between a particular and a general culture that are each always forming and never final (*Dubliners* 225).

One could say that this more interstitial location of Irish modernism is something of an inheritance from Irish modernism in its more "domestic" iteration, given that one of its central notions—that the irresolution of home at once inspires and materially suffuses the cosmic imagination—is also at the heart of W. B. Yeats's literary project. Indeed, it was Yeats who noted, as early as 1901, that Irish writers must both "re-create the ancient arts" in Ireland—a project that "an Englishman, with his belief in progress [and] instinctive preference for the cosmopolitan literature of the last century, may think . . . parochial"—and, at the same time, modernize those arts via subjective visions and an avant-garde aura of "strangeness" (384). For Yeats, the result is a symbolically evocative, Irish-world literature that would allow "Irishmen, even though they had gone thousands of miles away, [to] still be in their own country" (384).

Yeats's effort to articulate Irishness and worldliness simultaneously is never concluded, and only intensifies with his modernism, as is evident in his 1931 poem "Remorse for Intemperate Speech." Reflecting on his tenure as an Irish Free State Senator (1922–1928), during which he often played the strident contrarian to young republicans and "swept between France, Italy, England and Ireland" (Allen 2), Yeats aims to synthesize contrary wishes: to be the artist whose "fanatic" passions rendered him a kind of exile; and to have those same passions symbolize his indomitable Irishness:

Nothing said or done can reach
My fanatic heart.

Out of Ireland have we come.
Great hatred, little room,

Maimed us at the start.
I carry from my mother's womb
A fanatic heart. (lines 9–15)[1]

Yeats's early goal, to create in Ireland an internationally respected art grounded in a well-cultivated national consciousness, evolves here into the conviction that Irishness can only be located in a stance of resistance and, importantly, in the distance from home that such resistance produces "from the start." Ironically, the indefinite postponement of an organic or genuinely inhabited nationality, what Cheah calls a "spectral nationality," is all that survives *as* "Irish"—an opposition between national feeling and the present form of the state that Yeats sees, almost racially, as inherited from his "mother's womb." Disrupted from "the start," the location of home is therefore at once inexorable and nonfixable. Being "out of" Ireland—that is, being both Irish and unreconciled with a specific national abstract or form of statehood—becomes a mobile, nontranscendable point of origin in itself.

Even as Irish expatriate modernism elaborates many of the nation/world conundrums at the heart of the Irish Renaissance, so too does it anticipate the irresolute home/world dynamics expressed by such postcolonial-cosmopolitan authors as Salman Rushdie, Derek Walcott, Zadie Smith, Arundhati Roy, Michael Ondaatje, and J. M. Coetzee. Speaking collectively about many of these authors in her book *Cosmopolitan Fictions*, Katherine Stanton notes that they "uncouple certain conceptions, like citizenship, from nationality, and yet continue to attest to the persistence of the nation as, among other things, a structure of feeling. Their Cosmopolitical thinking is not post-national, in other words. Recognizing that borders are 'vacillating,' in Étienne Balibar's words, they do not claim they have disappeared" (4).

Similarly, Joyce, Bowen, and Beckett ask us to recognize a global society in which émigrés are not bearers of static traditions from home—tokens of preglobal cultural authenticity that certain First World metropolitans might covet to produce something called multiculturalism—but travelers whose attachments to home are too intellectual, complex, and dynamic to be thus commodified. Attachments that, too vital to be either fixed or ended, could be seen as embodied in Derek Walcott's interminable question, "How can I turn from Africa and live?" Noting this relationship between international Irish modernism and traveling postcolonial writers is not so much about the inclusion of Irish authors in postcolonial categories as it is about helping us to see that the so-called minority or alternative view of global and extra-national identity is in many ways closer to a majority view. More than a project of canon reorganization, it would mean relocating the philosophical center away from the default idea of the human subject as it exists "after history," and of the creative intellect as being crystallized in its emergence from national contexts, to the understanding that history and nation are invariably protean and that the human subject is forged, in full, during its perpetual negotiation with them.

Indeed, this more interstitial placement of the philosophical subject helps advance a sorely needed critique of modernity, for it radically challenges one of its most stubborn intellectual legacies: the grand narrative not simply of progress but of phased or sequential being. By this I mean the spatio-temporal plotting of the self that defaults to the "forward" and "outward" moves as the ones that supposedly reveal our ontological core, whether these are moves toward an ideal end or an irreversible displacement, a Kantian world government or a Conradian heart of darkness. Artists driven to voice the more shuttling, onward and returning, overlapping spatio-temporalities of postcolonial cosmopolitanism have often reminded us of the dire limitations of this sequential model of being. As Zadie Smith observes in *White Teeth*, "immigrants have always been particularly prone to repetition. . . . Even when you arrive, you're still going back and forth; . . . there's no proper term for it—*original sin* seems too harsh; maybe *original trauma* would be better" (135–36). As Smith ingeniously goes on to show, being subject to the repetitions of "original trauma" is not equivalent to being limited by history, but is rather a primer for the ability to see the continuousness of historical and geo-social identification as enduringly real, to recognize that these will *not* come to some grand and cosmic terminus.

This disinclination to believe in apocalypse and utopia alike is arguably the richest outcome of an intellectual journey that begins in a contested, colonial homeland. It is also, as I have tried to show, a powerful current within international Irish modernism—one that is always pushing back against the high modernist penchant for historical and geographic cataclysm. As the young heroine of Elizabeth Bowen's short story "Mysterious Kôr" so well puts it, looking across the ruins of London during the German blitz: "This war shows we've by no means come to the end. If you can blow whole places out of existence, you can blow whole places into it. I don't see why not" (*CS* 730).

In his late narrative "Company," Beckett puts the idea even more succinctly: "in the end you will utter again" (14). Indeed, there may be nothing more characteristic of Beckett than the idea that, in the midst of the apparent void, one inevitably stumbles upon the hope of socially connecting. All prospects seemingly exhausted, one utters again, admitting the absurd prospect of company. In a word, one goes "on." This most essential of Beckett words is, I would argue, less a sequential "on" (a call to move into or beyond some absolute aftermath) than an injunction to continue the unsettled condition that has existed from the start. In such a condition, we anticipate our origin, our grounding, as perpetually as we anticipate our end. As it reaches its fullest expression in Beckett, Irish Cosmopolitanism might thus be seen as the deep and continuous imagining of a more genuinely global citizenship, for it offers that the human essence is forged in the very midst of our perpetual creation and undoing of origin in a world without end.

NOTES

Introduction

1. In an article for the Trieste newspaper *Il Piccolo de la Sera*, Joyce used a similar image to symbolize the need for Irish sovereignty and improved international awareness of Irish affairs. He cites the story of an elderly Irish-speaking peasant, bewildered as he is unjustly sentenced to hang for his presumed role in an agrarian conflict, as an example of "the Irish nation at the bar of public opinion. . . . unable to appeal to the modern conscience of England and other countries" (*CW* 198).

2. In *At Home in the World: Cosmopolitanism Now*, Tim Brennan also insists that resisting relativism and essentialism are equally crucial projects. Bruce Robbins similarly admonishes that "new cosmopolitanism" will otherwise become a "comfortable [multicultural] piety [that] evade[s] the actual, pressing complexities" of minorities in the global economy (48).

3. Spelled "Cobh" in Irish, or, sometimes, "Cov" in English, but in both cases pronounced "kov," Cobh seaport, Co. Cork, is a particularly traumatic location. Called "Queenstown" until the Irish Free State renamed it Cobh in 1922, it was the primary port of departure during the famine (about 2.5 million emigrants left from that port), and, before and after the famine, it was the principal site for transporting Irish "criminals" to penal colonies in Australia. Under the much-disputed "treaty ports" clause in the Anglo-Irish treaty of 1921, Cobh also remained one of the four sovereign ports under U.K. control. Hamm's frequent command that Clov "Look at the sea" (30) reminds us that *Endgame*, in its entirety, takes place on the coast of a large body of water, possibly the Irish Sea. My thanks to Brian Richardson for pointing out the Kov/Cobh connection.

4. Anglo-Irish landlords and British officials essentially denied English grain to starving Irish tenants and itinerants through their slow and inefficient repeal of the "Corn Law" tariffs that kept up prices of grain in Ireland.

5. John Urry points out that "there are now 200 states [but] there are thought to be at least 2,000 'nation-peoples' all of which may suffer various kinds of displacement and ambiguous location" (qtd. in Brydon 700). Thus the so-called minority experience of globalization, in which transnational life precedes any achieved or normative sense of national life, is actually the majority experience.

Chapter 1. *Ulysses*, the Sea, and the Paradox of Irish Internationalism

1. The case of Liverpool, a hub for the slave trade and a site that funneled wealth into the hands of the British imperial state and its beneficiaries while channeling insignificant returns to the migrant working class that supplied its labor, is a fitting example. Like many coastal cases, it also has transoceanic echoes or correspondences: the dispersion of African peoples, the development of slave-dependent colonies in the Caribbean, and the ruthless drive to possess coastline and waterways in the European "scramble for Africa," to name but a few.

2. Implicit in this shift of attention is the broader concern, in modernist studies, for differentiating local conditions within global modernity and understanding how these local variations produce distinct modernisms. I am thinking, in particular, of Susan Stanford Friedman's call to "revisit the concept of modernist internationalism" by adopting "transnational strategies for reading a global landscape of mutually constitutive centers . . . that produce their own modernities and modernisms at different points in time" ("Toward" 35–36), and of Laura Doyle and Laura Winkiel's proposal that we "emplace modernism" by taking "a locational approach to [its] engagement[s] with cultural and political discourses of global modernity" (3).

3. The Martello towers were only one example of England's historically and geographically extensive practice of policing the Irish coast. As Patrick J. Duffy notes, "Coastguard stations are frequently imposing structures. . . . Like the RIC barracks, they were part of the fabric of the authority of the British state in the nineteenth century, the eyes and ears of Empire or Castle designed to stamp out smuggling, poitín making, plunder of wrecks and to maintain surveillance and security along the coast. . . . The Martello towers were erected (1804–1810) around the coast at strategically important points such as Cork harbor, Dublin Bay, the Shannon estuary, Galway Bay and Lough Foyle, as a signaling defensive network during the Napoleonic war" (136–37).

4. For the role of intranational rural migrations in the history of Joyce's working-class Dubliners, see Fairhall, chapter 3: "[M]any petty-bourgeois Dubliners,

the class depicted by Joyce, either were rural migrants themselves, or were their children or grandchildren" (75).

5. For extensive evidence of this position, as well as how Joyce's experiences in Trieste helped to shape it, see chapter 3 of John McCourt's *The Years of Bloom*, especially pp. 92–120.

6. Frederic Jameson would probably note that Bloom is here struggling with the "always already begun dynamic" of capitalism. Especially in its imperial phase, argues Jameson, it is "a synchronic system which, once in place, discredits the attempts . . . to conceive of its beginnings" (*Political* 280). After coming to Trieste, Joyce was increasingly concerned with Ireland's economic development vis-à-vis interstate capitalism, as is evident in a 1906 letter to his brother: "You ask me what I would substitute for parliamentary agitation in Ireland. I think the *Sinn Fein* policy would be more effective. Of course I see that its success would be to substitute Irish for English capital but no-one, I suppose, denies that capitalism is a stage of progress. The Irish proletariat has yet to be created" (*Letters* 125). Here, it sounds as if Joyce's sympathy for a socialist position that would see "capital" as the problem is preempted by the fact that capitalism, as a postfeudal "*stage of progress*," has not itself been fully realized in Ireland. The suggestion, once again, is that the time of postcolonial progress in Ireland is inherently out of joint.

7. Joseph Valente has recently noted that "the undeniable anti-nationalism of Joyce's Irish years and the budding nationalism of his early period in Italy [fostered by his interest in Italian irredentism and local misunderstanding of Irish nationalism] dialectically resolved themselves into an idiosyncratic cultural *transnationalism*, in which the localized attachments of and to the ethnos coincide, productively, with their cosmopolitan negation" (73).

8. As Ian Tyrell notes, in defining the aims of transnational historians, "Even when the nation-state becomes vital, that itself is produced transnationally. That is, the global context of security, economic competition, and demographic change means that the boundaries of the nation had to be made. They don't exist in isolation. National identities have been defined against other identities, including the transnational phenomena that impinge upon the nation as it is constructed" (paragraph 12).

9. Importantly, the ability to affirm these transnational realities, as opposed to the compulsion to suppress them, is an option available to the established state more so than the nation-in-process. As Louisa Schein argues, it is the state that has a "dialectical relation to the production of the transnational" because it is "crystallized in part through its engagement with that which breaches its border control, its putative sovereignty" (165).

10. As Rebecca Walkowitz has argued, Bloom's "utopian platitudes" betoken a

"detached idealism and universalist cosmopolitanism" that neglects the "living, contested present" of Irish nationhood introduced by his interlocutors (74–75).

11. One could argue that the critical history of *Ulysses* reflects the difficulty of seeing that the novel weighs both concerns equally: it begins in earnest when critics rescue the novel from negative receptions laced with English religious, class, and anti-Irish bias (for example, Virginia Woolf's claim that "[i]t is underbred, not only in the obvious sense, but in the literary sense" (*Diary* 48)) by demonstrating the immensity of its international significance and continental influences. This argument then sets in motion a "cosmopolitan" Joyce movement that underestimates the immensity of the Irish postcolonial concerns that are *also* a driving force behind the author's work.

12. Enda Duffy, for example, argues that *Ulysses* is "the starred text of an Irish national literature" because it is "*the* book of Irish postcolonial independence" (2–3). Andrew Gibson similarly maintains that "in *Ulysses*, Joyce works towards a liberation from the colonial power and its culture. He also takes his revenge on them" (13).

13. Tim Brennan's ongoing effort to point out the dangers of overlooking sovereign internationalism as we move from anticolonial nationalism to ideals of global hybridity also speaks volumes about Stephen's conundrum. "The existing nation-state system," argues Brennan, "contains the only structures through which transnational forms of solidarity might emerge in the only way they can— slowly and over many generations. . . . Internationalism should not [therefore] be mistaken for its dialectical other, the cosmopolitanism that is a product of . . . intricate theoretical edifices liable to weaken the very ability to imagine . . . a modicum of real sovereignty" in the developing world ("Cosmopolitanism and Internationalism" 48–49).

Chapter 2. "Forget! Remember!": Joyce's Voices and the Haunted Cosmos

1. On the postcolonial-cosmopolitan connection between Joyce and Walcott, see Pollard. For the similar challenges Joyce and Rushdie face as postcolonial writers trying to negotiate the problems of nationalism and postmodernism alike, see Tratner.

2. Suzette Henke proposes that *Finnegans Wake* represents the "fluid semio-texte" of *écriture feminine* by "introduc[ing] a lexical play-field that challenges the assumptions of traditional culture, including phallo-centric authority and logocentric discourse" (11)

3. Angela Bourke has described *caoineadh* as "an oral-formulaic poetic composition, produced in performance . . . by combining and recombining traditional motifs, [such as] [t]he lamenter address[ing] the dead person directly, prais[ing]

his beauty, his generosity and the splendor of his home, . . . pil[ing] image upon image of the desolation that will now follow his death" (72).

4. Yeats's aims for the Renaissance always had one eye on the international sphere, not only as a source of avant-garde forms but also as the milieu in which national arts would ultimately be validated.

Chapter 3. Elizabeth Bowen's Tenacious Cosmopolitanism

1. Especially in the case of Pound's "botched civilization," these excerpts exemplify Walter Mignolo's description of modernism as "a manifold geohistorical category which was interpreted chronologically within the reduced space of the heart of Europe" ("Human" 189).

2. Similarly, for Jessica Berman, British modernist fiction often "enacts notions of community that . . . undermine political versions of established consensus [and] blind universality [by] decenter[ing] belonging and challeng[ing] commonplace notions of the universal political subject" (22). They thus open themselves, and their readers, to "the possibility of a new cosmopolitanism, one that relies on the contingency of borders to open the community to a wider network of differences" and that "widens [the gap] between the theory of community and that of nationality, between a politics of connection and that of the modern nation-state" (15).

3. Jed Esty, in *A Shrinking Island*, points out that the "apocalyptic temporalities" (50) and expansive spatial abstractions of British modernism are more typical of early twentieth-century trends, just prior to the inward, "anthropological turn" (3) in British modernism of the 1930s to 1960s, during which the loss of empire and the concern for English nationhood as a phenomenon separate from empire become more of the focus. My analysis here is concerned with a particular aesthetic deployment of space and time that could be considered a component part of the early twentieth-century phase of British modernism that Esty describes. I would add, though, that these expansive, subjective representations of space and time indicate more than just the negative form, or imagined loss, of the expansive imperial worldview of the early century. They also reflect a presumptive linking of nation-state belonging with historically and geographically embedded life, and a more general, Eurocentric, conceptual sequence from achieved statehood to cosmopolitan life or thought.

4. For Jameson, the figure of an "ever-expanding grey placelessness" in British modernism is the result of an inability to imagine societal cohesion within the metropolitan heart of an expansive empire ("Modernism" 57–60). For Edward Said, the modernist "reformulation of . . . fragments drawn self consciously from disparate locations, sources, cultures" indicates a "[s]patiality [that has]

[become], ironically, the characteristic of an aesthetic rather than a political domination" (*Culture* 189–90). My suggestion is that spatial abstraction or conflation is inseparable from subjective or synchronic temporality and that this interdependence reflects the inclination of imperial state subjects to imagine local geographic and historical loss in universal terms, or as global in scope.

5. David Chandler and Timothy Brennan argue that cosmopolitanism has not changed much, at least with regard to its underestimation of the sovereign nation-state as the only proven guarantor of rights (Chandler 34–35; Brennan, "Cosmopolitanism" 42). For Brennan, it now merely means "the global entrance into a common hybrid self-consciousness by formerly subjugated peoples, without in the least disturbing the self-portraiture of the West" (45). Alternatively, Kwame Anthony Appiah proposes that the term "cosmopolitanism . . . can be rescued" to promote ethical cooperation in the contemporary global arena, given its core principles "that we have obligations to others [that] stretch beyond those to whom we are related by the ties of kith and kind, or even . . . shared citizenship," and "that we take seriously the value not just of human life but of particular human lives, which means taking an interest in the practices and beliefs which lend them significance" (*Cosmopolitanism* xiv–xv). Pheng Cheah notes that cosmopolitanism at its proper historical epitome (Immanuel Kant's promotion of the concept in 1795) had as its antonym "not nationalism but statism" and that, then as now, one's obligations to humanity at large and one's "affective and concrete" link to national processes, especially those "prior to [their] annexation of the territorial state," are not opposites ("Introduction" 22–25).

6. As Gita Rajan and Shailja Sharma put it, "new cosmopolitans [are] people who blur the edges of home and abroad by continuously moving physically, culturally, and socially, and by selectively using globalized forms of travel, communication, languages, and technology to position themselves in motion between at least two homes, sometimes even through dual forms of citizenship" (3).

7. Cheah clarifies, for example, that "cosmopolitanisms premised on the transcendence of the given [cultural and socioeconomic collective]" cannot account "for the majority who remain in peripheral space by choice or necessity"—those for whom "the nation-state, whatever its inconveniences, is a necessity," for whom the sovereign and equitable nation-state remains deferred, and for whom "postnationalism through migration is not an alternative" ("Given" 314).

8. For more on the historical and geographic insularity of the Ascendancy in general, see Foster, chapter 8. As Billy Gray puts it, "within a comparatively short historical period, the members of Protestant aristocracy who had been the original progenitors of Irish nationalism came to view themselves as exiles within their own country" (85).

9. As Maude Ellmann notes, "For Bowen, who believed that landed property protected her ancestors from the worst excesses of the will to power, Robert [Kelway]'s rootlessness is ominous [in that it] can boil over into fascism" (158). Bowen's claim in *Bowen's Court* that "we have everything to fear from the dispossessed" (455) reflects this idea, yet it also suggests that Catholic, republican Ireland—under serious suspicion in 1942 when she writes the book—is among the dangerously "dispossessed." The claim represents her guarded and biased view of the Catholic Irish, but it also squares with her tendency to validate their claims to statehood (their need for property, as it were) to international audiences inclined to see them only as insubordinate subjects of the crown.

10. As Beth Wightman observes, "The hole at the center of Lois's identity . . . is a fundamental function of place and space" in decolonizing Ireland: "Just as Anglo-Irish culture . . . struggles to connect with the land and people surrounding it, Lois cannot connect with a modern Irish nation-state, and she cannot conceive of an intact Irish space on any terms" (55).

11. As Robert Caserio notes, Bowen's narratives make us "feel the full impact of elemental contingency . . . and at the same time the solidarity among contingent and heterogeneous elements." "Historical and cultural context," argues Caserio, may thus appear vague or distant, but they ultimately "limit [her characters] freedom to be arbitrary and groundless." Bowen thus coaxes, but repeatedly rejects, "the full-throated modernist's positioning power, which sunders and dislocates itself from contexts to live out an allegory of freedom" (277–78).

12. As Neil Corcoran observes, the history of Anglo-Ireland and of the colonized, partitioned island more broadly is "still architecturally articulate on the land," embodied in such structures as the deteriorating mill and the silent, perplexed ruins of the Big Houses that the novel almost perpetually foreshadows. The suggestion is of a history that was decisively truncated but never itself understood. This combination, says Corcoran, "makes [the idea of an Anglo-Irish past] in some ways all the more insistent, with the insistence of the hauntingly irretrievable" (52).

13. As did many Anglo-Irish intellectuals, most notably W. B. Yeats and George Russell, in literary circles; Bowen, however, does not idealize particulars of the land and tenant economies and seems principally (though not stridently) concerned to define Ireland's thwarted, unrealized transnational past as a statewide concern.

14. Julia McElhattan Williams argues that *The Last September* itself enacts this renegotiation of Anglo-Irish presence within Irish history: "by placing fictional characters within a reconstructed past, Bowen offers one possible interpretation of the differences that have separated the Irish from the Anglo-Irish, not merely

as . . . self-interest, but [due to] conditions which stemmed from the mismanagement of Ireland under English colonial rule and victimized both the Irish and Anglo-Irish people" (227).

15. My thanks to Allan Hepburn, of McGill University, for bringing this article to my attention. Sean O'Faolain, in his inaugural editor's address for the magazine, stated the magazine's agenda thus: "Whoever you are, Gentile or Jew, Protestant or Catholic, priest or layman, Big House or Small House—the Bell is yours" (qtd. in Keogh).

Chapter 4. Crossings Still: Irish Interludes in Bowen's European Novels

1. In *The House in Paris*, the setting shifts from France to Ireland, ten years prior, but the ferry crossing that begins the flashback is actually that of Karen traveling to Cork from Holyhead, Wales.

2. Harriet Blodgett claims that "Stella's wartime rediscovery of her human identity is the novel's center. During wartime, the person becomes more sensitive to what matters to him under the threat of its diminution or loss; the individual self resists becoming equated with a political identity. . . . Meaning [thus] extends beyond temporality for *The Heat of the Day*. As is true for Eliot's *Four Quartets* there exists a pattern, its detail movement, but its core a still center" (154–55). Timothy Adams, in a more Bergsonian vein, proposes that *The House in Paris* enacts "the search for identity [through] an exercise in memory" (50).

3. W. J. McCormack addresses this history and proposes that the German counter-spy plot and "Kelway's fascism [are] Irish 'trace[s]' in the novel" (215).

4. Neil Corcoran notes that the novel's conclusion imagines "a new harmony of post-war interrelationship" between the "projected English future and the projected Irish future" (197). I would offer that such diplomacy is already taking shape in these scenes, and is expressed, too, in the novel's broader indecisiveness regarding the abstractions of time and history.

Chapter 5. "Haunt[ing] the Waterfront": Place and Displacement in *Echo's Bones* and *Les Nouvelles*

1. "The End," written first, in May 1946, was actually begun in English and finished in French.

2. Anna McMullan similarly notes that "Beckett's oeuvre can be seen as a sustained critique or parody of that sovereign consciousness which seeks to see, know, and record its objects" and that this is where his "aesthetics of radical dislocation intersect[s] with the cultural politics of the postcolonial" (95, 96).

3. As Minister for Agriculture Patrick Hogan noted in 1924, advocating the potential land reforms and subsidies of the Land Act of 1923, "there are about

500,000 tenants in Ireland; there are about one and a half million landless men and only about 30,000 holdings for them" (qtd. in Ferriter 314).

Chapter 6. Beckett, Setting, and Cosmopolitical Philosophy

1. Beckett's biographers disagree on the exact location between Dublin and Dalkey where this revelation occurred, but the ironic, self-effacing version of it that appears in *Krapp's Last Tape* is, as Beckett has confirmed, set upon the pier at Dún Laoghaire harbor, formerly Kingstown. I will consider the significance of this location later in the chapter.

2. James Knowlson and John Pilling focus on Beckett as a "cerebral artist [who] has been engaged in an unprecedented archaeological investigation [of the mind]" (xiii). For Rubin Rabinovitz, Beckett's later fiction uses "elaborate extended metaphors that suggest the enigmatic nature of the interaction between ideal and material reality. . . . Dante's metaphorical settings refer to a spiritual plane of existence, [while] Beckett's refer to existence on a mental level" (106).

3. As Cyraina Johnson-Roullier points out, the "[realm of] aesthetic perfection which has traditionally been that of Euro-American international modernism" assumes its own, deterritorialized "cultural space" (28).

4. The curricular guide to English television Channel 4's recent series "Beckett on Film" reminds us of how this dominant twentieth-century equation (immaterial setting = universal meaning) persists as a pedagogical imperative. The guide advises the Beckett newcomer that "[t]he focus is on the nature of human existence, regardless of where the characters are" ("*Waiting for Godot*: Setting").

5. Definitive and influential examples of this stance appear often in Richard Ellmann and Charles Feidelson's *The Modern Tradition*: "Modernism strongly implies some sort of historical discontinuity, either a liberation from inherited patterns or, at another extreme, deprivation and disinheritance. . . . Committed to everything in human experience that militates against custom . . . [modern literature] has made the most of its break with the past, its inborn challenge to established culture" (vi).

6. "Moulin à larmes" means "a tearmill" and is apparently Beckett's adaptation of the French for "windmill," "moulin à vent." This according to George Craig, the French translator for volume 1 of Beckett's letters (*Letters* 95).

7. For evidence of these particulars in the trilogy, see Eoin O'Brien's *The Beckett Country: Samuel Beckett's Ireland* and, especially for its accompanying critical analysis of "the hermeneutic treatment of place" in Beckett's novels, John Harrington's *The Irish Beckett*, 156–70.

8. In *Beckett/Beckett*, Vivian Mercier notes that the vast disparities of class and numerous homeless persons Beckett regularly witnessed when traveling from

Foxrock to surrounding points left a lasting impression on the author that persists in his depictions, and philosophical treatment, of tramps and vagabonds.

9. As John Harrington has pointed out, although Beckett's later prose "reduc[es] identifiable references to Ireland," it exaggerates a "hermeneutic treatment of place" and unresolved "dialectic of home and away" that is evident in his earlier novels *Mercier and Camier* and *Watt*, and important to modern Irish literature in general (158–59).

10. That police and hierarchies of state authority are integral to the alienation of Beckett's subjects is also evident in part two of *Molloy*, wherein Moran—who shares a surname with the zealous cultural nationalist Patrick Moran—tracks Molloy across "the Molloy country . . . called Bally," in service of "a cause that is not mine. . . . with hatred in my heart, and scorn, of my master and his designs" (132–33). A similar scenario is implied in *Malone Dies* (and therefore *The Unnamable*), via the hint that Malone's captivity relates to his memories of "kill[ing], [by] hitting them on the head or setting fire to . . . four [people], all unknowns," including an "old butler . . . in London" (236).

Epilogue

1. In a footnote to the poem, Yeats goes so far as to explain that "I pronounce 'fanatic' in what is, I suppose, the older and more Irish way, so that the last line of each stanza contains but two beats" (*Poems* 254). In so doing, he even further enhances the simultaneously national and exilic meaning of being "fanatic" at heart.

WORKS CITED

Ackerley, Chris J., and Stanley E. Gontarski. *The Grove Companion to Samuel Beckett*. New York: Grove, 2004.

Adams, Timothy Dow. "'Bend Sinister': Duration in Elizabeth Bowen's *The House in Paris*." *International Fiction Review* 7 (1980): 49–52.

Adorno, Theodor. *Notes to Literature, Volume One*. New York: Columbia University Press, 1991.

———. "Commitment." In *Aesthetics and Politics*, 177–95. London: Verso, 2007.

Allen, Nicholas. *Modernism, Ireland, and Civil War*. Cambridge, U.K.: Cambridge University Press, 2009.

Alvarez, Al. *Samuel Beckett*. New York: Viking, 1973.

Appiah, Kwame Anthony. *Cosmopolitanism: Ethics in a World of Strangers*. New York: Norton, 2007.

———. *The Ethics of Identity*. Princeton, N.J.: Princeton University Press, 2005.

Archibugi, Daniele, ed. *Debating Cosmopolitics*. London: Verso, 2003.

Bair, Deirdre. *Samuel Beckett*. London: Pan Books, 1980.

Baucom, Ian. *Out of Place: Englishness, Empire, and the Locations of Identity*. Ewing, N.J.: Princeton University Press, 1999.

Beckett, Samuel. *All That Fall*. In *Collected Shorter Plays*. New York: Grove, 1984.

———. "The Calmative." In *Stories and Texts for Nothing*. New York: Grove, 1967.

———. "Echo's Bones." In *Collected Poems in English and French*. New York: Grove, 1977.

———. "The End." In *Stories and Texts for Nothing*. New York: Grove, 1967.

———. *Endgame*. New York: Grove, 1958.

———. "The Expelled." In *Stories and Texts for Nothing*. New York: Grove, 1967.

———. *The Letters of Samuel Beckett, 1929–1940*. Edited by Martha Dow Fehsenfeld and Lois More Overbeck. Vol. 1. New York: Cambridge University Press, 2009.

———. *The Letters of Samuel Beckett, 1941–1956*. Edited by Martha Dow Fehsenfeld and Lois More Overbeck. Vol. 2. New York: Cambridge University Press, 2011.

———. *Nohow On*. New York: Grove, 1980.

———. *Three Novels by Samuel Beckett: Molloy, Malone Dies, The Unnamable*. Translated by Patrick Bowles. New York: Grove Weidenfeld, 1991.

———. *Waiting for Godot*. New York: Grove, 1954.

Benhabib, Seyla, with Jeremy Waldron, Bonnie Honig, and Will Kymlicka. *Another Cosmopolitanism: Hospitality, Sovereignty, and Democratic Iterations*. Edited by Robert Post. New York: Oxford University Press, 2006.

Bennet, Andrew, and Nicholas Royle. *Elizabeth Bowen and the Dissolution of the Novel*. New York: St. Martin's, 1995.

Ben-Zvi, Linda. *Samuel Beckett*. Boston: Twayne, 1986.

Benitez-Rojo, Antonio. *The Repeating Island: The Caribbean and the Postmodern Perspective*. Durham, N.C.: Duke University Press, 1996.

Berman, Jessica. *Modernist Fiction, Cosmopolitanism and the Politics of Community*. Cambridge, U.K.: Cambridge University Press, 2001.

Bhabha, Homi. "Unsatisfied: Notes on Vernacular Cosmopolitanism." In *Postcolonial Discourses: An Anthology*, edited by Gregory Castle, 39–52. Oxford, U.K.: Blackwell, 2001.

Bixby, Patrick. *Samuel Beckett and the Postcolonial Novel*. New York: Cambridge University Press, 2009.

Blodgett, Harriet. *Patterns of Reality: Elizabeth Bowen's Novels*. Paris: Mouton, 1975.

Boland, Eavan. *New Collected Poems*. New York: W. W. Norton, 2009.

———. *Object Lessons: The Life of the Woman and the Poet in Our Time*. New York: W. W. Norton, 1995.

Bourke, Angela. "Keening as Theatre: J. M. Synge and the Irish Lament Tradition." In *Interpreting Synge: Essays from the Synge Summer School, 1991–2000*, edited by Nicholas Grene, 67–79. Dublin: Lilliput Press, 2000.

Bowen, Elizabeth. *Bowen's Court*. New York: Ecco, 1979.

———. *Collected Impressions*. New York: Alfred A. Knopf, 1950.

———. *The Heat of the Day*. New York: Alfred A. Knopf, 1949.

———. *The House in Paris*. New York: Anchor/Random House, 2002.

———. "James Joyce." *The Bell* 1.6 (1941): 40–49.

———. *The Last September*. New York: Anchor/Random House, 2000.

———. *The Mulberry Tree: Writings of Elizabeth Bowen*. London: Virago, 1986.

———. "Mysterious Kôr." In *The Collected Stories of Elizabeth Bowen*, 728–40. New York: Alfred A. Knopf, 1981.

———. *Notes on Eire: Espionage Reports to Winston Churchill*. Cork: Aubane Historical Society, 1999.

Bradbury, Malcolm, and James McFarlane, eds. *Modernism: A Guide to European Literature 1890–1930*. London: Penguin, 1991.

Breckenridge, Carol A., Sheldon Pollock, Homi K. Bhabha, and Dipesh Chakrabarty, eds. *Cosmopolitanism (a Public Culture Book)*. Durham, N.C.: Duke University Press, 2002.

Brennan, Tim. *At Home in the World: Cosmopolitanism Now*. Cambridge, Mass.: Harvard University Press, 1997.

———. "Cosmopolitans and Celebrities." *Race and Class* 31.1 (1989): 1–19.

———. "Cosmopolitanism and Internationalism." In Archibugi, 40–50.

Brivic, Sheldon. *Joyce's Waking Women: An Introduction to "Finnegans Wake."* Madison: University of Wisconsin Press, 1995.

Brothers, Barbara. "Pattern and Void: Bowen's Irish Landscapes and *The Heat of the Day*." *Mosaic* 12 (1979): 129–38.

Brydon, Diana. "Post-colonialism Now: Autonomy, Cosmopolitanism, and Diaspora." *University of Toronto Quarterly* 73.2 (2004): 691–706.

Caserio, Robert L. "The Heat of the Day: Modernism and Narrative in Paul de Man and Elizabeth Bowen." *Modern Language Quarterly* 54.2 (1993): 263–84.

Chandler, David. "International Justice." In Archibugi, 27–39.

Corcoran, Neil. *Elizabeth Bowen: The Enforced Return*. New York: Oxford University Press, 2004.

Coughlin, Patricia. "'The Poetry is Another Pair of Sleeves': Beckett, Ireland and Modernist Lyric Poetry." In *Modernism and Ireland: The Poetry of the 1930s*, edited by Patricia Coughlan and Alex Davis. Cork: Cork University Press, 1995.

Cheah, Pheng. "Introduction Part II: The Cosmopolitical—Today." In *Cosmopolitics: Thinking and Feeling Beyond the Nation*, edited by Pheng Cheah and Bruce Robbins, 20–41. Cultural Politics 14. Minneapolis: University of Minnesota Press, 1998.

———. "Given Culture: Rethinking Cosmopolitical Freedom in Transnationalism." In Cheah and Robbins, 290–328.

———. *Spectral Nationality: Passages of Freedom from Kant to Postcolonial Literatures of Liberation*. New York: Columbia University Press, 2003.

Cheah, Pheng, and Bruce Robbins, eds. *Cosmopolitics: Thinking and Feeling Beyond the Nation*. Cultural Politics 14. Minneapolis: University of Minnesota Press, 1998.

Cheng, Vincent J. *Joyce, Race, and Empire*. Cambridge, U.K.: Cambridge University Press, 1995.

Cleary, Joe. "Misplaced Ideas?: Locating and Dislocating Ireland in Colonial and

Postcolonial Studies." In *Marxism, Modernity, and Postcolonial Studies*, edited by Crystal Bartolovich and Neil Lazarus, 101–24. Cambridge, U.K.: Cambridge University Press, 2002.

Clifford, James. "Travelling Cultures." In *Cultural Studies*, edited by Lawrence Grossberg, Cary Nelson, and Paula Treichle, 100–119. New York: Routledge, 1991.

Cohn, Ruby. "Joyce and Beckett, Irish Cosmopolitans." *James Joyce Quarterly* 8 (1971): 385–91.

Cronin, Anthony. *Samuel Beckett: The Last Modernist*. New York: Da Capo, 1999.

Darwhadker, Vinay, ed. *Cosmopolitan Geographies: New Locations in Literature and Culture*. New York: Routledge, 2001.

Davies, Paul. "Three Novels and Four 'Nouvelles': Giving Up the Ghost Be Born at Last." In *The Cambridge Companion to Beckett,* edited by John Pilling, 43–67. Cambridge, U.K.: Cambridge University Press, 1994.

Davis, Alex. "Reactions from their burg: Irish modernist poets of the 1930's." In *Locations of Literary Modernism: Region and Nation in British and American Modernist Poetry,* edited by Alex Davis and Lee M. Jenkins, 135–58. Cambridge, U.K.: Cambridge University Press, 2000.

Deane, Seamus. *Notes to "A Portrait of the Artist as a Young Man," by James Joyce*. New York: Penguin, 1993.

DiBattista, Maria. "Elizabeth Bowen's Troubled Modernism." In *Modernism and Colonialism: British and Irish Literature, 1899–1939,* edited by Richard Begam and Michael Valdez Moses, 226–45. Durham, N.C.: Duke University Press, 2007.

Doggett, Rob. "*In the Shadow of the Glen*: Gender, Nationalism, and 'A Woman Only.'" *ELH* 67.4 (2000): 1011–34.

Doyle, Laura, and Laura Winkiel. *Geomodernisms: Race, Modernism, Modernity*. Bloomington: Indiana University Press, 2006.

Dubow, Jessica. "The Mobility of Thought: Reflections on Blanchot and Benjamin." *Interventions* 6.2 (2004): 216–28.

Duckworth, Colin. *Angels of Darkness: Dramatic Effect in Beckett with Special Reference to Ionesco*. New York: Barnes and Noble, 1972.

Duffy, Enda. *The Subaltern Ulysses*. Minneapolis: University of Minnesota Press, 1994.

Duffy, Patrick J. *Exploring the History and Heritage of Irish Landscapes*. Maynooth Research Guides for Irish Local History 12. Dublin: Four Courts, 2007.

Eagleton, Terry. *Heathcliff and the Great Hunger: Studies in Irish Culture*. New York: Verso, 1995.

Eliot, T. S. *Four Quartets*. New York: Harcourt, 1988.

Ellmann, Maude. *Elizabeth Bowen: The Shadow across the Page*. Edinburgh: Edinburgh University Press, 2004.

Ellmann, Richard, and Charles Feidelson Jr., eds. *The Modern Tradition: Backgrounds of Modern Literature*. Oxford, U.K.: Oxford University Press, 1964.

Esty, Jed. *A Shrinking Island: Modernism and National Culture in England*. Princeton, N.J.: Princeton University Press, 2004.

Eysteinsson, Ástráður. *The Concept of Modernism*. Ithaca, N.Y.: Cornell University Press, 1990.

Fairhall, James. *James Joyce and the Question of History*. Cambridge, U.K.: Cambridge University Press, 1993.

Fanon, Frantz. *The Wretched of the Earth*. New York: Grove, 1963.

Ferriter, Diarmaid. *The Transformation of Ireland 1900–2000*. London: Profile Books, 2004.

Forster, E. M. *A Passage to India*. New York: Harcourt, 1984.

Foster, R. F. *Modern Ireland: 1600–1972*. New York: Penguin, 1989.

Friedman, Susan Stanford. "Cultural Parataxis and Transnational Landscapes of Reading: Toward a Locational Modernist Studies." In *Modernism*, edited by Ástráður Eysteinsson and Vivian Liska, 35–52. Vol. 1. Comparative History of Literatures in European Languages 21. Amsterdam: John Benjamins, 2007.

———. "Periodizing Modernism: Postcolonial Modernities and the Space/Time Borders of Modernist Studies." *Modernism/Modernity* 13.3 (2006): 425–43.

Gibbons, Luke. *Transformations in Irish Culture*. South Bend, Ind.: Notre Dame University Press, 1996.

Gibson, Andrew. *Joyce's Revenge: History, Politics, and Aesthetics in* Ulysses. New York: Oxford University Press, 2002.

Gifford, Don, with Robert J. Seidman. *"Ulysses" Annotated: Notes for James Joyce's "Ulysses."* 2nd ed. Berkeley: University of California Press, 1989.

Girvin, Brian. "The Republicanisation of Irish Society, 1932–48." In *A New History of Ireland: VII, Ireland 1921–84*, edited by J. R. Hill, 127–59. Oxford, U.K.: Oxford University Press, 2003.

Glendenning, Victoria. *Elizabeth Bowen*. New York: Avon, 1977.

Gontarski, S. E. *The Intent of "Undoing" in Samuel Beckett's Dramatic Texts*. Bloomington: Indiana University Press, 1985.

Gordon, Lois. *The World of Samuel Beckett, 1906–1946*. New Haven, Conn.: Yale University Press, 1998.

Gray, Billy. "'The Lukewarm Conviction of Temporary Lodgers': Hubert Butler and the Anglo-Irish Sense of Exile." *New Hibernia Review* 9.2 (2005): 84–89.

Greene, Graham. *The Heart of the Matter*. New York: Viking, 1948.

Hamilton, Alice, and Kenneth Hamilton. *Condemned to Life: The World of Samuel Beckett*. Grand Rapids, Mich.: Eerdmans, 1976.

Handbook to the City of Dublin and the Surrounding District. British Association for the Advancement of Science. 1908. Reprint. London: Forgotten Books, 2013.

Harper, Margaret Mills. "Sisters, Outsiders, Histories: First Principles and Last Things in Boland and Lorde." In *Representing Ireland,* edited by Susan Shaw Sailer, 181–93. Gainesville: University Press of Florida, 1997.

Harrington, John. *The Irish Beckett*. Syracuse, N.Y.: Syracuse University Press, 1991.

Harvey, Lawrence E. *Samuel Beckett: Poet and Critic*. Princeton, N.J.: Princeton University Press, 1970.

Henke, Suzette. *James Joyce and the Politics of Desire*. New York: Routledge, 1990.

Hobsbawm, E. J. *Industry and Empire*. New York: Penguin, 1978.

Innes, C. L. *Woman and Nation in Irish Literature and Society, 1880–1935*. Athens: University of Georgia Press, 1994.

Jameson, Frederic. "Modernism and Imperialism." In *Nationalism, Colonialism, and Literature,* by Terry Eagleton, Frederic Jameson, and Edward Said, 43–67. Minneapolis: University of Minnesota Press, 1990.

———. *The Political Unconscious: Narrative as a Socially Symbolic Act*. Ithaca, N.Y.: Cornell University Press, 1981.

Johnson-Roullier, Cyraina E. *Reading on the Edge: Exiles, Modernities, and Cultural Transformation in Proust, Joyce, and Baldwin*. Albany, N.Y.: SUNY Press, 2000.

Joyce, James. *Collected Poems*. New York: Viking, 1957.

———. *The Critical Writings of James Joyce*. Edited by Ellsworth Mason and Richard Ellmann. New York: Viking, 1959.

———. *Dubliners*. New York: Penguin, 1992.

———. *Finnegans Wake*. New York: Penguin, 1976.

———. *The Letters of James Joyce*. Edited by Stuart Gilbert and Richard Ellmann. Vol. 2. New York: Viking, 1966.

———. *Occasional, Critical, and Political Writing*. Oxford, U.K.: Oxford University Press, 2000.

———. *A Portrait of the Artist as a Young Man* New York: Penguin, 1993.

———. *Ulysses*. London: Penguin, 1986.

Kant, Immanuel. "Idea for a Universal History from a Cosmopolitan Point of View." Translated by Lewis White Beck. In *Immanuel Kant: Philosophical Writings,* edited by Ernst Behler, 249–62. New York: Continuum, 1986.

Kearney, Richard. *Postnationalist Ireland: Politics, Culture, Philosophy*. New York: Routledge, 1996.

Kelly, Marian. "The Power of the Past: Structural Nostalgia in Elizabeth Bowen's *The House in Paris* and *The Little Girls*." *Style* 36.1 (2002): 1–18.

Kennedy, Seán. "Does Beckett Studies Require a Subject?: Mourning Ireland in the *Texts for Nothing*." In Kennedy and Weiss, 11–30.

———. "'In the street I was lost': Cultural Dislocation in Samuel Beckett's 'The End.'" In *Beckett and Ireland*, edited by Seán Kennedy. Cambridge, U.K.: Cambridge University Press, 2010.

Kennedy, Seán, and Katherine Weiss, eds. *Samuel Beckett: History, Memory, Archive*. New York: Palgrave MacMillan, 2009.

Kenner, Hugh. *The Pound Era*. Berkeley: University of California Press, 1971.

Keogh, Dáire. "A World of Ideas Saved by the 'Bell' and the Jesuits." *Irish Times*, November 22, 2008. http://www.irishtimes.com. Accessed October 20, 2009.

Knowles, Sam. "Macrocosm-opolitanism? Gilroy, Appiah, and Bhabha: The Unsettling Generality of Cosmopolitan Ideas." *Postcolonial Text* 3.4 (2007): 1–11.

Knowlson, James. *Damned to Fame: The Life of Samuel Beckett*. New York: Simon and Schuster, 1996.

Knowlson, James, and John Pilling. *Frescoes of the Skull: The Later Prose and Drama of Samuel Beckett*. London: Calder, 1979.

Koshy, Susan. "Minority Cosmopolitanism." *PMLA* 126.3 (2011): 592–609.

Kristeva, Julia. *Strangers to Ourselves*. Trans. Leon S. Roudiez. New York: Columbia University Press, 1991.

Lee, Rachel C. "The Erasure of Places and the Re-Siting of Empire in Wendy Law-Yone's *The Coffin Tree*." *Cultural Critique* 35 (1996–1997): 149–78.

Levy, Eric P. *Beckett and the Voice of Species: A Study of the Prose Fiction*. New York: Barnes and Noble, 1980.

———. *Trapped in Thought: A Study of the Beckettian Mentality*. Syracuse, N.Y.: Syracuse University Press, 2007.

Lewis, Wyndham. "Vorticist Manifesto." In *The Longman Anthology of British Literature*, edited by Kevin J. H. Dettmar and Jennifer Wicke, 2310–24. Vol. 2C. 3rd ed. New York: Pearson/Longman, 2006.

Lloyd, David. *Anomalous States: Irish Writing and the Postcolonial Moment*. Durham, N.C.: Duke University Press, 1991.

———. "Ireland after History." In *A Companion to Postcolonial Studies*, edited by Sangeeta Ray and Henry Schwartz, 377–95. Malden, Mass.: Blackwell, 2000.

Mangan, James Clarence, trans. "Dark Rosaleen." Attributed to Owen Roe MacWard. In *The Book of Irish Verse: An Anthology of Irish Poetry from the Sixth*

Century to the Present, edited by John Montague, 125–27. New York: MacMillan, 1976.

McCabe, Colin. *James Joyce and the Revolution of the Word.* New York: Barnes and Noble, 1979.

McCormack, W. J. *Dissolute Characters: Irish Literary History through Balzac, Sheridan Le Fanu, Yeats, and Bowen.* New York: Manchester University Press, 1993.

McCourt, John. *The Years of Bloom: James Joyce in Trieste 1904–1920.* Madison: University of Wisconsin Press, 2000.

McMullan, Anna. "Irish/Postcolonial Beckett." In *Palgrave Advances in Samuel Becket Studies,* edited by Lois Oppenheim, 89–109. New York: Palgrave, 2004.

Mercier, Vivian. *Beckett/Beckett.* New York: Oxford, 1977.

Mignolo, Walter. "Human Understanding and (Latin) American Interests—The Politics and Sensibilities of Geohistorical Locations." In *A Companion to Postcolonial Studies,* edited by Henry Schwartz and Sangeeta Ray, 180–202. Malden, Mass.: Blackwell, 2000.

———. "The Many Faces of Cosmo-polis: Border Thinking and Critical Cosmopolitanism." In Breckenridge et al., 157–88.

Miller, Nicholas Andrew. *Modernism, Ireland, and the Erotics of Memory.* Cambridge, U.K.: Cambridge University Press, 2002.

Moore, Thomas. *Moore's Irish Melodies: The Illustrated 1846 Edition.* Illustrated by Daniel Maclise. Dublin: Courier Dover Publications, 2000.

Moran, D. P. *The Philosophy of Irish Ireland.* Dublin: James Duffy and Co., 1905.

Nolan, Emer. *James Joyce and Nationalism.* London: Routledge, 1995.

Norris, Margot. "Joyce's Noises." *Modernism/Modernity* 16.2 (2009): 377–82.

O'Brien, Eoin. *The Beckett Country: Samuel Beckett's Ireland.* Dublin: Black Cat Press, 1986.

O'Hara, J. D., ed. *Twentieth Century Interpretations of "Molloy," "Malone Dies," and "The Unnamable."* Englewood Cliffs, N.J.: Prentice-Hall, 1970.

Osborn, Susan. "Reconsidering Elizabeth Bowen." Rev. of *Elizabeth Bowen: The Enforced Return* by Neil Corcoran and *Elizabeth Bowen: The Shadow across the Page* by Maude Ellmann. *Modern Fiction Studies* 52.1 (2006): 187–97.

Pollard, Charles W. "Traveling with Joyce: Derek Walcott's Discrepant Cosmopolitan Modernism." *Twentieth Century Literature* 47.2 (2001): 197–216.

Pollock, Sheldon. "Cosmopolitanisms." In Breckenridge et al., 1–14.

Pound, Ezra. "Hugh Selwyn Mauberly: Life and Contacts." In *The Norton Anthology of Modern Poetry,* 2nd. ed., edited by Richard Ellmann and Robert O'Clair, 382–94. New York: W. W. Norton, 1988.

———. *Selected Poems.* New York: New Directions, 1957.

Quinones, Ricardo J. *Mapping Literary Modernism: Time and Development*. Princeton, N.J.: Princeton University Press, 1985.

Rabinovitz, Rubin. *Innovation in Samuel Beckett's Fiction*. Urbana: University of Illinois Press, 1993.

Rajan, Gita, and Shailja Sharma, eds. *New Cosmopolitanisms*. Stanford, Calif.: Stanford University Press, 2006.

Rao, Rahul. "Postcolonial Cosmopolitanism: Between Home and the World." PhD diss., University of Oxford, 2007.

Rée, Johnathan. "Cosmopolitanism and the Experience of Nationality." In Cheah and Robbins, 77–90.

Rickard, John. "Stephen Dedalus among Schoolchildren: The Schoolroom and the Riddle of Authority in Ulysses." *Studies in the Literary Imagination* 30.2 (1997): 17–36.

Robbins, Bruce. "Cosmopolitanism: New and Newer." *boundary 2* 34.3 (2007): 47–60.

———. "Introduction I: Actually Existing Cosmopolitanism." In Cheah and Robbins, 1–19.

Rushdie, Salman. *Shame*. New York: Aventura/Vintage, 1984.

Said, Edward. *Beginnings: Intention and Method*. New York: Columbia, 1975

———. *Culture and Imperialism*. New York: Vintage, 1994.

———. "Reflections on Exile." In *Reflections on Exile*. Cambridge, Mass.: Harvard University Press, 2000.

Schein, Louisa. "Importing Miao Brethren to Hmong America: A Not-So-Stateless Transnationalism." In *Cosmopolitics: Thinking and Feeling Beyond the Nation*, edited by Pheng Cheah and Bruce Robbins, 163–91. Cultural Politics 14. Minneapolis: University of Minnesota Press, 1998.

Smith, Zadie. *White Teeth*. New York: Vintage, 2001.

Sollers, Philippe. "Joyce and Co." *TriQuarterly* 38 (1977): 105–17.

Spender, Stephen. Introduction to *Under the Volcano*, by Malcolm Lowry. New York: New American Library, 1966.

Spivak, Gayatri Chakravorty. *In Other Worlds: Essays in Cultural Politics*. New York: Routledge, 1988.

Stanton, Katherine. *Cosmopolitan Fictions: Ethics, Politics, and Global Change in the Works of Kazuo Ishiguro, Michael Ondaatje, Jamaica Kincaid, and J. M. Coetzee*. New York: Routledge, 2009.

Synge, John Millington. *Collected Plays and Poems and The Aran Islands*. Edited by Allison Smith. London: J. M. Dent, 1992.

Tratner, Michael. "What's Wrong with Hybridity: The Impotence of Postmodern Political Ideals in *Ulysses* and *Midnight's Children*." In *Joyce, Imperialism, and Postcolonialism,* edited by Leonard Orr, 112–26. Syracuse, N.Y.: Syracuse University Press, 2008.

Tyrell, Ian. "What is transnational history?" http://www.iantyrell.wordpress.com. Accessed October 12, 2010.

Valente, Joseph. "Joyce's Politics: Race, Nation, and Transnationalism." In *Palgrave Advances in James Joyce Studies,* edited by Jean-Michel Rabaté, 73–96. Hampshire, U.K.: Palgrave MacMillan, 2005.

Vallega, Alejandro A. "Decoloniality and Philosophy, from a Latin American Perspective." Center of Study and Investigation for Global Dialogues. http://www.dialogoglobal.com/barcelona/texts/vallega/decoloniality-of-philosophy.pdf. Accessed May 27, 2012.

"*Waiting for Godot*: Setting." Channel 4 Learning. http://www.learning.channel4.com/support/programmenotes/netnotes/section/printyes/sectionid100664765_printyes.htm. Accessed May 26, 2008.

Walkowitz, Rebecca L. *Cosmopolitan Style: Modernism Beyond the Nation.* New York: Columbia University Press, 2006.

Webb, Eugene. *Samuel Beckett: A Study of His Novels.* Seattle: University of Washington Press, 1970.

Wightman, Beth. "Geopolitics and the Sight of the Nation: Elizabeth Bowen's *The Last September*." *LIT: Literature, Interpretation, Theory* 18 (2007): 37–64.

Williams, Julia McElhattan. "Fiction with the Texture of History: Elizabeth Bowen's *The Last September*." *Modern Fiction Studies* 41 (1995): 219–42.

Williams, Trevor. *Reading Joyce Politically.* Gainesville: University Press of Florida, 1997.

Woolf, Virginia. *To The Lighthouse.* New York: Harcourt, 1989.

———. *The Waves.* New York: Harcourt, 1931.

———. *A Writer's Diary.* Edited by Leonard Woolf. New York: Harcourt, 1982.

Yeats, William Butler. "Ireland and the Arts." In *The Yeats Reader: A Portable Compendium of Poetry, Drama, and Prose,* edited by Richard J. Finneran, 382–87. New York: Scribner, 2002.

———. *The Collected Poems of W.B. Yeats.* Edited by Richard J. Finneran. New York: Scribner, 1996.

INDEX

Abbey Theatre, 61

Abstract poetics, 123

Ackerley, C. J., 129

Adorno, Theodor, 130–31

Aisling poetry, 54–55, 57, 59

Alienation, 110; Beckett and, 15, 128

Allen, Nicholas, 147

All That Fall (Beckett), 134, 136–37

Anglo-Irish, 11, 157n12; Anglo-Irish War, 135–36; Bowen and, 72, 76, 83–84, 87, 116, 157n14

Anglophone modernism, 10, 54

Appiah, Kwame, 61

Ascendancy, 156n8; Bowen on, 72–73, 76, 79, 85, 93; Cork Ascendancy, 11; in *The Heat of the Day*, 88

Balibar, Étienne, 148

Baucom, Ian, 67

Beckett, Samuel, 1, 2, 11; abstract poetics, 123; aesthetic worldliness, 15; alienation and, 15, 128; belonging and, 119; bidirectional consciousness, 121; colonial expatriation and, 109–12; compassionate cosmopolitanism, 128; cosmopolitan exile, 145; cosmopolitical philosophy, 124–44; dialectic of non-identity, 105; dislocation and, 13–14; disorientation and, 105–6, 109, 122, 125, 139; Easter Rising and, 136;

global society and, 148; hope of socially connecting, 150; humanistic insight, 10; intellectual development, 14; interpretations of, 127–28; on Ireland, 135; Irish culture and, 128; Irish identity and, 125; Irishness of, 14–16; landscapes, 16–17; on Matisse, 112; minimalist style, 118, 124; minority cosmopolitanism and, 113–23; modernism, 102–3, 128, 129, 141; modernity and, 131; national feeling and, 147; as native exile, 117; place and displacement, 102–23; restless literary aesthetic, 101; revision process, 125; settings, 114, 124–44; supranational experimenter, 3; terrain, 143; unbelonging of, 108; understanding, 134; universe of, 112, 126–27; unknowing and, 141; vague landscapes, 103–6; on walking, 133

The Bell, 79, 80

Belonging, 68, 110, 115; Beckett and, 119; global, 131, 146; nation-state, 113, 155n3; unbelonging, 12, 108. *See also* Unbelonging

Benitez-Rojo, Antonio, 96

Bennett, Andrew, 90

Ben-Zvi, Linda, 117

Berman, Jessica, 68

Bhabha, Homi K., 25, 37–38, 41, 115

Bidirectional consciousness, 8, 121. *See also* Multidirectional sensibilities

NELS PEARSON, professor of English and director of the Humanities Institute at Fairfield University, is coeditor of *Detective Fiction in a Postcolonial and Transnational World*.